SPECIAL MESSAGE TO READERS

THE ULVERSCROFT FOUNDATION
(registered UK charity number 264873)
was established in 1972 to provide funds for research, diagnosis and treatment of eye diseases. Examples of major projects funded by the Ulverscroft Foundation are:-

- The Children's Eye Unit at Moorfields Eye Hospital, London
- The Ulverscroft Children's Eye Unit at Great Ormond Street Hospital for Sick Children
- Funding research into eye diseases and treatment at the Department of Ophthalmology, University of Leicester
- The Ulverscroft Vision Research Group, Institute of Child Health
- Twin operating theatres at the Western Ophthalmic Hospital, London
- The Chair of Ophthalmology at the Royal Australian College of Ophthalmologists

You can help further the work of the Foundation by making a donation or leaving a legacy. Every contribution is gratefully received. If you would like to help support the Foundation or require further information, please contact:

THE ULVERSCROFT FOUNDATION
The Green, Bradgate Road, Anstey
Leicester LE7 7FU, England
Tel: (0116) 236 4325

website: www.foundation.ulverscroft.com

Tara Westover was born in rural Idaho. She studied history at Brigham Young University and upon graduation was awarded a Gates Cambridge Scholarship. She received an MPhil in intellectual history from Trinity College, Cambridge in 2009, and a PhD in the same subject in 2014.

EDUCATED

Tara Westover grew up preparing for the End of Days, hoping that when the World of Men failed, her family would continue on, un-affected. She hadn't been registered for a birth certificate. She had no school records because she'd never set foot in a classroom, and no medical records because her father didn't believe in doctors or hospitals. According to the state and federal governments, she didn't exist. As she grew older, her father became more radical, and her brother more violent. At sixteen, Tara decided to educate herself. Her struggle for knowledge would take her far from her Idaho mountains, over oceans and across continents, to Harvard and to Cambridge. Only then would she wonder if she'd traveled too far. If there was still a way home.

TARA WESTOVER

EDUCATED

Complete and Unabridged

CHARNWOOD
Leicester

First published in Great Britain in 2018 by
Hutchinson
London

First Charnwood Edition
published 2018
by arrangement with
Hutchinson
Penguin Random House
London

The moral right of the author has been asserted

This book is a work of non-fiction based on the experiences and recollections of the author. In some cases the names of people and other identifying details have been changed to protect the privacy of others. The author has stated to the publishers that, except in such minor respects, not affecting the substantial accuracy of the work, the contents of this book are true.

A catalogue record for this book is available
from the British Library.

ISBN 978–1–4448–3841–1

Published by
F. A. Thorpe (Publishing)
Anstey, Leicestershire

Set by Words & Graphics Ltd.
Anstey, Leicestershire
Printed and bound in Great Britain by
T. J. International Ltd., Padstow, Cornwall

This book is printed on acid-free paper

For Tyler

The past is beautiful because one never rea-
lises an emotion at the time. It expands later,
& thus we don't have complete emotions about
the present, only about the past.

— Virginia Woolf

I believe finally that education must be
conceived as a continuing reconstruction of
experience; that the process and the goal
of education are one and the same thing.

— John Dewey

Contents

Author's Note

This story is not about Mormonism. Neither is it about any other form of religious belief. In it there are many types of people, some believers, some not; some kind, some not. The author disputes any correlation, positive or negative, between the two.

The following names, listed in alphabetical order, are pseudonyms: Aaron, Audrey, Benjamin, Emily, Erin, Faye, Gene, Jessica, Judy, Robert, Robin, Sadie, Shannon, Shawn, Susan, Vanessa.

Prologue

I'm standing on the red railway car that sits abandoned next to the barn. The wind soars, whipping my hair across my face and pushing a chill down the open neck of my shirt. The gales are strong this close to the mountain, as if the peak itself is exhaling. Down below, the valley is peaceful, undisturbed. Meanwhile our farm dances: the heavy conifer trees sway slowly, while the sagebrush and thistles quiver, bowing before every puff and pocket of air. Behind me a gentle hill slopes upward and stitches itself to the mountain base. If I look up, I can see the dark form of the Indian Princess.

The hill is paved with wild wheat. If the conifers and sagebrush are soloists, the wheat field is a corps de ballet, each stem following all the rest in bursts of movement, a million ballerinas bending, one after the other, as great gales dent their golden heads. The shape of that dent lasts only a moment, and is as close as anyone gets to seeing wind.

Turning toward our house on the hillside, I see movements of a different kind, tall shadows stiffly pushing through the currents. My brothers are awake, testing the weather. I imagine my mother at the stove, hovering over bran pancakes. I picture my father hunched by the back door, lacing his steel-toed boots and threading his callused hands into welding gloves. On the highway below,

1

the school bus rolls past without stopping.

I am only seven, but I understand that it is this fact, more than any other, that makes my family different: we don't go to school.

Dad worries that the Government will force us to go but it can't, because it doesn't know about us. Four of my parents' seven children don't have birth certificates. We have no medical records because we were born at home and have never seen a doctor or nurse.[1] We have no school records because we've never set foot in a class-room. When I am nine, I will be issued a Delayed Certificate of Birth, but at this moment, according to the state of Idaho and the federal government, I do not exist.

Of course I *did* exist. I had grown up preparing for the Days of Abomination, watching for the sun to darken, for the moon to drip as if with blood. I spent my summers bottling peaches and my winters rotating supplies. When the World of Men failed, my family would continue on, unaffected.

I had been educated in the rhythms of the mountain, rhythms in which change was never fundamental, only cyclical. The same sun appeared each morning, swept over the valley and dropped behind the peak. The snows that fell in winter always melted in the spring. Our lives were a cycle — the cycle of the day, the cycle of the seasons — circles of perpetual change that, when complete, meant nothing had changed at all. I believed my family was a part of this immortal pattern, that we were, in some sense, eternal. But eternity belonged only to the mountain.

2

There's a story my father used to tell about the peak. She was a grand old thing, a cathedral of a mountain. The range had other mountains, taller, more imposing, but Buck's Peak was the most finely crafted. Its base spanned a mile, its dark form swelling out of the earth and rising into a flawless spire. From a distance, you could see the impression of a woman's body on the mountain face: her legs formed of huge ravines, her hair a spray of pines fanning over the northern ridge. Her stance was commanding, one leg thrust forward in a powerful movement, more stride than step.

My father called her the Indian Princess. She emerged each year when the snows began to melt, facing south, watching the buffalo return to the valley. Dad said the nomadic Indians had watched for her appearance as a sign of spring, a signal the mountain was thawing, winter was over, and it was time to come home.

All my father's stories were about our mountain, our valley, our jagged little patch of Idaho. He never told me what to do if I left the mountain, if I crossed oceans and continents and found myself in strange terrain, where I could no longer search the horizon for the Princess. He never told me how I'd know when it was time to come home.

PART ONE

PART ONE

1

Choose the Good

My strongest memory is not a memory. It's something I imagined, then came to remember as if it had happened. The memory was formed when I was five, just before I turned six, from a story my father told in such detail that I and my brothers and sister had each conjured our own cinematic version, with gunfire and shouts. Mine had crickets. That's the sound I hear as my family huddles in the kitchen, lights off, hiding from the Feds who've surrounded the house. A woman reaches for a glass of water and her silhouette is lighted by the moon. A shot echoes like the lash of a whip and she falls. In my memory it's always Mother who falls, and she has a baby in her arms.

The baby doesn't make sense — I'm the youngest of my mother's seven children — but like I said, none of this happened.

★   ★   ★

A year after my father told us that story, we gathered one evening to hear him read aloud from Isaiah, a prophecy about Immanuel. He sat on our mustard-colored sofa, a large Bible open in his lap. Mother was next to him. The rest of us were strewn across the shaggy brown carpet.

'Butter and honey shall he eat,' Dad droned, low and monotone, weary from a long day hauling scrap. 'That he may know to refuse the evil, and choose the good.'

There was a heavy pause. We sat quietly.

My father was not a tall man but he was able to command a room. He had a presence about him, the solemnity of an oracle. His hands were thick and leathery — the hands of a man who'd been hard at work all his life — and they grasped the Bible firmly.

He read the passage aloud a second time, then a third, then a fourth. With each repetition the pitch of his voice climbed higher. His eyes, which moments before had been swollen with fatigue, were now wide and alert. There was a divine doctrine here, he said. He would inquire of the Lord.

The next morning Dad purged our fridge of milk, yogurt and cheese, and that evening when he came home, his truck was loaded with fifty gallons of honey.

'Isaiah doesn't say which is evil, butter or honey,' Dad said, grinning as my brothers lugged the white tubs to the basement. 'But if you ask, the Lord will tell you!'

When Dad read the verse to his mother, she laughed in his face. 'I got some pennies in my purse,' she said. 'You better take them. They'll be all the sense you got.'

Grandma had a thin, angular face and an endless store of faux Indian jewelry, all silver and turquoise, which hung in clumps from her spindly neck and fingers. Because she lived down the hill from us, near the highway, we called her Grandma-down-the-hill. This was to distinguish her from our mother's mother, who we called Grandma-over-in-town because she lived fifteen miles south, in the only town in the county, which had a single stoplight and a grocery store.

Dad and his mother got along like two cats with their tails tied together. They could talk for a week and not agree about anything, but they were tethered by their devotion to the mountain. My father's family had been living at the base of Buck's Peak for half a century. Grandma's daughters had married and moved away, but my father stayed, building a shabby yellow house, which he would never quite finish, just up the hill from his mother's, at the base of the mountain, and plunking a junkyard — one of several — next to her manicured lawn.

They argued daily, about the mess from the junkyard but more often about us kids. Grandma thought we should be in school and not, as she put it, 'roaming the mountain like savages.' Dad said public school was a ploy by the Government to lead children away from God. 'I may as well surrender my kids to the devil himself,' he said, 'as send them down the road to that school.'

God told Dad to share the revelation with the people who lived and farmed in the shadow of Buck's Peak. On Sundays, nearly everyone gathered at the church, a hickory-colored chapel just off the highway with the small, restrained steeple common to Mormon churches. Dad cornered fathers as they left their pews. He started with his cousin Jim, who listened good-naturedly while

9

Dad waved his Bible and explained the sinfulness of milk. Jim grinned, then clapped Dad on the shoulder and said no righteous God would deprive a man of homemade strawberry ice cream on a hot summer afternoon. Jim's wife tugged on his arm. As he slid past us I caught a whiff of manure. Then I remembered: the big dairy farm a mile north of Buck's Peak, that was Jim's.

★ ★ ★

After Dad took up preaching against milk, Grandma jammed her fridge full of it. She and Grandpa only drank skim but pretty soon it was all there — two percent, whole, even chocolate. She seemed to believe this was an important line to hold.

Breakfast became a test of loyalty. Every morning, my family sat around a large table of reworked red oak and ate either seven-grain cereal, with honey and molasses, or seven-grain pancakes, also with honey and molasses. Because there were nine of us, the pancakes were never cooked all the way through. I didn't mind the cereal if I could soak it in milk, letting the cream gather up the grist and seep into the pellets, but since the revelation we'd been having it with water. It was like eating a bowl of mud.

It wasn't long before I began to think of all that milk spoiling in Grandma's fridge. Then I got into the habit of skipping breakfast each morning and going straight to the barn. I'd slop the pigs and fill the trough for the cows and horses, then I'd hop over the corral fence, loop around the barn and step through Grandma's side door.

On one such morning, as I sat at the counter watching Grandma pour a bowl of cornflakes, she said, 'How would you like to go to school?'

'I wouldn't like it,' I said.

'How do you know,' she barked. 'You ain't never tried it.'

She poured the milk and handed me the bowl, then she perched at the bar, directly across from me, and watched as I shoveled spoonfuls into my mouth.

'We're leaving tomorrow for Arizona,' she told me, but I already knew. She and Grandpa always went to Arizona when the weather began to turn. Grandpa said he was too old for Idaho winters; the cold put an ache in his bones. 'Get yourself up real early,' Grandma said, 'around five, and we'll take you with us. Put you in school.'

I shifted on my stool. I tried to imagine school but couldn't. Instead I pictured Sunday school, which I attended each week and which I hated. A boy named Aaron had told all the girls that I couldn't read because I didn't go to school, and now none of them would talk to me.

'Dad said I can go?' I said.

'No,' Grandma said. 'But we'll be long gone by the time he realizes you're missing.' She set my bowl in the sink and gazed out the window.

Grandma was a force of nature — impatient, aggressive, self-possessed. To look at her was to take a step back. She dyed her hair black and this intensified her already severe features, especially her eyebrows, which she smeared on each morning in thick, inky arches. She drew them too large and this made her face seem stretched. They were also drawn too high and draped the rest of her features into an expression of boredom, almost sarcasm.

'You should be in school,' she said.

'Won't Dad just make you bring me back?' I said.

'Your dad can't make me do a damned thing.' Grandma stood, squaring herself. 'If he wants you, he'll have to come get you.' She hesitated, and for a moment looked ashamed. 'I talked to him yesterday. He won't be able to fetch you back for a long while. He's behind on that shed he's building in town. He can't pack up and drive to Arizona, not while the weather holds and he and the boys can work long days.'

Grandma's scheme was well plotted. Dad always worked from sunup until sundown in the weeks before the first snow, trying to stockpile enough money from hauling scrap and building barns to outlast the winter, when jobs were scarce. Even if his mother ran off with his youngest child, he wouldn't be able to stop working, not until the forklift was encased in ice.

'I'll need to feed the animals before we go,' I said. 'He'll notice I'm gone for sure if the cows break through the fence looking for water.'

★　★　★

I didn't sleep that night. I sat on the kitchen floor and watched the hours tick by. One A.M. Two. Three.

At four I stood and put my boots by the back door. They were caked in manure, and I was sure Grandma wouldn't let them into her car. I pictured them on her porch, abandoned, while I ran off shoeless to Arizona.

I imagined what would happen when my family discovered I was missing. My brother Richard and I often spent whole days on the mountain, so it was likely no one would notice until sundown, when Richard came home for dinner and I didn't. I pictured my brothers pushing out the door to search for me. They'd try the junkyard first, hefting iron slabs in case some stray sheet of metal had shifted and pinned me. Then they'd move outward, sweeping the farm, crawling up trees and into the barn attic. Finally, they'd turn to the mountain.

It would be past dusk by then — that moment just before night sets in, when the landscape is visible only as darkness and lighter darkness, and you feel the world around you more than you see it. I imagined my brothers spreading over the mountain, searching the black forests. No one would talk; everyone's thoughts would be the same. Things could go horribly wrong on the mountain. Cliffs appeared suddenly. Feral horses, belonging to my grandfather, ran wild over thick banks of water hemlock, and there were more than a few rattlesnakes. We'd done this search before when a calf went missing from the barn. In the valley you'd find an injured animal; on the mountain, a dead one.

I imagined Mother standing by the back door, her eyes sweeping the dark ridge, when my father came home to tell her they hadn't found me. My sister, Audrey, would suggest that someone ask Grandma, and Mother would say Grandma had left that morning for Arizona. Those words would hang in the air for a moment, then everyone would know where I'd gone. I imagined my father's face, his dark eyes shrinking, his mouth clamping into a frown as he turned to my mother. 'You think she chose to go?'

Low and sorrowful, his voice echoed. Then it was drowned out by sounds from another conjured remembrance — crickets, then gunfire, then silence.

★ ★ ★

The event was a famous one, I would later learn — like Wounded Knee or Waco — but when my father first told us the story, it felt like no one in the world knew about it except us.

It began near the end of canning season, which other kids probably called 'summer.' My family always spent the warm months bottling fruit for storage, which Dad said we'd need in the Days of Abomination. One evening, Dad was uneasy when he came in from the junkyard. He paced the kitchen during dinner, hardly touching a bite. We had to get everything in order, he said. There was little time.

We spent the next day boiling and skinning peaches. By sundown we'd filled dozens of Mason jars, which were set out in perfect rows, still warm from the pressure cooker. Dad surveyed our work, counting the jars and muttering to himself, then he turned to Mother and said, 'It's not enough.'

That night Dad called a family meeting, and we gathered around the kitchen table, because it was wide and long, and could seat all of us. We had a right to know what we were up against, he said. He was standing at the head of the table; the rest of us perched on benches, studying the thick planks of red oak.

'There's a family not far from here,' Dad said. 'They're freedom fighters. They wouldn't let the Government brainwash their kids in them public schools, so the Feds came after them.' Dad exhaled, long and slow. 'The Feds surrounded the family's cabin, kept them locked in there for weeks, and when a hungry child, a little boy, snuck out to go hunting, the Feds shot him dead.'

I scanned my brothers. I'd never seen fear on Luke's face before.

'They're still in the cabin,' Dad said. 'They keep the lights off, and they crawl on the floor, away from the doors and windows. I don't know how much food they got. Might be they'll starve before the Feds give up.'

No one spoke. Eventually Luke, who was twelve, asked if we could help. 'No,' Dad said. 'Nobody can. They're trapped in their own home. But they got their guns, you can bet that's why the Feds ain't charged in.' He paused to sit, folding himself onto the low bench in slow, stiff movements. He looked old to my eyes, worn out. 'We can't help them, but we can help ourselves. When the Feds come to Buck's Peak, we'll be ready.'

That night, Dad dragged a pile of old army bags up from the basement. He said they were our 'head for the hills' bags. We spent that night packing them with supplies — herbal medicines, water purifiers, flint and steel. Dad had bought several boxes of military MREs — Meals Ready-to-Eat — and we put as many as we could fit into our packs, imagining the moment when, having fled the house and hiding ourselves in the wild plum trees near the creek, we'd eat them. Some of my brothers stowed guns in their packs but I had only a small knife, and even so my pack was as big as me by the time we'd finished. I asked Luke to hoist it onto a shelf in my closet, but Dad told me to keep it low, where I could fetch it quick, so I slept with it in my bed.

I practiced slipping the bag onto my back and running with it — I didn't want to be left behind. I imagined our escape, a midnight flight to the safety of the Princess. The mountain, I understood, was our ally. To those who knew her she could be kind, but to intruders she was pure treachery, and this would give us an advantage. Then again, if we were going to take cover on the mountain when the Feds came, I didn't understand why we were canning all these peaches. We couldn't haul a thousand heavy Mason jars up the peak. Or did we need the peaches so we could bunker down in the house, like the Weavers, and fight it out?

Fighting it out seemed likely, especially a few days later when Dad came home with more than a dozen military-surplus rifles, mostly SKSs, their thin silver bayonets folded neatly under

16

their barrels. The guns arrived in narrow tin boxes and were packed in Cosmoline, a brownish substance the consistency of lard that had to be stripped away. After they'd been cleaned, my brother Tyler chose one and set it on a sheet of black plastic, which he folded over the rifle, sealing it with yards of silvery duct tape. Hoisting the bundle onto his shoulder, he carried it down the hill and dropped it next to the red railroad car. Then he began to dig. When the hole was wide and deep, he dropped the rifle into it, and I watched him cover it with dirt, his muscles swelling from the exertion, his jaw clenched.

Soon after, Dad bought a machine to manufacture bullets from spent cartridges. Now we could last longer in a standoff, he said. I thought of my 'head for the hills' bag, waiting in my bed, and of the rifle hidden near the railcar, and began to worry about the bullet-making machine. It was bulky and bolted to an iron workstation in the basement. If we were taken by surprise, I figured we wouldn't have time to fetch it. I wondered if we should bury it, too, with the rifle.

We kept on bottling peaches. I don't remember how many days passed or how many jars we'd added to our stores before Dad told us more of the story.

'Randy Weaver's been shot,' Dad said, his voice thin and erratic. 'He left the cabin to fetch his son's body, and the Feds shot him.' I'd never seen my father cry, but now tears were dripping in a steady stream from his nose. He didn't wipe them, just let them spill onto his shirt. 'His wife heard the shot and ran to the window, holding their baby. Then came the second shot.'

Mother was sitting with her arms folded, one hand across her chest, the other clamped over her mouth. I stared at our speckled linoleum while Dad told us how the baby had been lifted from its mother's arms, its face smeared with her blood.

Until that moment, some part of me had *wanted* the Feds to come, had craved the adventure. Now I felt real fear. I pictured my brothers crouching in the dark, their sweaty hands slipping down their rifles. I pictured Mother, tired and parched, drawing back away from the window. I pictured myself lying flat on the floor, still and silent, listening to the sharp chirp of crickets in the field. Then I saw Mother stand and reach for the kitchen tap. A white flash, the roar of gunfire, and she fell. I leapt to catch the baby.

Dad never told us the end of the story. We didn't have a TV or radio, so perhaps he never learned how it ended himself. The last thing I remember him saying about it was, 'Next time, it could be us.'

Those words would stay with me. I would hear their echo in the chirp of crickets, in the squish of peaches dropping into a glass jar, in the metallic *chink* of an SKS being cleaned. I would hear them every morning when I passed the railroad car and paused over the chickweed and bull thistle growing where Tyler had buried the rifle. Long after Dad had forgotten about the revelation in Isaiah, and Mother was again hefting

18

plastic jugs of 'Western Family 2%' into the fridge, I would remember the Weavers.

★　★　★

It was almost five a.m.

I returned to my room, my head full of crickets and gunfire. In the lower bunk, Audrey was snoring, a low, contented hum that invited me to do the same. Instead I climbed up to my bed, crossed my legs and looked out the window. Five passed. Then six. At seven, Grandma appeared and I watched her pace up and down her patio, turning every few moments to gaze up the hill at our house. Then she and Grandpa stepped into their car and pulled onto the highway.

When the car was gone, I got out of bed and ate a bowl of bran with water. Outside I was greeted by Luke's goat, Kamikaze, who nibbled my shirt as I walked to the barn. I passed the go-kart Richard was building from an old lawn mower. I slopped the pigs, filled the trough and moved Grandpa's horses to a new pasture.

After I'd finished I climbed the railway car and looked out over the valley. It was easy to pretend the car was moving, speeding away, that any moment the valley might disappear behind me. I'd spent hours playing that fantasy through in my head but today the reel wouldn't take. I turned west, away from the fields, and faced the peak.

The Princess was always brightest in spring, just after the conifers emerged from the snow, their deep green needles seeming almost black against the tawny browns of soil and bark. It was autumn now. I could still see her but she was fading: the reds and yellows of a dying summer obscured her dark form. Soon it would snow. In the valley that first snow would melt but on the mountain it would linger, burying the Princess until spring, when she would reappear, watchful.

2

The Midwife

'Do you have calendula?' the midwife said. 'I also need lobelia and witch hazel.'

She was sitting at the kitchen counter, watching Mother rummage through our birch wood cabinets. An electric scale sat on the counter between them, and occasionally Mother would use it to weigh dried leaves. It was spring. There was a morning chill despite the bright sunlight.

'I made a fresh batch of calendula last week,' Mother said. 'Tara, run and fetch it.'

I retrieved the tincture, and my mother packed it in a plastic grocery bag with the dried herbs. 'Anything else?' Mother laughed. The pitch was high, nervous. The midwife intimidated her, and when intimidated my mother took on a weightless quality, whisking about every time the midwife made one of her slow, solid movements.

The midwife surveyed her list. 'That will do.'

She was a short, plump woman in her late forties, with eleven children and a russet-colored wart on her chin. She had the longest hair I'd ever seen, a cascade the color of field mice that fell to her knees when she took it out of its tight bun. Her features were heavy, her voice thick with authority. She had no license, no certificates. She was a midwife entirely by the power of her own say-so, which was more than enough.

Mother was to be her assistant. I remember watching them that first day, comparing them. Mother with her rose-petal skin and her hair curled into soft waves that bounced about her shoulders. Her eyelids shimmered. Mother did her makeup every morning, but if she didn't have time she'd apologize all day, as if by not doing it, she had inconvenienced everyone.

The midwife looked as though she hadn't given a thought to her appearance in a decade, and the way she carried herself made you feel foolish for having noticed.

The midwife nodded goodbye, her arms full of Mother's herbs.

The next time the midwife came she brought her daughter Maria, who stood next to her mother, imitating her movements, with a baby wedged against her wiry nine-year-old frame. I stared hopefully at her. Besides Audrey, I hadn't met many other girls like me, who didn't go to school. I edged closer, trying to draw her attention, but she was wholly absorbed in listening to her mother, who was explaining how cramp bark and motherwort should be administered to treat post-birth contractions. Maria's head bobbed in agreement; her eyes never left her mother's face.

I trudged down the hall to my room, alone, but when I turned to shut the door she was standing in it, still toting the baby on her hip. He was a meaty box of flesh, and her torso bent sharply at the waist to offset his bulk.

'Are you going?' she said.

I didn't understand the question.

'I always go,' she said. 'Have you seen a baby get born?'

'No.'

'I have, lots of times. Do you know what it means when a baby comes breech?'

'No.' I said it like an apology.

★ ★ ★

The first time Mother assisted with a birth she was gone for two days. Then she wafted through the back door, so pale she seemed translucent, and drifted to the couch, where she stayed, trembling. 'It was awful,' she whispered. 'Even Judy said she was scared.' Mother closed her eyes. 'She didn't *look* scared.'

Mother rested for several minutes, until she regained some color, then she told the story. The labor had been long, grueling, and when the baby finally came the mother had torn, and badly. There was blood everywhere. The hemorrhage wouldn't stop. That's when Mother realized the umbilical cord had wrapped around the baby's throat. He was purple, so still Mother thought he was dead. As Mother recounted these details, the blood drained from her face until she sat, pale as an egg, her arms wrapped around herself.

Audrey made chamomile tea and we put our mother to bed. When Dad came home that night, Mother told him the same story. 'I can't do it,' she said. 'Judy can, but I can't.' Dad put an arm on her shoulder. 'This is a calling from the Lord,' he said. 'And sometimes the Lord asks for hard things.'

Mother didn't want to be a midwife. Midwifery had been Dad's idea, one of his schemes for self-reliance. There was nothing he hated more than our being dependent on the Government. Dad said one day we would be completely off the grid. As soon as he could get the money together, he planned to build a pipeline to bring water down from the mountain, and after that he'd install solar panels all over the farm. That way we'd have water and electricity in the End of Days, when everyone else was drinking from puddles and living in darkness. Mother was an herbalist so she could tend our health, and if she learned to midwife she would be able to deliver the grandchildren when they came along.

The midwife came to visit Mother a few days after the first birth. She brought Maria, who again followed me to my room. 'It's too bad your mother got a bad one her first time,' she said, smiling. 'The next one will be easier.'

A few weeks later, this prediction was tested. It was midnight. Because we didn't have a phone, the midwife called Grandma-down-the-hill, who walked up the hill, tired and ornery, and barked that it was time for Mother to go 'play doctor.' She stayed only minutes but woke the whole house. 'Why you people can't just go to a hospital like everyone else is beyond me,' she shouted, slamming the door on her way out.

Mother retrieved her overnight bag and the tackle box she'd filled with dark bottles of tincture, then she walked slowly out the door. I was anxious and slept badly, but when Mother came home the next morning, hair deranged and dark circles under her eyes, her lips were parted in a wide smile. 'It was a girl,' she said. Then she went to bed and slept all day.

Months passed in this way, Mother leaving the house at all hours and coming home, trembling, relieved to her core that it was over. By the time the leaves started to fall she'd helped with a dozen births. By the end of winter, several dozen. In the spring she told my father she'd had enough, that she could deliver a baby if she had to, if it was the End of the World. Now she could stop.

Dad's face sank when she said this. He reminded her that this was God's will, that it would bless our family. 'You need to be a midwife,' he said. 'You need to deliver a baby on your own.'

Mother shook her head. 'I can't,' she said. 'Besides, who would hire me when they could hire Judy?'

She'd jinxed herself, thrown her gauntlet before God. Soon after, Maria told me her father had a new job in Wyoming. 'Mom says your mother should take over,' Maria said. A thrilling image took shape in my imagination, of me in Maria's role, the midwife's daughter, confident, knowledgeable. But when I turned to look at my mother standing next to me, the image turned to vapor.

Midwifery was not illegal in the state of Idaho, but it had not yet been sanctioned. This meant that if a delivery went wrong, a midwife might face charges for practicing medicine without a license; if things went very wrong, she could face criminal charges for manslaughter, even prison time. Few women would take such a risk, so midwives were scarce: on the day Judy left for Wyoming, Mother became the only midwife for a hundred miles.

Women with swollen bellies began coming to the house and begging Mother to deliver their babies. Mother crumpled at the thought. One woman sat on the edge of our faded yellow sofa, her eyes cast downward, as she explained that her husband was out of work and they didn't have money for a hospital. Mother sat quietly, eyes focused, lips tight, her whole expression momentarily solid. Then the expression dissolved and she said, in her small voice, 'I'm not a midwife, just an assistant.'

The woman returned several times, perching on our sofa again and again, describing the uncomplicated births of her other children. Whenever Dad saw the woman's car from the junkyard, he'd often come into the house, quietly, through the back door, on the pretense of getting water; then he'd stand in the kitchen taking slow, silent sips, his ear bent toward the living room. Each time the woman left Dad could hardly contain his excitement, so that finally, succumbing to either the woman's desperation or to Dad's elation, or to both, Mother gave way.

The birth went smoothly. Then the woman had a friend who was also pregnant, and Mother delivered her baby as well. Then that woman had a friend. Mother took on an assistant. Before long she was delivering so many babies that

Audrey and I spent our days driving around the valley with her, watching her conduct prenatal exams and prescribe herbs. She became our teacher in a way that, because we rarely held school at home, she'd never been before. She explained every remedy and palliative. If So-and-so's blood pressure was high, she should be given hawthorn to stabilize the collagen and dilate the coronary blood vessels. If Mrs. Someone-or-other was having premature contractions, she needed a bath in ginger to increase the supply of oxygen to the uterus.

Midwifing changed my mother. She was a grown woman with seven children, but this was the first time in her life that she was, without question or caveat, the one in charge. Sometimes, in the days after a birth, I detected in her something of Judy's heavy presence, in a forceful turn of her head, or the imperious arch of an eyebrow. She stopped wearing makeup, then she stopped apologizing for not wearing it.

Mother charged about five hundred dollars for a delivery, and this was another way midwifing changed her: suddenly she had money. Dad didn't believe that women should work, but I suppose he thought it was all right for Mother to be paid for midwifing, because it undermined the Government. Also, we needed the money. Dad worked harder than any man I knew, but scrapping and building barns and hay sheds didn't bring in much, and it helped that Mother could buy groceries with the envelopes of small bills she kept in her purse. Sometimes, if we'd spent the whole day flying about the valley, delivering herbs and doing prenatal exams, Mother would use that money to take me and Audrey out to eat. Grandma-over-in-town had given me a journal, pink with a caramel-colored teddy bear on the cover, and in it I recorded the first time Mother took us to a restaurant, which I described as 'real fancy with menus and everything.' According to the entry, my meal came to $3.30.

Mother also used the money to improve herself as a midwife. She bought an oxygen tank in case a baby came out and couldn't breathe, and she took a suturing class so she could stitch the women who tore. Judy had always sent women to the hospital for stitches, but Mother was determined to learn. *Self-reliance*, I imagine her thinking.

With the rest of the money, Mother put in a phone line.[2] One day a white van appeared, and a handful of men in dark overalls began climbing over the utility poles by the highway. Dad burst through the back door demanding to know what the hell was going on. 'I thought you *wanted* a phone,' Mother said, her eyes so full of surprise they were irreproachable. She went on, talking fast. 'You said there could be trouble if someone goes into labor and Grandma isn't home to take the call. I thought, He's right, we need a phone! Silly me! Did I misunderstand?'

Dad stood there for several seconds, his mouth open. Of course a midwife needs a phone, he said. Then he went back to the junkyard and that's all that was ever said about it. We hadn't had a telephone for as long as I could remember, but the next day there it was, resting in a lime-green cradle, its glossy finish looking out of place next to the murky jars of cohosh and skullcap.

★　★　★

Luke was fifteen when he asked Mother if he could have a birth certificate. He wanted to enroll in Driver's Ed because Tony, our oldest brother, was making good money driving rigs hauling gravel, which he could do because he had a license. Shawn and Tyler, the next oldest after Tony, had birth certificates; it was only the youngest four — Luke, Audrey, Richard and me — who didn't.

Mother began to file the paperwork. I don't know if she talked it over with Dad first. If she did, I can't explain what changed his mind — why suddenly a ten-year policy of not registering with the Government ended without a struggle — but I think maybe it was that telephone. It was almost as if my father had come to accept that if he were really going to do battle with the Government, he would have to take certain risks. Mother's being a midwife would subvert the Medical Establishment, but in order to be a midwife she needed a phone. Perhaps the same logic was extended to Luke: Luke would need income to support a family, to buy supplies and prepare for the End of Days, so he needed a birth certificate. The other possibility is that Mother didn't ask Dad. Perhaps she just decided, on her own, and he accepted her decision. Perhaps even he

— charismatic gale of a man that he was — was temporarily swept aside by the force of her.

Once she had begun the paperwork for Luke, Mother decided she might as well get birth certificates for all of us. It was harder than she expected. She tore the house apart looking for documents to prove we were her children. She found nothing. In my case, no one was sure when I'd been born. Mother remembered one date, Dad another, and Grandma-down-the-hill, who went to town and swore an affidavit that I was her granddaughter, gave a third date.

Mother called the church headquarters in Salt Lake City. A clerk there found a certificate from my christening, when I was a baby, and another from my baptism, which, as with all Mormon children, had occurred when I was eight. Mother requested copies. They arrived in the mail a few days later. 'For Pete's sake!' Mother said when she opened the envelope. Each document gave a different birth date, and neither matched the one Grandma had put on the affidavit.

That week Mother was on the phone for hours every day. With the receiver wedged against her shoulder, the cord stretched across the kitchen, she cooked, cleaned, and strained tinctures of goldenseal and blessed thistle, while having the same conversation over and over.

'Obviously I should have registered her when she was born, but I didn't. So here we are.'

Voices murmured on the other end of the line.

'I've already *told* you — *and* your subordinate, *and* your subordinate's subordinate, and *fifty* other people this week — she doesn't *have*

30

school or medical records. She doesn't have them! They weren't lost. I can't ask for copies. They don't exist!'

'Her birthday? Let's say the twenty-seventh.'

'No, I'm not sure.'

'No, I don't have documentation.'

'Yes, I'll hold.'

The voices always put Mother on hold when she admitted that she didn't know my birthday, passing her up the line to their superiors, as if not knowing what day I was born delegitimized the entire notion of my having an identity. You can't be a person without a birthday, they seemed to say. I didn't understand why not. Until Mother decided to get my birth certificate, not knowing my birthday had never seemed strange. I knew I'd been born near the end of September, and each year I picked a day, one that didn't fall on a Sunday because it's no fun spending your birthday in church. Sometimes I wished Mother would give me the phone so I could explain. 'I have a birthday, same as you,' I wanted to tell the voices. 'It just changes. Don't you wish you could change your birthday?'

Eventually, Mother persuaded Grandma-down-the-hill to swear a new affidavit claiming I'd been born on the twenty-seventh, even though Grandma still believed it was the twenty-ninth, and the state of Idaho issued a Delayed Certificate of Birth. I remember the day it came in the mail. It felt oddly dispossessing, being handed this first legal proof of my personhood: until that moment, it had never occurred to me that proof was required.

In the end, I got my birth certificate long before Luke got his. When Mother had told the voices on the phone that she thought I'd been born sometime in the last week of September, they'd been silent. But when she told them she wasn't exactly sure whether Luke had been born in May or June, that set the voices positively buzzing.

★ ★ ★

That fall, when I was nine, I went with Mother on a birth. I'd been asking to go for months, reminding her that Maria had seen a dozen births by the time she was my age. 'I'm not a nursing mother,' she said. 'I have no reason to take you. Besides, you wouldn't like it.'

Eventually, Mother was hired by a woman who had several small children. It was arranged; I would tend them during the birth.

The call came in the middle of the night. The mechanical ring drilled its way down the hall, and I held my breath, hoping it wasn't a wrong number. A minute later Mother was at my bedside. 'It's time,' she said, and together we ran to the car.

For ten miles Mother rehearsed with me what I was to say if the worst happened and the Feds came. Under no circumstances was I to tell them that my mother was a midwife. If they asked why we were there, I was to say nothing. Mother called it 'the art of shutting up.' 'You just keep saying you were asleep and you didn't see anything and you don't know anything and you can't remember why we're here,' she said. 'Don't give them any more rope to hang me with than they already have.'

Mother fell into silence. I studied her as she drove. Her face was illuminated by the lights in the dashboard, and it appeared ghostly white set against the utter blackness of country roads. Fear was etched into her features, in the bunching of her forehead and the tightening of her lips. Alone with just me, she put aside the persona she displayed for others. She was her old self again, fragile, breathy.

I heard soft whispers and realized they were coming from her. She was chanting what-ifs to herself. What if something went wrong? What if there was a medical history they hadn't told her about, some complication? Or what if it was something ordinary, a common crisis, and she panicked, froze, failed to stop the hemorrhage in time? In a few minutes we would be there, and she would have two lives in her small, trembling hands. Until that moment, I'd never understood the risk she was taking. 'People die in hospitals,' she whispered, her fingers clenching the wheel, wraithlike. 'Sometimes God calls them home, and there's nothing anyone can do. But if it happens to a midwife — ' She turned, speaking directly to me. 'All it takes is one mistake, and you'll be visiting me in prison.'

We arrived and Mother transformed. She issued a string of commands, to the father, to the mother, and to me. I almost forgot to do what she asked, I couldn't take my eyes off her. I realize now that that night I was seeing her for the first time, the secret strength of her.

She barked orders and we moved wordlessly to follow them. The baby was born without complications. It was mythic and romantic, being an intimate witness to this turn in life's cycle, but Mother had been right, I didn't like it. It was long and exhausting, and smelled of groin sweat.

I didn't ask to go on the next birth. Mother returned home pale and shaking. Her voice quivered as she told me and my sister the story: how the unborn baby's heart rate had dropped dangerously low, to a mere tremor; how she'd called an ambulance, then decided they couldn't wait and taken the mother in her own car. She'd driven at such speed that by the time she made it to the hospital, she'd acquired a police escort. In the ER, she'd tried to give the doctors the information they needed without seeming too knowledgeable, without making them suspect that she was an unlicensed midwife.

An emergency cesarean was performed. The mother and baby remained in the hospital for several days, and by the time they were released Mother had stopped trembling. In fact, she seemed exhilarated and had begun to tell the story differently, relishing the moment she'd been pulled over by the policeman, who was surprised to find a moaning woman, obviously in labor, in the backseat. 'I slipped into the scatterbrained-woman routine,' she told me and Audrey, her voice growing louder, catching hold. 'Men like to think they're saving some brain-dead woman who's got herself into a scrape. All I had to do was step aside and let *him* play the hero!'

The most dangerous moment for Mother had come minutes later, in the hospital, after the woman had been wheeled away. A doctor stopped Mother and asked why she'd been at the birth in the first place. She smiled at the memory. 'I asked him the dumbest questions I could think of.' She put on a high, coquettish voice very unlike her own. 'Oh! Was that the baby's head? Aren't babies supposed to come out feet-first?' The doctor was persuaded that she couldn't possibly be a midwife.

★   ★   ★

There were no herbalists in Wyoming as good as Mother, so a few months after the incident at the hospital, Judy came to Buck's Peak to restock. The two women chatted in the kitchen, Judy perched on a barstool, Mother leaning across the counter, her head resting lazily in her hand. I took the list of herbs to the storeroom. Maria, lugging a different baby, followed. I pulled dried leaves and clouded liquids from the shelves, all the while gushing about Mother's exploits, finishing with the confrontation in the hospital. Maria had her own stories about dodging Feds, but when she began to tell one I interrupted her.

'Judy is a fine midwife,' I said, my chest rising. 'But when it comes to doctors and cops, *nobody* plays stupid like my mother.'

3

Cream Shoes

My mother, Faye, was a mailman's daughter. She grew up in town, in a yellow house with a white picket fence lined with purple irises. Her mother was a seamstress, the best in the valley some said, so as a young woman Faye wore beautiful clothes, all perfectly tailored, from velvet jackets and polyester trousers to woolen pantsuits and gabardine dresses. She attended church and participated in school and community activities. Her life had an air of intense order, normalcy, and unassailable respectability.

That air of respectability was carefully concocted by her mother. My grandmother, LaRue, had come of age in the 1950s, in the decade of idealistic fever that burned after World War II. LaRue's father was an alcoholic in a time before the language of addiction and empathy had been invented, when alcoholics weren't called alcoholics, they were called drunks. She was from the 'wrong kind' of family but embedded in a pious Mormon community that, like many communities, visited the crimes of the parents on the children. She was deemed unmarriageable by the respectable men in town. When she met and married my grandfather — a good-natured young man just out of the navy — she dedicated herself to constructing the

36

perfect family, or at least the appearance of it. This would, she believed, shield her daughters from the social contempt that had so wounded her.

One result of this was the white picket fence and the closet of handmade clothes. Another was that her eldest daughter married a severe young man with jet-black hair and an appetite for unconventionality.

That is to say, my mother responded willfully to the respectability heaped upon her. Grandma wanted to give her daughter the gift she herself had never had, the gift of coming from a *good* family. But Faye didn't want it. My mother was not a social revolutionary — even at the peak of her rebellion she preserved her Mormon faith, with its devotion to marriage and motherhood — but the social upheavals of the 1970s did seem to have at least one effect on her: she didn't want the white picket fence and gabardine dresses.

My mother told me dozens of stories of her childhood, of Grandma fretting about her oldest daughter's social standing, about whether her piqué dress was the proper cut, or her velvet slacks the correct shade of blue. These stories nearly always ended with my father swooping in and trading out the velvet for blue jeans. One telling in particular has stayed with me. I am seven or eight and am in my room dressing for church. I have taken a damp rag to my face, hands and feet, scrubbing only the skin that will be visible. Mother watches me pass a cotton dress over my head, which I have chosen for its long sleeves so I won't have to wash my arms, and a jealousy lights her eyes.

'If you were Grandma's daughter,' she says, 'we'd have been up at the crack of dawn preening your hair. Then the rest of the morning would be spent agonizing over which shoes, the white or the cream, would give the right impression.'

Mother's face twists into an ugly smile. She's grasping for humor but the memory is jaundiced. 'Even after we finally chose the cream, we'd be late, because at the last minute Grandma would panic and drive to Cousin Donna's to borrow *her* cream shoes, which had a lower heel.'

Mother stares out the window. She has retreated into herself.

'White or cream?' I say. 'Aren't they the same color?' I owned only one pair of church shoes. They were black, or at least they'd been black when they belonged to my sister.

With the dress on, I turn to the mirror and sand away the crusty dirt around my neckline, thinking how lucky Mother is to have escaped a world in which there was an important difference between white and cream, and where such questions might consume a perfectly good morning, a morning that might otherwise be spent plundering Dad's junkyard with Luke's goat.

★ ★ ★

My father, Gene, was one of those young men who somehow manage to seem both solemn and mischievous. His physical appearance was striking — ebony hair, a strict, angular face, nose

38

like an arrow pointing toward fierce, deep-set eyes. His lips were often pressed together in a jocular grin, as if all the world were his to laugh at.

Although I passed my childhood on the same mountain that my father had passed his, slopping pigs in the same iron trough, I know very little about his boyhood. He never talked about it, so all I have to go on are hints from my mother, who told me that, in his younger years, Grandpa-down-the-hill had been violent, with a hair-trigger temper. Mother's use of the words 'had been' always struck me as funny. We all knew better than to cross Grandpa. He had a short fuse, that was just fact and anybody in the valley could have told you as much. He was weatherworn inside and out, as taut and rugged as the horses he ran wild on the mountain.

Dad's mother worked for the Farm Bureau in town. As an adult, Dad would develop fierce opinions about women working, radical even for our rural Mormon community. 'A woman's place is in the home,' he would say every time he saw a married woman working in town. Now I'm older, I sometimes wonder if Dad's fervor had more to do with his own mother than with doctrine. I wonder if he just wished that *she* had been home, so he wouldn't have been left for all those long hours with Grandpa's temper.

Running the farm consumed Dad's childhood. I doubt he expected to go to college. Still, the way Mother tells it, back then Dad was bursting with energy, laughter and panache. He drove a baby-blue Volkswagen Beetle, wore outlandish suits cut from colorful fabrics, and showcased a thick, fashionable mustache.

They met in town. Faye was waitressing at the bowling alley one Friday night when Gene wandered in with a pack of his friends. She'd never seen him before, so she knew immediately that he wasn't from town and must have come from the mountains surrounding the valley. Farm life had made Gene different from other young men: he was serious for his age, more physically impressive and independent-minded.

There's a sense of sovereignty that comes from life on a mountain, a perception of privacy and isolation, even of dominion. In that vast space you can sail unaccompanied for hours, afloat on pine and brush and rock. It's a tranquility born of sheer immensity; it calms with its very magnitude, which renders the merely human of no consequence. Gene was formed by this alpine hypnosis, this hushing of human drama.

In the valley, Faye tried to stop her ears against the constant gossip of a small town, whose opinions pushed in through the windows and crept under the doors. Mother often described herself as a pleaser: she said she couldn't stop herself from speculating what people wanted her to be, and from contorting herself, compulsively, unwillingly, into whatever it was. Living in her respectable house in the center of town, crowded by four other houses, each so near anyone could peer through the windows and whisper a judgment, Faye felt trapped.

I've often imagined the moment when Gene took Faye to the top of Buck's Peak and she was, for the first time, unable to see the faces or hear the voices of the people in the town below. They were far away. Dwarfed by the mountain, hushed by the wind.

They were engaged soon after.

★   ★   ★

Mother used to tell a story from the time before she was married. She had been close to her brother Lynn, so she took him to meet the man she hoped would be her husband. It was summer, dusk, and Dad's cousins were rough-housing the way they did after a harvest. Lynn arrived and, seeing a room of bowlegged ruffians shouting at each other, fists clenched, swiping at the air, thought he was witnessing a brawl straight out of a John Wayne film. He wanted to call the police.

'I told him to listen,' Mother would say, tears in her eyes from laughing. She always told this story the same way, and it was such a favorite that if she departed in any way from the usual script, we'd tell it for her. 'I told him to pay attention to the actual words they were shouting. Everyone *sounded* mad as hornets, but really they were having a lovely conversation. You had to listen to *what* they were saying, not *how* they were saying it. I told him, That's just how Westovers talk!'

By the time she'd finished we were usually on the floor. We'd cackle until our ribs hurt, imagining our prim, professorial uncle meeting Dad's unruly crew. Lynn found the scene so

41

distasteful he never went back, and in my whole life I never saw him on the mountain. Served him right, we thought, for his meddling, for trying to draw Mother back into that world of gabardine dresses and cream shoes. We understood that the dissolution of Mother's family was the inauguration of ours. The two could not exist together. Only one could have her.

Mother never told us that her family had opposed the engagement but we knew. There were traces the decades hadn't erased. My father seldom set foot in Grandma-over-in-town's house, and when he did he was sullen and stared at the door. As a child I scarcely knew my aunts, uncles or cousins on my mother's side. We rarely visited them — I didn't even know where most of them lived — and it was even rarer for them to visit the mountain. The exception was my aunt Angie, my mother's youngest sister, who lived in town and insisted on seeing my mother.

What I know about the engagement has come to me in bits and pieces, mostly from the stories Mother told. I know she had the ring before Dad served a mission — which was expected of all faithful Mormon men — and spent two years proselytizing in Florida. Lynn took advantage of this absence to introduce his sister to every marriageable man he could find this side of the Rockies, but none could make her forget the stern farm boy who ruled over his own mountain.

Gene returned from Florida and they were married.

LaRue sewed the wedding dress.

42

I've only seen a single photograph from the wedding. It's of my parents posing in front of a gossamer curtain of pale ivory. Mother is wearing a traditional dress of beaded silk and venetian lace, with a neckline that sits above her collarbone. An embroidered veil covers her head. My father wears a cream suit with wide black lapels. They are both intoxicated with happiness, Mother with a relaxed smile, Dad with a grin so large it pokes out from under the corners of his mustache.

It is difficult for me to believe that the untroubled young man in that photograph is my father. Fearful and anxious, he comes into focus for me as a weary middle-aged man stockpiling food and ammunition.

I don't know when the man in that photograph became the man I know as my father. Perhaps there was no single moment. Dad married when he was twenty-one, had his first son, my brother Tony, at twenty-two. When he was twenty-four, Dad asked Mother if they could hire an herbalist to midwife my brother Shawn. She agreed. Was that the first hint, or was it just Gene being Gene, eccentric and unconventional, trying to shock his disapproving in-laws? After all, when Tyler was born twenty months later, the birth took place in a hospital. When Dad was twenty-seven, Luke was born, at home, delivered by a midwife. Dad decided not to file for a birth certificate, a decision he repeated with Audrey, Richard and me. A few years later, around the time he turned thirty, Dad pulled my brothers out of school. I don't remember it, because it was before I was born, but I wonder if perhaps that was a turning point. In the four years that followed, Dad got rid of the telephone and chose not to renew his license to drive. He stopped registering and insuring the family car. Then he began to hoard food.

This last part sounds like my father, but it is not the father my older brothers remember. Dad had just turned forty when the Feds laid siege to the Weavers, an event that confirmed his worst fears. After that he was at war, even if the war was only in his head. Perhaps that is why Tony looks at that photo and sees his father, and I see a stranger.

Fourteen years after the incident with the Weavers, I would sit in a university classroom and listen to a professor of psychology describe something called bipolar disorder. Until that moment I had never heard of mental illness. I knew people could go crazy — they'd wear dead cats on their heads or fall in love with a turnip — but the notion that a person could be functional, lucid, persuasive, and something could still be wrong, had never occurred to me.

The professor recited facts in a dull, earthy voice: the average age of onset is twenty-five; there may be no symptoms before then.

The irony was that if Dad was bipolar — or had any of a dozen disorders that might explain his behavior — the same paranoia that was a symptom of the illness would prevent its ever being diagnosed and treated. No one would ever know.

Grandma-over-in-town died three years ago, age eighty-six.

I didn't know her well.

All those years I was passing in and out of her kitchen, and she never told me what it had been like for her, watching her daughter shut herself away, walled in by phantoms and paranoias.

When I picture her now I conjure a single image, as if my memory is a slide projector and the tray is stuck. She's sitting on a cushioned bench. Her hair pushes out of her head in tight curls, and her lips are pulled into a polite smile, which is welded in place. Her eyes are pleasant but unoccupied, as if she's observing a staged drama.

That smile haunts me. It was constant, the only eternal thing, inscrutable, detached, dispassionate. Now that I'm older and I've taken the trouble to get to know her, mostly through my aunts and uncles, I know she was none of those things.

I attended the memorial. It was open casket and I found myself searching her face. The embalmers hadn't gotten her lips right — the gracious smile she'd worn like an iron mask had been stripped away. It was the first time I'd seen her without it and that's when it finally occurred to me: that Grandma was the only person who might have understood what was happening to me. How the paranoia and fundamentalism were carving up my life, how they were taking from me the people I cared about and leaving only degrees and certificates — an air of respectability — in their place. What was happening now had happened before. This was the second severing of mother and daughter. The tape was playing in a loop.

4

Apache Women

No one saw the car leave the road. My brother Tyler, who was seventeen, fell asleep at the wheel. It was six in the morning and he'd been driving in silence for most of the night, piloting our station wagon through Arizona, Nevada and Utah. We were in Cornish, a farming town twenty miles south of Buck's Peak, when the station wagon drifted over the center line into the other lane, then left the highway. The car jumped a ditch, smashed through two utility poles of thick cedar, and was finally brought to a stop only when it collided with a row-crop tractor.

★   ★   ★

The trip had been Mother's idea.

A few months earlier, when crisp leaves had begun slipping to the ground, signaling the end of summer, Dad had been in high spirits. His feet tapped show tunes at breakfast, and during dinner he often pointed at the mountain, his eyes shining, and described where he would lay the pipes to bring water down to the house. Dad promised that when the first snow fell, he'd build the biggest snowball in the state of Idaho. What he'd do, he said, was hike to the mountain base

47

and gather a small, insignificant ball of snow, then roll it down the hillside, watching it triple in size each time it raced over a hillock or down a ravine. By the time it reached the house, which was atop the last hill before the valley, it'd be big as Grandpa's barn and people on the highway would stare up at it, amazed. We just needed the right snow. Thick, sticky flakes. After every snowfall, we brought handfuls to him and watched him rub the flakes between his fingers. That snow was too fine. This, too wet. After Christmas, he said. That's when you get the *real* snow.

But after Christmas Dad seemed to deflate, to collapse in on himself. He stopped talking about the snowball, then he stopped talking altogether. A darkness gathered in his eyes until it filled them. He walked with his arms limp, shoulders slumping, as if something had hold of him and was dragging him to the earth.

By January Dad couldn't get out of bed. He lay flat on his back, staring blankly at the stucco ceiling with its intricate pattern of ridges and veins. He didn't blink when I brought his dinner plate each night. I'm not sure he knew I was there.

That's when Mother announced we were going to Arizona. She said Dad was like a sunflower — he'd die in the snow — and that come February he needed to be taken away and planted in the sun. So we piled into the station wagon and drove for twelve hours, winding through canyons and speeding over dark freeways, until we arrived at the mobile home in the parched Arizona desert where my grandparents were waiting out the winter.

We arrived a few hours after sunrise. Dad made it as far as Grandma's porch, where he stayed for the rest of the day, a knitted pillow under his head, a callused hand on his stomach. He kept that posture for two days, eyes open, not saying a word, still as a bush in that dry, windless heat.

On the third day he seemed to come back into himself, to become aware of the goings-on around him, to listen to our mealtime chatter rather than staring, unresponsive, at the carpet. After dinner that night, Grandma played her phone messages, which were mostly neighbors and friends saying hello. Then a woman's voice came through the speaker to remind Grandma of her doctor's appointment the following day. That message had a dramatic effect on Dad.

At first Dad asked Grandma questions: what was the appointment for, who was it with, why would she see a doctor when Mother could give her tinctures.

Dad had always believed passionately in Mother's herbs, but that night felt different, like something inside him was shifting, a new creed taking hold. Herbalism, he said, was a spiritual doctrine that separated the wheat from the tares, the faithful from the faithless. Then he used a word I'd never heard before: Illuminati. It sounded exotic, powerful, whatever it was. Grandma, he said, was an unknowing agent of the Illuminati.

God couldn't abide faithlessness, Dad said.

That's why the most hateful sinners were those who wouldn't make up their minds, who used herbs and medication both, who came to Mother on Wednesday and saw their doctor on Friday — or, as Dad put it, 'Who worship at the altar of God one day and offer a sacrifice to Satan the next.' These people were like the ancient Israelites because they'd been given a true religion but hankered after false idols.

'Doctors and pills,' Dad said, nearly shouting. 'That's their god, and they whore after it.'

Mother was staring at her food. At the word 'whore' she stood, threw Dad an angry look, then walked into her room and slammed the door. Mother didn't always agree with Dad. When Dad wasn't around, I'd heard her say things that he — or at least this new incarnation of him — would have called sacrilege, things like, 'Herbs are supplements. For something serious, you should go to a doctor.'

Dad took no notice of Mother's empty chair. 'Those doctors aren't trying to save you,' he told Grandma. 'They're trying to *kill* you.'

When I think of that dinner, the scene comes back to me clearly. I'm sitting at the table. Dad is talking, his voice urgent. Grandma sits across from me, chewing her asparagus again and again in her crooked jaw, the way a goat might, sipping from her ice water, giving no indication that she's heard a word Dad has said, except for the occasional vexed glare she throws the clock when it tells her it's still too early for bed. 'You're a knowing participant in the plans of Satan,' Dad says.

50

This scene played every day, sometimes several times a day, for the rest of the trip. All followed a similar script. Dad, his fervor kindled, would drone for an hour or more, reciting the same lines over and over, fueled by some internal passion that burned long after the rest of us had been lectured into a cold stupor.

Grandma had a memorable way of laughing at the end of these sermons. It was a sort of sigh, a long, drawn-out leaking of breath, that finished with her eyes rolling upward in a lazy imitation of exasperation, as if she wanted to throw her hands in the air but was too tired to complete the gesture. Then she'd smile — not a soothing smile for someone else but a smile for herself, of baffled amusement, a smile that to me always seemed to say, *Ain't nothin' funnier than real life, I tell you what.*

★ ★ ★

It was a scorching afternoon, so hot you couldn't walk barefoot on the pavement, when Grandma took me and Richard for a drive through the desert, having wrestled us into seat-belts, which we'd never worn before. We drove until the road began to incline, then kept driving as the asphalt turned to dust beneath our tires, and still we kept going, Grandma weaving higher and higher into the bleached hills, coming to a stop only when the dirt road ended and a hiking trail began. Then we walked. Grandma was winded after a few minutes, so she sat on a flat red stone and pointed to a sandstone rock formation in the distance, formed of crumbling spires, each a little ruin, and told us to hike to it. Once there, we were to hunt for nuggets of black rock.

'They're called Apache tears,' she said. She reached into her pocket and pulled out a small black stone, dirty and jagged, covered in veins of gray and white like cracked glass. 'And this is how they look after they've been polished a bit.' From her other pocket she withdrew a second stone, which was inky black and so smooth it felt soft.

Richard identified both as obsidian. 'These are volcanic rock,' he said in his best encyclopedic voice. 'But this isn't.' He kicked a washed-out stone and waved at the formation. 'This is sediment.' Richard had a talent for scientific trivia. Usually I ignored his lecturing but today I was gripped by it, and by this strange, thirsty terrain. We hiked around the formation for an hour, returning to Grandma with our shirt-fronts sagging with stones. Grandma was pleased; she could sell them. She put them in the trunk, and as we made our way back to the trailer, she told us the legend of the Apache tears.

According to Grandma, a hundred years ago a tribe of Apaches had fought the U.S. Cavalry on those faded rocks. The tribe was outnumbered: the battle lost, the war over. All that was left to do was wait to die. Soon after the battle began, the warriors became trapped on a ledge. Unwilling to suffer a humiliating defeat, cut down one by one as they tried to break through the cavalry, they mounted their horses and charged off the face of the mountain. When the

Apache women found their broken bodies on the rocks below, they cried huge, desperate tears, which turned to stone when they touched the earth.

Grandma never told us what happened to the women. The Apaches were at war but had no warriors, so perhaps she thought the ending too bleak to say aloud. The word 'slaughter' came to mind, because slaughter is the word for it, for a battle when one side mounts no defense. It's the word we used on the farm. We slaughtered chickens, we didn't fight them. A slaughter was the likely outcome of the warriors' bravery. They died as heroes, their wives as slaves.

As we drove to the trailer, the sun dipping in the sky, its last rays reaching across the highway, I thought about the Apache women. Like the sandstone altar on which they had died, the shape of their lives had been determined years before — before the horses began their gallop, their sorrel bodies arching for that final collision. Long before the warriors' leap it was decided how the women would live and how they would die. By the warriors, by the women themselves. Decided. Choices, numberless as grains of sand, had layered and compressed, coalescing into sediment, then into rock, until all was set in stone.

★ ★ ★

I had never before left the mountain and I ached for it, for the sight of the Princess etched in pine across the massif. I found myself glancing at the

53

vacant Arizona sky, hoping to see her black form swelling out of the earth, laying claim to her half of the heavens. But she was not there. More than the sight of her, I missed her caresses — the wind she sent through canyons and ravines to sweep through my hair every morning. In Arizona, there was no wind. There was just one heat-stricken hour after another.

I spent my days wandering from one side of the trailer to the other, then out the back door, across the patio, over to the hammock, then around to the front porch, where I'd step over Dad's semiconscious form and back inside again. It was a great relief when, on the sixth day, Grandpa's four-wheeler broke down and Tyler and Luke took it apart to find the trouble. I sat on a large barrel of blue plastic, watching them, wondering when we could go home. When Dad would stop talking about the Illuminati. When Mother would stop leaving the room whenever Dad entered it.

That night after dinner, Dad said it was time to go. 'Get your stuff,' he said. 'We're hitting the road in a half hour.' It was early evening, which Grandma said was a ridiculous time to begin a twelve-hour drive. Mother said we should wait until morning, but Dad wanted to get home so he and the boys could scrap the next morning. 'I can't afford to lose any more work days,' he said.

Mother's eyes darkened with worry, but she said nothing.

★ ★ ★

54

I awoke when the car hit the first utility pole. I'd been asleep on the floor under my sister's feet, a blanket over my head. I tried to sit up but the car was shaking, lunging — it felt like it was coming apart — and Audrey fell on top of me. I couldn't see what was happening but I could feel and hear it. Another loud *thud*, a lurch, my mother screaming, 'Tyler!' from the front seat, and a final violent jolt before everything stopped and silence set in.

Several seconds passed in which nothing happened.

Then I heard Audrey's voice. She was calling our names one by one. Then she said, 'Everyone's here except Tara!'

I tried to shout but my face was wedged under the seat, my cheek pressed to the floor. I struggled under Audrey's weight as she shouted my name. Finally, I arched my back and pushed her off, then stuck my head out of the blanket and said, 'Here.'

I looked around. Tyler had twisted his upper body so that he was practically climbing into the backseat, his eyes bulging as he took in every cut, every bruise, every pair of wide eyes. I could see his face but it didn't look like his face. Blood gushed from his mouth and down his shirt. I closed my eyes, trying to forget the twisted angles of his bloodstained teeth. When I opened them again, it was to check everyone else. Richard was holding his head, a hand over each ear like he was trying to block out a noise. Audrey's nose was strangely hooked and blood was streaming from it down her arm. Luke was

55

shaking but I couldn't see any blood. I had a gash on my forearm from where the seat's frame had caught hold of me.

'Everyone all right?' My father's voice. There was a general mumble.

'There are power lines on the car,' Dad said. 'Nobody gets out till they've shut them off.' His door opened, and for a moment I thought he'd been electrocuted, but then I saw he'd pitched himself far enough so that his body had never touched the car and the ground at the same time. I remember peering at him through my shattered window as he circled the car, his red cap pushed back so the brim reached upward, licking the air. He looked strangely boyish.

He circled the car then stopped, crouching low, bringing his head level with the passenger seat. 'Are you okay?' he said. Then he said it again. The third time he said it, his voice quivered.

I leaned over the seat to see who he was talking to, and only then realized how serious the accident had been. The front half of the car had been compressed, the engine arched, curving back over itself, like a fold in solid rock.

There was a glare on the windshield from the morning sun. I saw crisscrossing patterns of fissures and cracks. The sight was familiar. I'd seen hundreds of shattered windshields in the junkyard, each one unique, with its particular spray of gossamer extruding from the point of impact, a chronicle of the collision. The cracks on our windshield told their own story. Their epicenter was a small ring with fissures circling outward. The ring was directly in front of the passenger seat.

'You okay?' Dad pleaded. 'Honey, can you hear me?'

Mother was in the passenger seat. Her body faced away from the window. I couldn't see her face, but there was something terrifying in the way she slumped against her seat.

'Can you hear me?' Dad said. He repeated this several times. Eventually, in a movement so small it was almost imperceptible, I saw the tip of Mother's ponytail dip as she nodded.

Dad stood, looking at the active power lines, looking at the earth, looking at Mother. Looking helpless. 'Do you think — should I call an ambulance?'

I *think* I heard him say that. And if he did, which surely he must have, Mother must have whispered a reply, or maybe she wasn't able to whisper anything, I don't know. I've always imagined that she asked to be taken home.

I was told later that the farmer whose tractor we'd hit rushed from his house. He'd called the police, which we knew would bring trouble because the car wasn't insured, and none of us had been wearing seatbelts. It took perhaps twenty minutes after the farmer informed Utah Power of the accident for them to switch off the deadly current pulsing through the lines. Then Dad lifted Mother from the station wagon and I saw her face — her eyes, hidden under dark circles the size of plums, and the swelling distorting her soft features, stretching some, compressing others.

I don't know how we got home, or when, but I

remember that the mountain face glowed orange in the morning light. Once inside, I watched Tyler spit streams of crimson down the bathroom sink. His front teeth had smashed into the steering wheel and been displaced, so that they jutted backward toward the roof of his mouth.

Mother was laid on the sofa. She mumbled that the light hurt her eyes. We closed the blinds. She wanted to be in the basement, where there were no windows, so Dad carried her downstairs and I didn't see her for several hours, not until that evening, when I used a dull flashlight to bring her dinner. When I saw her, I didn't know her. Both eyes were a deep purple, so deep they looked black, and so swollen I couldn't tell whether they were open or closed. She called me Audrey, even after I corrected her twice. 'Thank you, Audrey, but just dark and quiet, that's fine. Dark. Quiet. Thank you. Come check on me again, Audrey, in a little while.'

Mother didn't come out of the basement for a week. Every day the swelling worsened, the black bruises turned blacker. Every night I was sure her face was as marked as it was possible for a face to be, but every morning it was somehow darker, more tumid. After a week, when the sun went down, we turned off the lights and Mother came upstairs. She looked as if she had two objects strapped to her forehead, large as apples, black as olives.

There was never any more talk of a hospital. The moment for such a decision had passed, and to return to it would be to return to all the fury and fear of the accident itself. Dad said doctors

58

couldn't do anything for her anyhow. She was in God's hands.

In the coming months, Mother called me by many names. When she called me Audrey I didn't worry, but it was troubling when we had conversations in which she referred to me as Luke or Tony, and in the family it has always been agreed, even by Mother herself, that she's never been quite the same since the accident. We kids called her Raccoon Eyes. We thought it was a great joke, once the black rings had been around for a few weeks, long enough for us to get used to them and make them the subject of jokes. We had no idea it was a medical term. Raccoon eyes. A sign of serious brain injury.

Tyler's guilt was all-consuming. He blamed himself for the accident, then kept on blaming himself for every decision that was made thereafter, every repercussion, every reverberation that clanged down through the years. He laid claim to that moment and all its consequences, as if time itself had commenced the instant our station wagon left the road, and there was no history, no context, no agency of any kind until he began it, at the age of seventeen, by falling asleep at the wheel. Even now, when Mother forgets any detail, however trivial, that look comes into his eyes — the one he had in the moments after the collision, when blood poured from his own mouth as he took in the scene, raking his eyes over what he imagined to be the work of his hands and his hands only.

Me, I never blamed anyone for the accident, least of all Tyler. It was just one of those things.

59

A decade later my understanding would shift, part of my heavy swing into adulthood, and after that the accident would always make me think of the Apache women, and of all the decisions that go into making a life — the choices people make, together and on their own, that combine to produce any single event. Grains of sand, incalculable, pressing into sediment, then rock.

5

Honest Dirt

The mountain thawed and the Princess appeared on its face, her head brushing the sky. It was Sunday, a month after the accident, and everyone had gathered in the living room. Dad had begun to expound a scripture when Tyler cleared his throat and said he was leaving.

'I'm g-g-going to c-college,' he said, his face rigid. A vein in his neck bulged as he forced the words out, appearing and disappearing every few seconds, a great, struggling snake.

Everyone looked at Dad. His expression was folded, impassive. The silence was worse than shouting.

Tyler would be the third of my brothers to leave home. My oldest brother, Tony, drove rigs, hauling gravel or scrap, trying to scrape together enough money to marry the girl down the road. Shawn, the next oldest, had quarreled with Dad a few months before and taken off. I hadn't seen him since, though Mother got a hurried call every few weeks telling her he was fine, that he was welding or driving rigs. If Tyler left too, Dad wouldn't have a crew, and without a crew he couldn't build barns or hay sheds. He would have to fall back on scrapping.

'What's college?' I said.

'College is extra school for people too dumb

to learn the first time around,' Dad said. Tyler stared at the floor, his face tense. Then his shoulders dropped, his face relaxed and he looked up; it seemed to me that he'd stepped out of himself. His eyes were soft, pleasant. I couldn't see him in there at all.

He listened to Dad, who settled into a lecture. 'There's two kinds of them college professors,' Dad said. 'Those who know they're lying, and those who think they're telling the truth.' Dad grinned. 'Don't know which is worse, come to think of it, a bona fide agent of the Illuminati, who at least knows he's on the devil's payroll, or a high-minded professor who thinks his wisdom is greater than God's.' He was still grinning. The situation wasn't serious; he just needed to talk some sense into his son.

Mother said Dad was wasting his time, that nobody could talk Tyler out of anything once his mind was made up. 'You may as well take a broom and start sweeping dirt off the mountain,' she said. Then she stood, took a few moments to steady herself, and trudged downstairs.

She had a migraine. She nearly always had a migraine. She was still spending her days in the basement, coming upstairs only after the sun had gone down, and even then she rarely stayed more than an hour before the combination of noise and exertion made her head throb. I watched her slow, careful progress down the steps, her back bent, both hands gripping the rail, as if she were blind and had to feel her way. She waited for both feet to plant solidly on one step before reaching for the next. The swelling in her face was nearly gone, and she almost looked like herself again, except for the rings, which had gradually faded from black to dark purple, and were now a mix of lilac and raisin.

An hour later Dad was no longer grinning. Tyler had not repeated his wish to go to college, but he had not promised to stay, either. He was just sitting there, behind that vacant expression, riding it out. 'A man can't make a living out of books and scraps of paper,' Dad said. 'You're going to be the head of a family. How can you support a wife and children with *books?*'

Tyler tilted his head, showed he was listening, and said nothing.

'A son of mine, standing in line to get brainwashed by socialists and Illuminati spies — '

'The s-s-school's run by the ch-ch-church,' Tyler interrupted. 'How b-bad can it b-be?'

Dad's mouth flew open and a gust of air rushed out. 'You don't think the Illuminati have infiltrated the church?' His voice was booming; every word reverberated with a powerful energy. 'You don't think the first place they'd go is that school, where they can raise up a whole generation of socialist Mormons? I raised you better than that!'

I will always remember my father in this moment, the potency of him, and the desperation. He leans forward, jaw set, eyes narrow, searching his son's face for some sign of agreement, some crease of shared conviction. He doesn't find it.

★ ★ ★

63

The story of how Tyler decided to leave the mountain is a strange one, full of gaps and twists. It begins with Tyler himself, with the bizarre fact of him. It happens sometimes in families: one child who doesn't fit, whose rhythm is off, whose meter is set to the wrong tune. In our family, that was Tyler. He was waltzing while the rest of us hopped a jig; he was deaf to the raucous music of our lives, and we were deaf to the serene polyphony of his.

Tyler liked books, he liked quiet. He liked organizing and arranging and labeling. Once, Mother found a whole shelf of matchboxes in his closet, stacked by year. Tyler said they contained his pencil shavings from the past five years, which he had collected to make fire starters for our 'head for the hills' bags. The rest of the house was pure confusion: piles of unwashed laundry, oily and black from the junkyard, littered the bedroom floors; in the kitchen, murky jars of tincture lined every table and cabinet, and these were only cleared away to make space for even messier projects, perhaps to skin a deer carcass or strip Cosmoline off a rifle. But in the heart of this chaos, Tyler had half a decade's pencil shavings, cataloged by year.

My brothers were like a pack of wolves. They tested each other constantly, with scuffles breaking out every time some young pup hit a growth spurt and dreamed of moving up. When I was young these tussles usually ended with Mother screaming over a broken lamp or vase, but as I got older there were fewer things left to break. Mother said we'd owned a TV once, when

64

I was a baby, until Shawn had put Tyler's head through it.

While his brothers wrestled, Tyler listened to music. He owned the only boom box I had ever seen, and next to it he kept a tall stack of CDs with strange words on them, like 'Mozart' and 'Chopin.' One Sunday afternoon, when he was perhaps sixteen, he caught me looking at them. I tried to run, because I thought he might wallop me for being in his room, but instead he took my hand and led me to the stack. 'W-which one do y-you like best?' he said.

One was black, with a hundred men and women dressed in white on the cover. I pointed to it. Tyler eyed me skeptically. 'Th-th-this is ch-ch-choir music,' he said.

He slipped the disc into the black box, then sat at his desk to read. I squatted on the floor by his feet, scratching designs into the carpet. The music began: a breath of strings, then a whisper of voices, chanting, soft as silk, but somehow piercing. The hymn was familiar to me — we'd sung it at church, a chorus of mismatched voices raised in worship — but *this* was different. It was worshipful, but it was also something else, something to do with study, discipline and collaboration. Something I didn't yet understand.

The song ended and I sat, paralyzed, as the next played, and the next, until the CD finished. The room felt lifeless without the music. I asked Tyler if we could listen to it again, and an hour later, when the music stopped, I begged him to restart it. It was very late, and the house quiet, when Tyler stood from his desk and pushed play, saying this was the last time.

'W-w-we can l-l-listen again tomorrow,' he said.

Music became our language. Tyler's speech impediment kept him quiet, made his tongue heavy. Because of that, he and I had never talked much; I had not known my brother. Now, every evening when he came in from the junkyard, I would be waiting for him. After he'd showered, scrubbing the day's grime from his skin, he'd settle in at his desk and say, 'W-w-what shall we l-l-listen t-t-to tonight?' Then I would choose a CD, and he would read while I lay on the floor next to his feet, eyes fixed on his socks, and listened.

I was as rowdy as any of my brothers, but when I was with Tyler I transformed. Maybe it was the music, the grace of it, or maybe it was *his* grace. Somehow he made me see myself through his eyes. I tried to remember not to shout. I tried to avoid fights with Richard, especially the kind that ended with the two of us rolling on the floor, him pulling my hair, me dragging my fingernails through the softness of his face.

I should have known that one day Tyler would leave. Tony and Shawn had gone, and they'd belonged on the mountain in a way that Tyler never did. Tyler had always loved what Dad called 'book learning,' which was something the rest of us, with the exception of Richard, were perfectly indifferent to.

There had been a time, when Tyler was a boy, when Mother had been idealistic about education. She used to say that we were kept at home so we could get a *better* education than other kids. But it was only Mother who said that, as Dad thought we should learn more practical skills. When I was very young, that was the battle between them: Mother trying to hold school every morning, and Dad herding the boys into the junkyard the moment her back was turned.

But Mother would lose that battle, eventually. It began with Luke, the fourth of her five sons. Luke was smart when it came to the mountain — he worked with animals in a way that made it seem like he was talking to them — but he had a severe learning disability and struggled to learn to read. Mother spent five years sitting with him at the kitchen table every morning, explaining the same sounds again and again, but by the time he was twelve, it was all Luke could do to cough out a sentence from the Bible during family scripture study. Mother couldn't understand it. She'd had no trouble teaching Tony and Shawn to read, and everyone else had just sort of picked it up. Tony had taught me to read when I was four, to win a bet with Shawn, I think.

Once Luke could scratch out his name and read short, simple phrases, Mother turned to math. What math I was ever taught I learned doing the breakfast dishes and listening to Mother explain, over and over, what a fraction is or how to use negative numbers. Luke never made any progress, and after a year Mother gave up. She stopped talking about us getting a better education than other kids. She began to echo Dad. 'All that really matters,' she said to me one morning, 'is that you kids learn to read. That

67

other twaddle is just brainwashing.' Dad started coming in earlier and earlier to round up the boys until, by the time I was eight, and Tyler sixteen, we'd settled into a routine that omitted school altogether.

Mother's conversion to Dad's philosophy was not total, however, and occasionally she was possessed of her old enthusiasm. On those days, when the family was gathered around the table, eating breakfast, Mother would announce that today we were *doing school*. She kept a bookshelf in the basement, stocked with books on herbalism, along with a few old paperbacks. There were a few textbooks on math, which we shared, and an American history book that I never saw anyone read except Richard. There was also a science book, which must have been for young children because it was filled with glossy illustrations.

It usually took half an hour to find all the books, then we would divide them up and go into separate rooms to 'do school.' I have no idea what my siblings did when they did school, but when I did it I opened my math book and spent ten minutes turning pages, running my fingers down the center fold. If my finger touched fifty pages, I'd report to Mother that I'd done fifty pages of math.

'Amazing!' she'd say. 'You see? That pace would never be possible in the public school. You can only do that at home, where you can sit down and really focus, with no distractions.'

Mother never delivered lectures or administered exams. She never assigned essays. There was a computer in the basement with a program called Mavis Beacon, which gave lessons on typing.

Sometimes, when she was delivering herbs, if we'd finished our chores, Mother would drop us at the Carnegie library in the center of town. The basement had a room full of children's books, which we read. Richard even took books from upstairs, books for adults, with heavy titles about history and science.

Learning in our family was entirely self-directed: you could learn anything you could teach yourself, after your work was done. Some of us were more disciplined than others. I was one of the least disciplined, so by the time I was ten, the only subject I had studied systematically was Morse code, because Dad insisted that I learn it. 'If the lines are cut, we'll be the only people in the valley who can communicate,' he said, though I was never quite sure, if we were the only people learning it, who we'd be communicating with.

The older boys — Tony, Shawn and Tyler — had been raised in a different decade, and it was almost as if they'd had different parents. Their father had never heard of the Weavers; he never talked about the Illuminati. He'd enrolled his three oldest sons in school, and even though he'd pulled them out a few years later, vowing to teach them at home, when Tony had asked to go back, Dad had let him. Tony had stayed in school through high school, although he missed so many days working in the junkyard that he wasn't able to graduate.

69

Because Tyler was the third son, he barely remembered school and was happy to study at home. Until he turned thirteen. Then, perhaps because Mother was spending all her time teaching Luke to read, Tyler asked Dad if he could enroll in the eighth grade.

Tyler stayed in school that whole year, from the fall of 1991 through the spring of 1992. He learned algebra, which felt as natural to his mind as air to his lungs. Then the Weavers came under siege that August. I don't know if Tyler would have gone back to school, but I know that after Dad heard about the Weavers, he never again allowed one of his children to set foot in a public classroom. Still, Tyler's imagination had been captured. With what money he had he bought an old trigonometry textbook and continued to study on his own. He wanted to learn calculus next but couldn't afford another book, so he went to the school and asked the math teacher for one. The teacher laughed in his face. 'You can't teach yourself calculus,' he said. 'It's impossible.' Tyler pushed back. 'Give me a book, I think I can.' He left with the book tucked under his arm.

The real challenge was finding time to study. Every morning at seven, my father gathered his sons, divided them into teams and sent them out to tackle the tasks of the day. It usually took about an hour for Dad to notice that Tyler was not among his brothers. Then he'd burst through the back door and stride into the house to where Tyler sat studying in his room. 'What the hell are you doing?' he'd shout, tracking clumps of dirt onto Tyler's spotless carpet. 'I got Luke loading

70

I-beams by himself — one man doing a two-man job — and I come in here and find you sitting on your ass?'

If Dad had caught me with a book when I was supposed to be working, I'd have skittered, but Tyler was steady. 'Dad,' he'd say. 'I'll w-w-work after l-l-lunch. But I n-n-need the morning to s-st-study.' Most mornings they'd argue for a few minutes, then Tyler would surrender his pencil, his shoulders slumping as he pulled on his boots and welding gloves. But there were other mornings — mornings that always astonished me — when Dad huffed out the back door, alone.

★ ★ ★

I didn't believe Tyler would really go to college, that he would ever abandon the mountain to join the Illuminati. I figured Dad had all summer to bring Tyler to his senses, which he tried to do most days when the crew came in for lunch. The boys would putter around the kitchen, dishing up seconds and thirds, and Dad would stretch himself out on the hard linoleum — because he was tired and needed to lie down, but was too dirty for Mother's sofa — and begin his lecture about the Illuminati.

One lunch in particular has lodged in my memory. Tyler is assembling tacos from the fixings Mother has laid out: he lines up the shells on his plate, three in a perfect row, then adds the hamburger, lettuce and tomatoes carefully, measuring the amounts, perfectly distributing the sour cream. Dad drones steadily. Then, just as Dad reaches the end of his lecture and takes a breath to begin again, Tyler slides all three of the flawless tacos into Mother's juicer, the one she uses to make tinctures, and turns it on. A loud roar howls through the kitchen, imposing a kind of silence. The roar ceases; Dad resumes. Tyler pours the orange liquid into a glass and begins to drink, carefully, delicately, because his front teeth are still loose, still trying to jump out of his mouth. Many memories might be summoned to symbolize this period of our lives, but this is the one that has stayed with me: of Dad's voice rising up from the floor while Tyler drinks his tacos.

As spring turned to summer, Dad's resolve turned to denial — he acted as if the argument were over and he had won. He stopped talking about Tyler's leaving and refused to hire a hand to replace him.

One warm afternoon, Tyler took me to visit Grandma- and Grandpa-over-in-town, who lived in the same house where they'd raised Mother, a house that could not have been more different from ours. The decor was not expensive but it was well cared for — creamy white carpet on the floors, soft floral paper on the walls, thick, pleated curtains in the windows. They seldom replaced anything. The carpet, the wallpaper, the kitchen table and countertops — everything was the same as it was in the slides I'd seen of my mother's childhood.

Dad didn't like us spending time there. Before he retired Grandpa had been a mailman, and Dad said no one worth our respect would have worked for the Government. Grandma was even worse, Dad said. She was frivolous. I didn't know what that word meant, but he said it so often that I'd come to associate it with her — with her creamy carpet and soft petal wallpaper.

Tyler loved it there. He loved the calm, the order, the soft way my grandparents spoke to each other. There was an aura in that house that made me feel instinctively, without ever being told, that I was not to shout, not to hit anyone or tear through the kitchen at full speed. I *did* have to be told, and told repeatedly, to leave my muddy shoes by the door.

'Off to college!' Grandma said once we were settled onto the floral-print sofa. She turned to me. 'You must be so proud of your brother!' Her eyes squinted to accommodate her smile. I could see every one of her teeth. *Leave it to Grandma to think getting yourself brainwashed is something to celebrate*, I thought.

'I need the bathroom,' I said.

Alone in the hall I walked slowly, pausing with each step to let my toes sink into the carpet. I smiled, remembering that Dad had said Grandma could keep her carpet so white only because Grandpa had never done any real work. 'My hands might be dirty,' Dad had said, winking at me and displaying his blackened fingernails. 'But it's honest dirt.'

★ ★ ★

Weeks passed and it was full summer. One Sunday Dad called the family together. 'We've

73

got a good supply of food,' he said. 'We've got fuel and water stored away. What we don't got is money.' Dad took a twenty from his wallet and crumpled it. 'Not this fake money. In the Days of Abomination, this won't be worth a thing. People will trade hundred-dollar bills for a roll of toilet paper.'

I imagined a world where green bills littered the highway like empty soda cans. I looked around. Everyone else seemed to be imagining that too, especially Tyler. His eyes were focused, determined. 'I've got a little money saved,' Dad said. 'And your mother's got some tucked away. We're going to change it into silver. That's what people will be wishing they had soon, silver and gold.'

A few days later Dad came home with the silver, and even some gold. The metal was in the form of coins, packed in small, heavy boxes, which he carried through the house and piled in the basement. He wouldn't let me open them. 'They aren't for playing,' he said.

Sometime after Tyler took several thousand dollars — nearly all the savings he had left after he'd paid the farmer for the tractor and Dad for the station wagon — and bought his own pile of silver, which he stacked in the basement next to the gun cabinet. He stood there for a long time, considering the boxes, as if suspended between two worlds.

Tyler was a softer target: I begged and he gave me a silver coin as big as my palm. The coin soothed me. It seemed to me that Tyler's buying it was a declaration of loyalty, a pledge to our family that despite the madness that had hold of him, that made him want to go to school, ultimately he would choose us. Fight on our side when the End came. By the time the leaves began to change, from the juniper greens of summer to the garnet reds and bronzed golds of autumn, that coin shimmered even in the lowest light, polished by a thousand finger strokes. I'd taken comfort in the raw physicality of it, certain that if the coin was real, Tyler's leaving could not be.

★　★　★

I awoke one morning in August to find Tyler packing his clothes, books and CDs into boxes. He'd nearly finished by the time we sat down to breakfast. I ate quickly, then went into his room and looked at his shelves, now empty except for a single CD, the black one with the image of the people dressed in white, which I now recognized as the Mormon Tabernacle Choir. Tyler appeared in the doorway. 'I'm l-l-leaving that f-f-for you,' he said. Then he walked outside and hosed down his car, blasting away the Idaho dust until it looked as though it had never seen a dirt road.

Dad finished his breakfast and left without a word. I understood why. The sight of Tyler loading boxes into his car made me crazed. I wanted to scream but instead I ran, out the back door and up through the hills toward the peak. I ran until the sound of blood pulsing in my ears was louder than the thoughts in my head; then I turned around and ran back, swinging around the pasture to the red railroad car. I scrambled onto its roof just in time to see Tyler close his trunk and turn in a circle, as if he wanted to say goodbye but there was no one to say goodbye to. I imagined him calling my name and pictured his face falling when I didn't answer.

He was in the driver's seat by the time I'd climbed down, and the car was rumbling down the dirt road when I leapt out from behind an iron tank. Tyler stopped, then got out and hugged me — not the crouching hug that adults often give children but the other kind, both of us standing, him pulling me into him and bringing his face close to mine. He said he would miss me, then he let me go, stepping into his car and speeding down the hill and onto the highway. I watched the dust settle.

Tyler rarely came home after that. He was building a new life for himself across enemy lines. He made few excursions back to our side. I have almost no memory of him until five years later, when I am fifteen, and he bursts into my life at a critical moment. By then we are strangers.

It would be many years before I would understand what leaving that day had cost him, and how little he had understood about where he was going. Tony and Shawn had left the mountain, but they'd left to do what my father had taught them to do: drive semis, weld, scrap. Tyler stepped into a void. I don't know why he did it and neither does he. He can't explain where the conviction came from, or how it burned brightly enough to shine through the black uncertainty. But I've always supposed it was the music in his head, some hopeful tune the rest of us couldn't hear, the same secret melody he'd been humming when he bought that trigonometry book, or saved all those pencil shavings.

★ ★ ★

Summer waned, seeming to evaporate in its own heat. The days were still hot but the evenings had begun to cool, the frigid hours after sunset claiming more of each day. Tyler had been gone a month.

I was spending the afternoon with Grandma-over-in-town. I'd had a bath that morning, even though it wasn't Sunday, and I'd put on special clothes with no holes or stains so that, scrubbed and polished, I could sit in Grandma's kitchen and watch her make pumpkin cookies. The autumn sun poured in through gossamer curtains and onto marigold tiles, giving the whole room an amber glow.

After Grandma slid the first batch into the oven, I went to the bathroom. I passed through the hallway, with its soft white carpet, and felt a stab of anger when I remembered that the last time I'd seen it, I'd been with Tyler. The bathroom felt foreign. I took in the pearly sink, the rosy tint of the carpet, the peach-colored rug. Even the toilet peeked out from under a primrose covering. I took in my own reflection, framed by creamy tiles. I looked nothing like myself, and I wondered for a moment if *this* was what Tyler wanted, a pretty house with a pretty bathroom and a pretty sister to visit him. Maybe this was what he'd left for. I hated him for that.

Near the tap there were a dozen pink and white soaps, shaped like swans and roses, resting in an ivory-tinted shell. I picked up a swan, feeling its soft shape give under pressure from my fingers. It was beautiful and I wanted to take it. I pictured it in our basement bathroom, its delicate wings set against the coarse cement. I imagined it lying in a muddy puddle on the sink, surrounded by strips of curling yellowed wallpaper. I returned it to its shell.

Coming out, I walked into Grandma, who'd been waiting for me in the hall.

'Did you wash your hands?' she asked, her tone sweet and buttery.

'No,' I said.

My reply soured the cream in her voice. 'Why not?'

'They weren't dirty.'

'You should always wash your hands after you use the toilet.'

'It can't be that important,' I said. 'We don't even have soap in the bathroom at home.'

'That's not true,' she said. 'I raised your mother better than that.'

I squared my stance, ready to argue, to tell Grandma again that we didn't use soap, but when I looked up, the woman I saw was not the woman I expected to see. She didn't seem frivolous, didn't seem like the type who'd waste an entire day fretting over her white carpet. In that moment she was transformed. Maybe it was something in the shape of her eyes, the way they squinted at me in disbelief, or maybe it was the hard line of her mouth, which was clamped shut, determined. Or maybe it was nothing at all, just the same old woman looking like herself and saying the things she always said. Maybe her transformation was merely a temporary shift in my perspective — for that moment, perhaps the perspective was *his*, that of the brother I hated, and loved.

Grandma led me into the bathroom and watched as I washed my hands, then directed me to dry them on the rose-colored towel. My ears burned, my throat felt hot.

Dad picked me up soon after on his way home from a job. He pulled up in his truck and honked for me to come out, which I did, my head bent low. Grandma followed. I rushed into the passenger seat, displacing a toolbox and welding gloves, while Grandma told Dad about my not washing. Dad listened, sucking on his cheeks while his right hand fiddled with the gearshift. A laugh was bubbling up inside him.

Having returned to my father, I felt the power of his person. A familiar lens slid over my eyes and Grandma lost whatever strange power she'd had over me an hour before.

'Don't you teach your children to wash after they use the toilet?' Grandma said.

Dad shifted the truck into gear. As it rolled forward he waved and said, 'I teach them not to piss on their hands.'

6

Shield and Buckler

The winter after Tyler left, Audrey turned fifteen. She picked up her driver's license from the county courthouse and, on her way home, got a job flipping burgers. Then she took a second job milking cows at four A.M. every morning. For a year she'd been fighting with Dad, bucking under the restraints he put on her. Now she had money; she had her own car; we hardly saw her. The family was shrinking, the old hierarchy compressing.

Dad didn't have enough of a crew to build hay sheds, so he went back to scrapping. With Tyler gone, the rest of us were promoted: Luke, at sixteen, became the eldest son, my father's right hand, and Richard and I took his place as grunts.

I remember the first morning I entered the junkyard as one of my father's crew. The earth was ice, even the air felt stiff. We were in the yard above the lower pasture, which was overrun by hundreds of cars and trucks. Some were old and broken down but most had been wrecked and they looked it — bent, arched, twisted, the impression they gave was of crumpled paper, not steel. In the center of the yard there was a lake of debris, vast and deep: leaking car batteries, tangles of insulated copper wire, abandoned transmissions, rusted sheets of corrugated tin, antique faucets, smashed radiators, serrated lengths of luminous brass pipe, and on and on. It was endless, a formless mass.

Dad led me to its edge.

'You know the difference between aluminum and stainless steel?' he said.

'I think so.'

'Come here.' His tone was impatient. He was used to dictating to grown men. Having to explain his trade to a ten-year-old girl somehow made us both feel small.

He yanked out a chunk of shimmering metal. 'This here's aluminum,' he said. 'See how it shines? Feel how light it is?' Dad put the piece into my hand. He was right; it was not as heavy as it looked. Next Dad handed me a dented pipe. 'This here's steel,' he said.

We began to sort the debris into piles — aluminum, iron, steel, copper — so it could be sold. I picked up a piece of iron. It was dense with bronze rust, and its jagged angles nibbled at my palms. I had a pair of leather gloves, but when Dad saw them he said they'd slow me down. 'You'll get calluses real quick,' he promised as I handed them over. I'd found a hard hat in the shop, but Dad took that, too. 'You'll move slower trying to balance this silly thing on your head,' he said.

Dad lived in fear of time. He felt it stalking him. I could see it in the worried glances he gave the sun as it moved across the sky, in the anxious way he appraised every length of pipe or cut of steel. Dad saw every piece of scrap as the money it could be sold for, minus the time needed to

81

sort, cut and deliver it. Every slab of iron, every ring of copper tubing was a nickel, a dime, a dollar — less if it took more than two seconds to extract and classify — and he constantly weighed these meager profits against the hourly expense of running the house. He figured that to keep the lights on, the house warm, he needed to work at breakneck speed. I never saw Dad carry anything to a sorting bin; he just chucked it, with all the strength he had, from wherever he was standing.

The first time I saw him do it, I thought it was an accident, a mishap that would be corrected. I hadn't yet grasped the rules of this new world. I had bent down, and was reaching for a copper coil, when something massive cut through the air next to me. When I turned to see where it had come from, I caught a steel cylinder full in the stomach.

The impact knocked me to the ground. 'Oops!' Dad hollered. I rolled over on the ice, winded. By the time I'd scrambled to my feet, Dad had launched something else. I ducked but lost my footing and fell. This time I stayed down. I was shaking but not from cold. My skin was alive and tingling with the certainty of danger, yet when I looked for the source of that danger, all I could see was a tired old man, tugging on a broken light fixture.

I remembered all the times I'd seen one of my brothers burst through the back door, howling, pinching some part of his body that was gashed or squashed or broken or burned. I remembered two years before, when a man named Robert, who worked for Dad, had lost a finger. I remembered the otherworldly pitch of his scream as he ran to the house. I remembered staring at the bloody stump, and then at the severed finger, which Luke brought in and placed on the counter. It looked like a prop from a magic trick. Mother put it on ice and rushed Robert to town so the doctors could sew it back on. Robert's was not the only finger the junkyard had claimed. A year before Robert, Shawn's girlfriend, Emma, had come through the back door shrieking. She'd been helping Shawn and lost half her index. Mother had rushed Emma to town, too, but the flesh had been crushed, and there was nothing they could do.

I looked at my own pink fingers, and in that moment the junkyard shifted. As children, Richard and I had passed countless hours in the debris, jumping from one mangled car to the next, looting some, leaving others. It had been the backdrop for a thousand imagined battles — between demons and wizards, fairies and goons, trolls and giants. Now it was changed. It had ceased to be my childhood playground and had become its own reality, one whose physical laws were mysterious, hostile.

I was remembering the strange pattern the blood had made as it streaked down Emma's wrist, smearing across her forearm, when I stood and, still shaking, tried to pry loose the small length of copper tubing. I almost had it when Dad flung a catalytic converter. I leapt aside, cutting my hand on the serrated edge of a punctured tank. I wiped the blood on my jeans and shouted, 'Don't throw them here! *I'm* here!'

Dad looked up, surprised. He'd forgotten I was there. When he saw the blood, he walked over to me and put a hand on my shoulder. 'Don't worry, honey,' he said. 'God and his angels are here, working right alongside us. They won't let you get hurt.'

★ ★ ★

I wasn't the only one whose feet were searching for solid ground. For six months after the car accident, Mother had improved steadily and we'd thought she would fully recover. The headaches had become less frequent, so that she was shutting herself in the basement only two or three days a week. Then the healing had slowed. Now it had been nine months. The headaches persisted, and Mother's memory was erratic. At least twice a week she'd ask me to cook breakfast long after everyone had eaten and the dishes had been cleared. She'd tell me to weigh a pound of yarrow for a client, and I'd remind her that we'd delivered the yarrow the day before. She'd begin mixing a tincture, then a minute later couldn't remember which ingredients she'd added, so that the whole batch had to be tossed. Sometimes she would ask me to stand next to her and watch, so I could say, 'You already added the lobelia. Next is the blue vervain.'

Mother began to doubt whether she would ever midwife again, and while she was saddened by this, Dad was devastated. His face sagged every time Mother turned a woman away. 'What if I have a migraine when she goes into labor?'

84

she told him. 'What if I can't remember what herbs I've given her, or the baby's heart rate?'

In the end it wasn't Dad who convinced Mother to midwife again. She convinced herself, perhaps because it was a part of herself she couldn't surrender without some kind of struggle. That winter, she midwifed two babies that I remember. After the first she came home sickly and pale, as if bringing that life into the world had taken a measure of her own. She was shut in the basement when the second call came. She drove to the birth in dark glasses, trying to peer through the waves distorting her vision. By the time she arrived the headache was blinding, pulsing, driving out all thought. She locked herself in a back room and her assistant delivered the baby. After that, Mother was no longer the Midwife. On the next birth, she used the bulk of her fee to hire a second midwife, to supervise her. Everyone was supervising her now, it seemed. She had been an expert, an uncontested power; now she had to ask her ten-year-old daughter whether she'd eaten lunch. That winter was long and dark, and I wondered if sometimes Mother was staying in bed even when she didn't have a migraine.

At Christmas, someone gave her an expensive bottle of blended essential oils. It helped her headaches, but at fifty dollars for a third of an ounce, we couldn't afford it. Mother decided to make her own. She began buying single, unmixed oils — eucalyptus and helichrysum, sandalwood and ravensara — and the house, which for years had smelled of earthy bark and bitter leaves, suddenly smelled of lavender and chamomile.

She spent whole days blending oils, making adjustments to achieve specific fragrances and attributes. She worked with a pad and pen so she could record every step as she took it. The oils were much more expensive than the tinctures; it was devastating when she had to throw out a batch because she couldn't remember whether she'd added the spruce. She made an oil for migraines and an oil for menstrual cramps, one for sore muscles and one for heart palpitations. In the coming years she would invent dozens more.

To create her formulas, Mother took up something called 'muscle testing,' which she explained to me as 'asking the body what it needs and letting it answer.' Mother would say to herself, aloud, 'I have a migraine. What will make it better?' Then she would pick up a bottle of oil, press it to her chest and, with her eyes closed, say, 'Do I need *this*?' If her body swayed forward it meant yes, the oil would help her headache. If her body swayed backward it meant no, and she would test something else.

As she became more skilled, Mother went from using her whole body to only her fingers. She would cross her middle and index fingers, then flex slightly to try to uncross them, asking herself a question. If the fingers remained entwined that meant yes; if they parted it was no. The sound produced by this method was faint but unmistakable: each time the pad of her middle finger slipped across the nail of her index, there was a fleshy *click*.

Mother used muscle testing to experiment with other methods of healing. Diagrams of chakras and pressure points appeared around the house, and she began charging clients for something called 'energy work.' I didn't know what that meant until one afternoon when Mother called me and Richard into the back room. A woman named Susan was there. Mother's eyes were closed and her left hand was resting on Susan's. The fingers on her other hand were crossed, and she was whispering questions to herself. After a few she turned to the woman and said, 'Your relationship with your father is damaging your kidneys. Think of him while we adjust the chakra.' Mother explained that energy work is most effective when several people are present. 'So we can draw from everyone's energy,' she said. Mother pointed to my forehead and told me to tap the center, between my eyebrows, while with my other hand I was to grab Susan's arm. Richard was to tap a pressure point on his chest while reaching out to me with his other hand, and Mother was to hold a point in her palm while touching Richard with her foot. 'That's it,' she said as I took my brother's arm. We stood in silence for ten minutes, a human chain.

When I think of that afternoon, what I remember first is the awkwardness of it: Mother said she could feel the hot energy moving through our bodies, but I felt nothing. Mother and Richard stood still, eyes shut, breath shallow. They could feel the energy and were transported by it. I fidgeted. I tried to focus, then worried that I was ruining things for Susan, that I was a break in the chain, that Mother and Richard's healing power would never reach her because I was failing to conduct it. When the ten minutes were up, Susan gave Mother twenty dollars and the next customer came in.

If I was skeptical, my skepticism was not entirely my fault. It was the result of my not being able to decide which of my mothers to trust. A year before the accident, when Mother had first heard of muscle testing and energy work, she'd dismissed both as wishful thinking. 'People want a miracle,' she'd told me. 'They'll swallow anything if it brings them hope, if it lets them believe they're getting better. But there's no such thing as magic. Nutrition, exercise and a careful study of herbal properties, that's all there is. But when they're suffering, people can't accept that.'

Now Mother said that healing was spiritual and limitless. Muscle testing, she explained to me, was a kind of prayer, a divine supplication. An act of faith in which God spoke through her fingers. In some moments I believed her, this wise woman with an answer to every question; but I could never quite forget the words of that other woman, that other mother, who was also wise. *There's no such thing as magic.*

One day Mother announced that she had reached a new skill level. 'I no longer need to say the question aloud,' she said. 'I can just think it.'

That's when I began to notice Mother moving around the house, her hand resting lightly on various objects as she muttered to herself, her fingers flexing in a steady rhythm. If she was making bread and wasn't sure how much flour she'd added. *Click click click.* If she was mixing oils and couldn't remember whether she'd added frankincense. *Click click click.* She'd sit down to read her scriptures for thirty minutes, forget what time she'd started, then muscle-test how long it had been. *Click click click.*

Mother began to muscle-test compulsively, unaware she was doing it, whenever she grew tired of a conversation, whenever the ambiguities of her memory, or even just those of normal life, left her unsatisfied. Her features would slacken, her face become vacant, and her fingers would click like crickets at dusk.

Dad was rapturous. 'Them doctors can't tell what's wrong just by touching you,' he said, glowing. 'But Mother can!'

★ ★ ★

The memory of Tyler haunted me that winter. I remembered the day he left, how strange it was to see his car bumping down the hill loaded with boxes. I couldn't imagine where he was now, but sometimes I wondered if perhaps school was less evil than Dad thought, because Tyler was the least evil person I knew, and he loved school — loved it more, it seemed, than he loved us.

The seed of curiosity had been planted; it needed nothing more than time and boredom to grow. Sometimes, when I was stripping copper from a radiator or throwing the five hundredth chunk of steel into the bin, I'd find myself imagining the classrooms where Tyler was spending his days. My interest grew more acute with every deadening hour in the junkyard, until one day I had a bizarre thought: that I should enroll in the public school.

Mother had always said we could go to school if we wanted. We just had to ask Dad, she said. Then we could go.

But I didn't ask. There was something in the hard line of my father's face, in the quiet sigh of supplication he made every morning before he began family prayer, that made me think my curiosity was an obscenity, an affront to all he'd sacrificed to raise me.

I made some effort to keep up my schooling in the free time I had between scrapping and helping Mother make tinctures and blend oils. Mother had given up homeschooling by then, but still had a computer, and there were books in the basement. I found the science book, with its colorful illustrations, and the math book I remembered from years before. I even located a faded green book of history. But when I sat down to study I nearly always fell asleep. The pages were glossy and soft, made softer by the hours I'd spent hauling scrap.

When Dad saw me with one of those books, he'd try to get me away from them. Perhaps he was remembering Tyler. Perhaps he thought if he could just distract me for a few years, the danger would pass. So he made up jobs for me to do, whether they needed doing or not. One afternoon, after he'd caught me looking at the math book, he and I spent an hour hauling buckets of water across the field to his fruit trees, which wouldn't have been at all unusual except it was during a rainstorm.

But if Dad was trying to keep his children from being overly interested in school and books — from being seduced by the Illuminati, like Tyler had been — he would have done better to turn his attention to Richard. Richard was also supposed to spend his afternoons making tinctures for Mother, but he almost never did. Instead, he'd disappear. I don't know if Mother knew where he went, but I did. In the afternoons, Richard could nearly always be found in the dark basement, wedged in the crawl space between the couch and the wall, an encyclopedia propped open in front of him. If Dad happened by he'd turn the light off, muttering about wasted electricity. Then I'd find some excuse to go downstairs so I could turn it back on. If Dad came through again, a snarl would sound through the house, and Mother would have to sit through a lecture on leaving lights on in empty rooms. She never scolded me, which makes me wonder if she did know where Richard was. If I couldn't get back down to turn on the light, Richard would pull the book to his nose and read in the dark; he wanted to read that badly. He wanted to read the *encyclopedia* that badly.

★ ★ ★

Tyler was gone. There was hardly a trace he'd ever lived in the house, except one: every night, after dinner, I would close the door to my room and pull Tyler's old boom box from under my bed. I'd drag his desk into my room, and while the choir sang I would settle into his chair and study, just as I'd seen him do on a thousand nights. I didn't study history or math. I studied religion.

I read the Book of Mormon twice. I read the New Testament, once quickly, then a second time more slowly, pausing to make notes, to cross-reference, and even to write short essays on doctrines like faith and sacrifice. No one read the essays; I wrote them for myself, the way I imagined Tyler had studied for himself and himself only. I worked through the Old Testament next, then I read Dad's books, which were mostly compilations of the speeches, letters and journals of the early Mormon prophets. Their language was of the nineteenth century — stiff, winding, but exact — and at first I understood nothing. But over time my eyes and ears adjusted, so that I began to feel at home with those fragments of my people's history: stories of pioneers, my ancestors, striking out across the American wilderness. While the stories were vivid, the lectures were abstract, treatises on obscure philosophical subjects, and it was to these abstractions that I devoted most of my study.

In retrospect, I see that *this* was my education, the one that would matter: the hours I spent sitting at a borrowed desk, struggling to parse narrow strands of Mormon doctrine in mimicry of a brother who'd deserted me. The skill I was learning was a crucial one, the patience to read things I could not yet understand.

★ ★ ★

By the time the snow on the mountain began to melt, my hands were thickly callused. A season in the junkyard had honed my reflexes: I'd learned to listen for the low grunt that escaped Dad's lips whenever he tossed something heavy, and when I heard it I hit the dirt. I spent so much time flat in the mud, I didn't salvage much. Dad joked I was as slow as molasses running uphill.

The memory of Tyler had faded, and with it had faded his music, drowned out by the crack of metal crashing into metal. Those were the sounds that played in my head at night now — the jingle of corrugated tin, the short tap of copper wire, the thunder of iron.

I had entered into the new reality. I saw the world through my father's eyes. I saw the angels, or at least I imagined I saw them, watching us scrap, stepping forward and catching the car batteries or jagged lengths of steel tubing that Dad launched across the yard. I'd stopped shouting at Dad for throwing them. Instead, I prayed.

I worked faster when I salvaged alone, so one morning when Dad was in the northern tip of the yard, near the mountain, I headed for the southern tip, near the pasture. I filled a bin with two thousand pounds of iron; then, my arms aching, I ran to find Dad. The bin had to be emptied, and I couldn't operate the loader — a massive forklift with a telescopic arm and wide, black wheels that were taller than I was. The loader would raise the bin some twenty-five feet into the air and then, with the boom extended, tilt the forks so the scrap could slide out, raining down into the trailer with a tremendous clamor. The trailer was a fifty-foot flatbed rigged for scrapping, essentially a giant bucket. Its walls were made of thick iron sheets that reached eight feet from the bed. The trailer could hold between fifteen and twenty bins, or about forty thousand pounds of iron.

I found Dad in the field, lighting a fire to burn the insulation from a tangle of copper wires. I told him the bin was ready, and he walked back with me and climbed into the loader. He waved at the trailer. 'We'll get more in if you settle the iron after it's been dumped. Hop in.'

I didn't understand. He wanted to dump the bin with me in it? 'I'll climb up after you've dumped the load,' I said.

'No, this'll be faster,' Dad said. 'I'll pause when the bin's level with the trailer wall so you can climb out. Then you can run along the wall and perch on top of the cab until the dump is finished.'

I settled myself on a length of iron. Dad jammed the forks under the bin, then lifted me and the scrap and began driving, full throttle, toward the trailer's head. I could barely hold on. On the last turn, the bucket swung with such force that a spike of iron was flung toward me. It pierced the inside of my leg, an inch below my knee, sliding into the tissue like a knife into warm butter. I tried to pull it out but the load had shifted, and it was partially buried. I heard the soft groaning of hydraulic pumps as the boom extended. The groaning stopped when the bin was level with the trailer. Dad was giving me time to climb onto the trailer wall but I was pinned. 'I'm stuck!' I shouted, only the growl of the loader's engine was too loud. I wondered if Dad would wait to dump the bin until he saw me sitting safely on the semi's cab, but even as I wondered I knew he wouldn't. Time was still stalking.

The hydraulics groaned and the bin raised another eight feet. Dumping position. I shouted again, higher this time, then lower, trying to find a pitch that would pierce through the drone of the engine. The bin began its tilt, slowly at first, then quickly. I was pinned near the back. I wrapped my hands around the bin's top wall, knowing this would give me a ledge to grasp when the bin was vertical. As the bin continued to pitch, the scrap at the front began to slide forward, bit by bit, a great iron glacier breaking apart. The spike was still embedded in my leg, dragging me downward. My grip had slipped and I'd begun to slide when the spike finally ripped from me and fell away, smashing into the trailer with a tremendous crash. I was now free, but falling. I flailed my arms, willing them to seize something that wasn't plunging downward. My palm caught hold of the bin's side wall, which was now nearly vertical. I pulled myself toward it and hoisted my body over its edge, then continued my fall. Because I was now falling from the side of the bin and not the front, I hoped — I prayed — that I was falling toward the ground and not toward the trailer, which was at that moment a fury of grinding metal. I sank, seeing only blue sky, waiting to feel either the stab of sharp iron or the jolt of solid earth.

My back struck iron: the trailer's wall. My feet snapped over my head and I continued my graceless plunge to the ground. The first fall was seven or eight feet, the second perhaps ten. I was relieved to taste dirt.

I lay on my back for perhaps fifteen seconds before the engine growled to silence and I heard Dad's heavy step.

'What happened?' he said, kneeling next to me.

'I fell out,' I wheezed. The wind had been knocked out of me, and there was a powerful throbbing in my back, as if I'd been cut in two.

'How'd you manage that?' Dad said. His tone was sympathetic but disappointed. I felt stupid. *I should have been able to do it*, I thought. *It's a simple thing*.

Dad examined the gash in my leg, which had been ripped wide as the spike had fallen away. It looked like a pothole; the tissue had simply sunk out of sight. Dad slipped out of his flannel shirt and pressed it to my leg. 'Go on home,' he said. 'Mother will stop the bleeding.'

I limped through the pasture until Dad was out of sight, then collapsed in the wheatgrass. I was shaking, gulping mouthfuls of air that never made it to my lungs. I didn't understand why I was crying. I was alive. I would be fine. The angels had done their part. So why couldn't I stop trembling?

I was light-headed when I crossed the last field and approached the house, but I burst through the back door, as I'd seen my brothers do, as

Robert and Emma had done, shouting for Mother. When she saw the crimson footprints streaked across the linoleum, she fetched the homeopathic she used to treat hemorrhages and shock, called Rescue Remedy, and put twelve drops of the clear, tasteless liquid under my tongue. She rested her left hand lightly on the gash and crossed the fingers of her right. Her eyes closed. *Click click click.* 'There's no tetanus,' she said. 'The wound will close. Eventually. But it'll leave a nasty scar.'

She turned me onto my stomach and examined the bruise — a patch of deep purple the size of a human head — that had formed a few inches above my hip. Again her fingers crossed and her eyes closed. *Click click click.*

'You've damaged your kidney,' she said. 'We'd better make a fresh batch of juniper and mullein flower.'

★ ★ ★

The gash below my knee had formed a scab — dark and shiny, a black river flowing through pink flesh — when I came to a decision.

I chose a Sunday evening, when Dad was resting on the couch, his Bible propped open in his lap. I stood in front of him for what felt like hours, but he didn't look up, so I blurted out what I'd come to say: 'I want to go to school.'

He seemed not to have heard me.

'I've prayed, and I want to go,' I said.

Finally, Dad looked up and straight ahead, his gaze fixed on something behind me. The silence settled, its presence heavy. 'In this family,' he said, 'we obey the commandments of the Lord.'

He picked up his Bible and his eyes twitched as they jumped from line to line. I turned to leave, but before I reached the doorway Dad spoke again. 'You remember Jacob and Esau?'

'I remember,' I said.

He returned to his reading, and I left quietly. I did not need any explanation; I knew what the story meant. It meant that I was not the daughter he had raised, the daughter of faith. I had tried to sell my birthright for a mess of pottage.

7

The Lord Will Provide

It was a rainless summer. The sun blazed across the sky each afternoon, scorching the mountain with its arid, desiccating heat, so that each morning when I crossed the field to the barn, I felt stalks of wild wheat crackle and break beneath my feet.

I spent an amber morning making the Rescue Remedy homeopathic for Mother. I would take fifteen drops from the base formula — which was kept in Mother's sewing cupboard, where it would not be used or polluted — and add them to a small bottle of distilled water. Then I would make a circle with my index finger and my thumb, and push the bottle through the circle. The strength of the homeopathic, Mother said, depended on how many passes the bottle made through my fingers, how many times it drew on my energy. Usually I stopped at fifty.

Dad and Luke were on the mountain, in the junkyard above the upper pasture, a quarter mile from the house. They were preparing cars for the crusher, which Dad had hired for later that week. Luke was seventeen. He had a lean, muscular build and, when outdoors, an easy smile. Luke and Dad were draining gasoline from the tanks. The crusher won't take a car with the fuel tank attached, because there's a risk of explosion, so every tank had to be drained and removed. It was slow work, puncturing the tank with a hammer and stake, then waiting for the fuel to drip out so the tank could be safely removed with a cutting torch. Dad had devised a shortcut: an enormous skewer, eight feet tall, of thick iron. Dad would lift a car with the forklift, and Luke would guide him until the car's tank was suspended directly over the spike. Then Dad would drop the forks. If all went well, the car would be impaled on the spike and gasoline would gush from the tank, streaming down the spike and into the flat-bottom container Dad had welded in place to collect it.

By noon, they had drained somewhere between thirty and forty cars. Luke had collected the fuel in five-gallon buckets, which he began to haul across the yard to Dad's flatbed. On one pass he stumbled, drenching his jeans in a gallon of gas. The summer sun dried the denim in a matter of minutes. He finished hauling the buckets, then went home for lunch.

I remember that lunch with unsettling clarity. I remember the clammy smell of beef-and-potato casserole, and the jingle of ice cubes tumbling into tall glasses, which sweated in the summer heat. I remember Mother telling me I was on dish duty, because she was leaving for Utah after lunch to consult for another midwife on a complicated pregnancy. She said she might not make it home for dinner but there was hamburger in the freezer.

I remember laughing the whole hour. Dad lay on the kitchen floor cracking jokes about an ordinance that had recently passed in our little farming village. A stray dog had bitten a boy and everyone was up in arms. The mayor had decided to limit dog ownership to two dogs per family, even though the attacking dog hadn't belonged to anybody at all.

'These genius socialists,' Dad said. 'They'd drown staring up at the rain if you didn't build a roof over them.' I laughed so hard at that my stomach ached.

Luke had forgotten all about the gasoline by the time he and Dad walked back up the mountain and readied the cutting torch, but when he jammed the torch into his hip and struck flint to steel, flames burst from the tiny spark and engulfed his leg.

The part we would remember, would tell and retell so many times it became family folklore, was that Luke was unable to get out of his gasoline-soaked jeans. That morning, like every morning, he had hitched up his trousers with a yard of baling twine, which is smooth and slippery, and needs a horseman's knot to stay in place. His footwear didn't help, either: bulbous steel-toed boots so tattered that for weeks he'd been duct-taping them on each morning, then cutting them off each night with his pocketknife. Luke might have severed the twine and hacked through the boots in a matter of seconds, but he went mad with panic and took off, dashing like a marked buck, spreading fire through the sagebrush and wheat grass, which were baked and brittle from the parched summer.

★   ★   ★

I'd stacked the dirty dishes and was filling the kitchen sink when I heard it — a shrill, strangled cry that began in one key and ended in another. There was no question it was human. I'd never heard an animal bellow like that, with such fluctuations in tone and pitch.

I ran outside and saw Luke hobbling across the grass. He screamed for Mother, then collapsed. That's when I saw that the jeans on his left leg were gone, melted away. Parts of the leg were livid, red and bloody; others were bleached and dead. Papery ropes of skin wrapped delicately around his thigh and down his calf, like wax dripping from a cheap candle.

His eyes rolled back in his head.

I bolted back into the house. I'd packed the new bottles of Rescue Remedy, but the base formula still sat on the counter. I snatched it and ran outside, then dumped half the bottle between Luke's twitching lips. There was no change. His eyes were marble white.

One brown iris slipped into view, then the other. He began to mumble, then to scream. 'It's on fire! It's on fire!' he roared. A chill passed through him and his teeth clattered; he was shivering.

I was only ten, and in that moment I felt very much a child. Luke was my big brother; I thought he would know what to do, so I grabbed his shoulders and shook him, hard. 'Should I make you cold or make you hot?' I shouted. He answered with a gasp.

The burn was the injury, I reasoned. It made sense to treat it first. I fetched a pack of ice from

102

the chest freezer on the patio, but when the pack touched his leg he screamed — a back-arching, eye-popping scream that made my brain claw at my skull. I needed another way to cool the leg. I considered unloading the chest freezer and putting Luke inside it, but the freezer would work only if the lid was shut, and then he'd suffocate.

I mentally searched the house. We had a large garbage can, a blue whale of a bin. It was splattered with bits of rotted food, so rank we kept it shut away in a closet. I sprinted into the house and emptied it onto the linoleum, noting the dead mouse Richard had tossed in the day before, then I carried the bin outside and sprayed it out with the garden hose. I knew I should clean it more thoroughly, maybe with dish soap, but looking at Luke, the way he was writhing on the grass, I didn't feel I had time. With the last bit of slop blasted away, I righted the bin and filled it with water.

Luke was scrambling toward me to put his leg in when I heard an echo of my mother's voice. She was telling someone that the real worry with a burn isn't the damaged tissue, but infection.

'Luke!' I shouted. 'Don't! Don't put your leg in!'

He ignored me and continued crawling toward the bin. He had a cold look in his eye that said nothing mattered except the fire burning from his leg into his brain. I moved quickly. I shoved the bin, and a great wave of water heaved over the grass. Luke made a gargled noise, as if he were choking.

I ran back into the kitchen and found the bags that fit the can, then held one open for Luke and told him to put his leg in. He didn't move, but he allowed me to pull the bag over the raw flesh. I righted the can and stuffed the garden hose inside. While the bin filled, I helped Luke balance on one foot and lower his burned leg, now wrapped in black plastic, into the garbage can. The afternoon air was sweltering; the water would warm quickly; I tossed in the pack of ice.

It didn't take long — twenty minutes, maybe thirty — before Luke seemed in his right mind, calm and able to prop himself up. Then Richard wandered up from the basement. The garbage can was smack in the middle of the lawn, ten feet from any shade, and the afternoon sun was strong. Full of water, the can was too heavy for us to move, and Luke refused to take out his leg, even for a minute. I fetched a straw sombrero Grandma had given us in Arizona. Luke's teeth were still chattering so I also brought a wool blanket. And there he stood, a sombrero on his head, a wool blanket around his shoulders, and his leg in a garbage can. He looked something between homeless and on vacation.

The sun warmed the water; Luke began to shift uncomfortably. I returned to the chest freezer but there was no more ice, just a dozen bags of frozen vegetables, so I dumped them in. The result was a muddy soup with bits of peas and carrots.

Dad wandered home sometime after this, I couldn't say how long, a gaunt, defeated look on his face. Quiet now, Luke was resting, or as near

104

to resting as he could be standing up. Dad wheeled the bin into the shade because, despite the hat, Luke's hands and arms had turned red with sunburn. Dad said the best thing to do was leave the leg where it was until Mother came home.

Mother's car appeared on the highway around six. I met her halfway up the hill and told her what had happened. She rushed to Luke and said she needed to see the leg, so he lifted it out, dripping. The plastic bag clung to the wound. Mother didn't want to tear the fragile tissue, so she cut the bag away slowly, carefully, until the leg was visible. There was very little blood and even fewer blisters, as both require skin and Luke didn't have much. Mother's face turned a grayish yellow, but she was calm. She closed her eyes and crossed her fingers, then asked aloud whether the wound was infected. *Click click click.*

'You were lucky this time, Tara,' she said. 'But what were you thinking, putting a burn into a *garbage* can?'

Dad carried Luke inside and Mother fetched her scalpel. It took her and Dad most of the evening to cut away the dead flesh. Luke tried not to scream, but when they pried up and stretched bits of his skin, trying to see where the dead flesh ended and the living began, he exhaled in great gusts and tears slid from his eyes.

Mother dressed the leg in mullein and comfrey salve, her own recipe. She was good with burns — they were a specialty of hers — but I could tell she was worried. She said she'd never seen one as bad as Luke's. She didn't know what would happen.

* * *

Mother and I stayed by Luke's bed that first night. He barely slept, he was so delirious with fever and pain. For the fever we put ice on his face and chest; for the pain we gave him lobelia, blue vervain and skullcap. This was another of Mother's recipes. I'd taken it after I'd fallen from the scrap bin, to dull the throbbing in my leg while I waited for the gash to close, but as near as I could tell it had no effect.

I believed hospital drugs were an abomination to God, but if I'd had morphine that night, I'd have given it to Luke. The pain robbed him of breath. He lay propped up in his bed, beads of sweat falling from his forehead onto his chest, holding his breath until he turned red, then purple, as if depriving his brain of oxygen was the only way he could make it through the next minute. When the pain in his lungs overtook the pain of the burn, he would release the air in a great, gasping cry — a cry of relief for his lungs, of agony for his leg.

I tended him alone the second night so Mother could rest. I slept lightly, waking at the first sounds of fussing, at the slightest shifting of weight, so I could fetch the ice and tinctures before Luke became fully conscious and the pain gripped him. On the third night, Mother tended him and I stood in the doorway, listening to his gasps, watching Mother watch him, her face hollow, her eyes

106

swollen with worry and exhaustion.

When I slept, I dreamed. I dreamed about the fire I hadn't seen. I dreamed it was me lying in that bed, my body wrapped in loose bandages, mummified. Mother knelt on the floor beside me, pressing my plastered hand the way she pressed Luke's, dabbing my forehead, praying.

Luke didn't go to church that Sunday, or the Sunday after that, or the one after that. Dad told us to tell people Luke was sick. He said there'd be trouble if the Government found out about Luke's leg, that the Feds would take us kids away. That they would put Luke in a hospital, where his leg would get infected and he would die.

About three weeks after the fire, Mother announced that the skin around the edges of the burn had begun to grow back, and that she had hope for even the worst patches. By then Luke was sitting up, and a week later, when the first cold spell hit, he could stand for a minute or two on crutches. Before long, he was thumping around the house, thin as a string bean, swallowing buckets of food to regain the weight he'd lost. By then, the twine was a family fable.

'A man ought to have a real belt,' Dad said at breakfast on the day Luke was well enough to return to the junkyard, handing him a leather strap with a steel buckle.

'Not Luke,' Richard said. 'He prefers twine, you know how fashionable he is.'

Luke grinned. 'Beauty's everything,' he said.

★ ★ ★

For eighteen years I never thought of that day, not in any probing way. The few times my reminiscing carried me back to that torrid afternoon, what I remembered first was the belt. *Luke,* I would think. *You wild dog. I wonder, do you still wear twine?*

Now, at age twenty-nine, I sit down to write, to reconstruct the incident from the echoes and shouts of a tired memory. I scratch it out. When I get to the end, I pause. There's an inconsistency, a ghost in this story.

I read it. I read it again. And there it is.

Who put out the fire?

A long-dormant voice says, *Dad did.*

But Luke was alone when I found him. If Dad had been with Luke on the mountain, he would have brought him to the house, would have treated the burn. Dad was away on a job somewhere, that's why Luke had had to get himself down the mountain. Why his leg had been treated by a ten-year-old. Why it had ended up in a garbage can.

I decide to ask Richard. He's older than I, and has a sharper memory. Besides, last I heard, Luke no longer has a telephone.

I call. The first thing Richard remembers is the twine, which, true to his nature, he refers to as a 'baling implement.' Next he remembers the spilled gasoline. I ask how Luke managed to put out the fire and get himself down the mountain, given that he was in shock when I found him. Dad was with him, Richard says flatly.

Right.

Then why wasn't Dad at the house?

Richard says, Because Luke had run through the weeds and set the mountain afire. You remember that summer. Dry, scorching. You can't go starting forest fires in farm country during a dry summer. So Dad put Luke in the truck and told him to drive to the house, to Mother. Only Mother was gone.

Right.

I think it over for a few days, then sit back down to write. Dad is there in the beginning — Dad with his funny jokes about socialists and dogs and the roof that keeps liberals from drowning. Then Dad and Luke go back up the mountain, Mother drives away and I turn the tap to fill the kitchen sink. Again. For the third time it feels like.

On the mountain something is happening. I can only imagine it but I see it clearly, more clearly than if it were a memory. The cars are stacked and waiting, their fuel tanks ruptured and drained. Dad waves at a tower of cars and says, 'Luke, cut off those tanks, yeah?' And Luke says, 'Sure thing, Dad.' He lays the torch against his hip and strikes flint. Flames erupt from nowhere and take him. He screams, fumbles with the twine, screams again, and takes off through the weeds.

Dad chases him, orders him to stand still. It's probably the first time in his whole life that Luke doesn't do something when Dad is telling him to. Luke is fast but Dad is smart. He takes a shortcut through a pyramid of cars and tackles Luke, slamming him to the ground.

I can't picture what happens next, because

nobody ever told me how Dad put out the fire on Luke's leg. Then a memory surfaces — of Dad, that night in the kitchen, wincing as Mother slathers salve on his hands, which are red and blistering — and I know what he must have done.

Luke is no longer on fire.

I try to imagine the moment of decision. Dad looks at the weeds, which are burning fast, thirsty for flame in that quivering heat. He looks at his son. He thinks if he can choke the flames while they're young, he can prevent a wildfire, maybe save the house.

Luke seems lucid. His brain hasn't processed what's happened; the pain hasn't set in. *The Lord will provide*, I imagine Dad thinking. *God left him conscious.*

I imagine Dad praying aloud, his eyes drawn heavenward, as he carries his son to the truck and sets him in the driver's seat. Dad shifts the engine into first, the truck starts its roll. It's going at a good speed now, Luke is gripping the wheel. Dad jumps from the moving truck, hits the ground hard and rolls, then runs back toward the brushfire, which has spread wider and grown taller. *The Lord will provide*, he chants, then he takes off his shirt and begins to beat back the flames.[3]

8

Tiny Harlots

I wanted to get away from the junkyard and there was only one way to do that, which was the way Audrey had done it: by getting a job so I wouldn't be at the house when Dad rounded up his crew. The trouble was, I was eleven.

I biked a mile into the dusty center of our little village. There wasn't much there, just a church, a post office and a gas station called Papa Jay's. I went into the post office. Behind the counter was an older lady whose name I knew was Myrna Moyle, because Myrna and her husband Jay (Papa Jay) owned the gas station. Dad said they'd been behind the city ordinance limiting dog ownership to two dogs per family. They'd proposed other ordinances, too, and now every Sunday Dad came home from church shouting about Myrna and Jay Moyle, and how they were from Monterey or Seattle or wherever and thought they could impose West Coast socialism on the good people of Idaho.

I asked Myrna if I could put a card up on the board. She asked what the card was for. I said I hoped I could find jobs babysitting.

'What times are you available?' she said.

'Anytime, all the time.'

'You mean after school?'

'I mean all the time.'

111

Myrna looked at me and tilted her head. 'My daughter Mary needs someone to tend her youngest. I'll ask her.'

Mary taught nursing at the school, which Dad said was just about as brainwashed as a person could get, to be working for the Medical Establishment *and* the Government both. I thought maybe he wouldn't let me work for her, but he did, and pretty soon I was babysitting Mary's daughter every Monday, Wednesday and Friday morning. Then Mary had a friend, Eve, who needed a babysitter for her three children on Tuesdays and Thursdays.

A mile down the road, a man named Randy ran a business out of his home, selling cashews, almonds and macadamias. He stopped by the post office one afternoon and chatted with Myrna about how tired he was of packing the boxes himself, how he wished he could hire some kids but they were all tied up with football and band.

'There's at least one kid in this town who isn't,' Myrna said. 'And I think she'd be real eager.' She pointed to my card, and soon I was babysitting from eight until noon Monday to Friday, then going to Randy's to pack cashews until supper. I wasn't paid much, but as I'd never been paid anything before, it felt like a lot.

People at church said Mary could play the piano beautifully. They used the word 'professional.' I didn't know what that meant until one Sunday when Mary played a piano solo for the congregation. The music stopped my breath. I'd heard the piano played countless times before, to

112

accompany hymns, but when Mary played it, the sound was nothing like that formless clunking. It was liquid, it was air. It was rock one moment and wind the next.

The next day, when Mary returned from the school, I asked her if instead of money she would give me lessons. We perched on the piano bench and she showed me a few finger exercises. Then she asked what else I was learning besides the piano. Dad had told me what to say when people asked about my schooling. 'I do school every day,' I said.

'Do you meet other kids?' she asked. 'Do you have friends?'

'Sure,' I said. Mary returned to the lesson. When we'd finished and I was ready to go, she said, 'My sister Caroline teaches dance every Wednesday in the back of Papa Jay's. There are lots of girls your age. You could join.'

That Wednesday, I left Randy's early and pedaled to the gas station. I wore jeans, a large gray T-shirt, and steel-toed boots; the other girls wore black leotards and sheer, shimmering skirts, white tights and tiny ballet shoes the color of taffy. Caroline was younger than Mary. Her makeup was flawless and gold hoops flashed through chestnut curls.

She arranged us in rows, then showed us a short routine. A song played from a boom box in the corner. I'd never heard it before but the other girls knew it. I looked in the mirror at our reflection, at the twelve girls, sleek and shiny, pirouetting blurs of black, white and pink. Then at myself, large and gray.

113

When the lesson finished, Caroline told me to buy a leotard and dance shoes.

'I can't,' I said.

'Oh.' She looked uncomfortable. 'Maybe one of the girls can lend you one.'

She'd misunderstood. She thought I didn't have money. 'It isn't modest,' I said. Her lips parted in surprise. *These Californian Moyles*, I thought.

'Well, you can't dance in boots,' she said. 'I'll talk to your mother.'

A few days later, Mother drove me forty miles to a small shop whose shelves were lined with exotic shoes and strange acrylic costumes. Not one was modest. Mother went straight to the counter and told the attendant we needed a black leotard, white tights and jazz shoes.

'Keep those in your room,' Mother said as we left the store. She didn't need to say anything else. I already understood that I should not show the leotard to Dad.

That Wednesday, I wore the leotard and tights with my gray T-shirt over the top. The T-shirt reached almost to my knees, but even so I was ashamed to see so much of my legs. Dad said a righteous woman never shows anything above her ankle.

The other girls rarely spoke to me, but I loved being there with them. I loved the sensation of conformity. Learning to dance felt like learning to belong. I could memorize the movements and, in doing so, step into their minds, lunging when they lunged, reaching my arms upward in time with theirs. Sometimes, when I glanced at the

114

mirror and saw the tangle of our twirling forms, I couldn't immediately discern myself in the crowd. It didn't matter that I was wearing a gray T-shirt — a goose among swans. We moved together, a single flock.

We began rehearsals for the Christmas recital, and Caroline called Mother to discuss the costume. 'The skirt will be how long?' Mother said. 'And sheer? No, that's not going to work.' I heard Caroline say something about what the other girls in the class would want to wear. 'Tara can't wear that,' Mother said. 'If that's what the other girls are wearing, she will stay home.'

On the Wednesday after Caroline called Mother, I arrived at Papa Jay's a few minutes early. The younger class had just finished, and the store was flooded with six-year-olds, prancing for their mothers in red velvet hats and skirts sparkling with sequins of deep scarlet. I watched them wiggle and leap through the aisles, their thin legs covered only by sheer tights. I thought they looked like tiny harlots.

The rest of my class arrived. When they saw the outfits, they rushed into the studio to see what Caroline had for *them*. Caroline was standing next to a cardboard box full of large gray sweatshirts. She began handing them out. 'Here are your costumes!' she said. The girls held up their sweatshirts, eyebrows raised in disbelief. They had expected chiffon or ribbon, not Fruit of the Loom. Caroline had tried to make the sweatshirts more appealing by sewing large Santas, bordered with glitter, on the fronts, but this only made the dingy cotton seem dingier.

115

Mother hadn't told Dad about the recital, and neither had I. I didn't ask him to come. There was an instinct at work in me, a learned intuition. The day of the recital, Mother told Dad I had a 'thing' that night. Dad asked a lot of questions, which surprised Mother, and after a few minutes she admitted it was a dance recital. Dad grimaced when Mother told him I'd been taking lessons from Caroline Moyle, and I thought he was going to start talking about California socialism again, but he didn't. Instead he got his coat and the three of us walked to the car.

The recital was held at the church. Everyone was there, with flashing cameras and bulky camcorders. I changed into my costume in the same room where I attended Sunday school. The other girls chatted cheerfully; I pulled on my sweatshirt, trying to stretch the material a few more inches. I was still tugging it downward when we lined up on the stage.

Music played from a stereo on the piano and we began to dance, our feet tapping in sequence. Next we were supposed to leap, reach upward and spin. My feet remained planted. Instead of flinging my arms above my head, I lifted them only to my shoulders. When the other girls crouched to slap the stage, I tilted; when we were to cartwheel, I swayed, refusing to allow gravity to do its work, to draw the sweatshirt any higher up my legs.

The music ended. The girls glared at me as we left the stage — I had ruined the performance — but I could barely see them. Only one person in that room felt real to me, and that was Dad. I searched the audience and recognized him easily. He was standing in the back, the lights from the stage flickering off his square glasses. His expression was stiff, impassive, but I could see anger in it.

The drive home was only a mile; it felt like a hundred. I sat in the backseat and listened to my father shout. How could Mother have let me sin so openly? Was this why she'd kept the recital from him? Mother listened for a moment, chewing her lip, then threw her hands in the air and said that she'd had no idea the costume would be so immodest. 'I'm furious with Caroline Moyle!' she said.

I leaned forward to see Mother's face, wanting her to look at me, to see the question I was mentally asking her, because I didn't understand, not at all. I knew Mother wasn't furious with Caroline, because I knew Mother had seen the sweatshirt days before. She had even called Caroline and thanked her for choosing a costume I could wear. Mother turned her head toward the window.

I stared at the gray hairs on the back of Dad's head. He was sitting quietly, listening to Mother, who continued to insult Caroline, to say how shocking the costumes were, how obscene. Dad nodded as we bumped up the icy driveway, becoming less angry with every word from Mother.

The rest of the night was taken up by my father's lecture. He said Caroline's class was one of Satan's deceptions, like the public school, because it claimed to be one thing when really it was another. It *claimed* to teach dance, but instead it taught immodesty, promiscuity. Satan was shrewd, Dad said. By calling it 'dance,' he had convinced good Mormons to accept the sight of their daughters jumping about like whores in the Lord's house. That fact offended Dad more than anything else: that such a lewd display had taken place in a church.

After he had worn himself out and gone to bed, I crawled under my covers and stared into the black. There was a knock at my door. It was Mother. 'I should have known better,' she said. 'I should have seen that class for what it was.'

★ ★ ★

Mother must have felt guilty after the recital, because in the weeks that followed she searched for something else I could do, something Dad wouldn't forbid. She'd noticed the hours I spent in my room with Tyler's old boom box, listening to the Mormon Tabernacle Choir, so she began looking for a voice teacher. It took a few weeks to find one, and another few weeks to persuade the teacher to take me. The lessons were much more expensive than the dance class had been, but Mother paid for them with the money she made selling oils.

The teacher was tall and thin, with long fingernails that clicked as they flew across the piano keys. She straightened my posture by pulling the hair at the base of my neck until I'd tucked in my chin, then she stretched me out on

118

the floor and stepped on my stomach to strengthen my diaphragm. She was obsessed with balance and often slapped my knees to remind me to stand powerfully, to take up my own space.

After a few lessons, she announced that I was ready to sing in church. It was arranged, she said. I would sing a hymn in front of the congregation that Sunday.

The days slipped away quickly, as days do when you're dreading something. On Sunday morning, I stood at the pulpit and stared into the faces of the people below. There was Myrna and Papa Jay, and behind them Mary and Caroline. They looked sorry for me, like they thought I might humiliate myself.

Mother played the introduction. The music paused; it was time to sing. I might have had any number of thoughts at that moment. I might have thought of my teacher and her techniques — square stance, straight back, dropped jaw. Instead I thought of Tyler, and of lying on the carpet next to his desk, staring at his woolen-socked feet while the Mormon Tabernacle Choir chanted and trilled. He'd filled my head with their voices, which to me were more beautiful than anything except Buck's Peak.

Mother's fingers hovered over the keys. The pause had become awkward; the congregation shifted uncomfortably. I thought of the voices, of their strange contradictions — of the way they made sound float on air, of how that sound was soft like a warm wind, but so sharp it pierced. I reached for those voices, reached into my mind — and there they were. Nothing had ever felt so natural; it was as if I *thought* the sound, and by thinking it brought it into being. But reality had never yielded to my thoughts before.

The song finished and I returned to our pew. A prayer was offered to close the service, then the crowd rushed me. Women in floral prints smiled and clasped my hand, men in square black suits clapped my shoulder. The choir director invited me to join the choir, Brother Davis asked me to sing for the Rotary Club, and the bishop — the Mormon equivalent of a pastor — said he'd like me to sing my song at a funeral. I said yes to all of them.

Dad smiled at everyone. There was scarcely a person in the church that Dad hadn't called a gentile — for visiting a doctor or for sending their kids to the public school — but that day he seemed to forget about California socialism and the Illuminati. He stood next to me, a hand on my shoulder, graciously collecting compliments. 'We're very blessed,' he kept saying. 'Very blessed.' Papa Jay crossed the chapel and paused in front of our pew. He said I sang like one of God's own angels. Dad looked at him for a moment, then his eyes began to shine and he shook Papa Jay's hand like they were old friends.

I'd never seen this side of my father, but I would see it many times after — every time I sang. However long he'd worked in the junkyard, he was never too tired to drive across the valley to hear me. However bitter his feelings toward socialists like Papa Jay, they were never so bitter that, should those people praise my voice, Dad wouldn't put aside the great battle he was fighting against the Illuminati long enough to say, 'Yes, God has blessed us, we're very blessed.' It was as if, when I sang, Dad forgot for a moment that the world was a frightening place, that it would corrupt me, that I should be kept safe, sheltered, at home. He wanted my voice to be heard.

The theater in town was putting on a play, *Annie*, and my teacher said that if the director heard me sing, he would give me the lead. Mother warned me not to get my hopes up. She said we couldn't afford to drive the twelve miles to town four nights a week for rehearsals, and that even if we could, Dad would never allow me to spend time in town, alone, with who knows what kind of people.

I practiced the songs anyway because I liked them. One evening, I was in my room singing, 'The sun'll come out tomorrow,' when Dad came in for supper. He chewed his meatloaf quietly, and listened.

'I'll find the money,' he told Mother when they went to bed that night. 'You get her to that audition.'

9

Perfect in His Generations

The summer I sang the lead for *Annie* it was 1999. My father was in serious preparedness mode. Not since I was five, and the Weavers were under siege, had he been so certain that the Days of Abomination were upon us.

Dad called it Y2K. On January 1, he said, computer systems all over the world would fail. There would be no electricity, no telephones. All would sink into chaos, and this would usher in the Second Coming of Christ.

'How do you know the day?' I asked.

Dad said that the Government had programmed the computers with a six-digit calendar, which meant the year had only two digits. 'When nine-nine becomes oh-oh,' he said, 'the computers won't know what year it is. They'll shut down.'

'Can't they fix it?'

'Nope, can't be done,' Dad said. 'Man trusted his own strength, and his strength was weak.'

At church, Dad warned everyone about Y2K. He advised Papa Jay to get strong locks for his gas station, and maybe some defensive weaponry. 'That store will be the first thing looted in the famine,' Dad said. He told Brother Mumford that every righteous man should have, at minimum, a ten-year supply of food, fuel, guns and gold. Brother Mumford just whistled. 'We can't all be as righteous as you, Gene,' he said. 'Some of us are sinners!' No one listened. They went about their lives in the summer sun.

Meanwhile, my family boiled and skinned peaches, pitted apricots and churned apples into sauce. Everything was pressure-cooked, sealed, labeled, and stored away in a root cellar Dad had dug out in the field. The entrance was concealed by a hillock; Dad said I should never tell anybody where it was.

One afternoon, Dad climbed into the excavator and dug a pit next to the old barn. Then, using the loader, he lowered a thousand-gallon tank into the pit and buried it with a shovel, carefully planting nettles and sow thistle in the freshly tossed dirt so they would grow and conceal the tank. He whistled 'I Feel Pretty' from *West Side Story* while he shoveled. His hat was tipped back on his head, and he wore a brilliant smile. 'We'll be the only ones with fuel when The End comes,' he said. 'We'll be driving when everyone else is hotfooting it. We'll even make a run down to Utah, to fetch Tyler.'

★ ★ ★

I had rehearsals most nights at the Worm Creek Opera House, a dilapidated theater near the only stoplight in town. The play was another world. Nobody talked about Y2K.

The interactions between people at Worm Creek were not at all what I was used to in my family. Of course I'd spent time with people outside my family, but they were like us: women

123

who'd hired Mother to midwife their babies, or who came to her for herbs because they didn't believe in the Medical Establishment. I had a single friend, named Jessica. A few years before, Dad had convinced her parents, Rob and Diane, that public schools were little more than Government propaganda programs, and since then they had kept her at home. Before her parents had pulled Jessica from school, she was one of *them*, and I never tried to talk to her; but after, she was one of *us*. The normal kids stopped including her, and she was left with me.

I'd never learned how to talk to people who weren't like us — people who went to school and visited the doctor. Who weren't preparing, every day, for the End of the World. Worm Creek was full of these people, people whose words seemed ripped from another reality. That was how it felt the first time the director spoke to me, like he was speaking from another dimension. All he said was, 'Go find FDR.' I didn't move.

He tried again. 'President Roosevelt. FDR.'

'Is that like a JCB?' I said. 'You need a forklift?'

Everyone laughed.

I'd memorized all my lines, but at rehearsals I sat alone, pretending to study my black binder. When it was my turn onstage, I would recite my lines loudly and without hesitation. That made me feel a kind of confidence. If *I* didn't have anything to say, at least Annie did.

A week before opening night, Mother dyed my brown hair cherry red. The director said it was perfect, that all I needed now was to finish my costumes before the dress rehearsal on Saturday.

In our basement I found an oversized knit sweater, stained and hole-ridden, and an ugly blue dress, which Mother bleached to a faded brown. The dress was perfect for an orphan, and I was relieved at how easy finding the costumes had been, until I remembered that in act two Annie wears beautiful dresses, which Daddy Warbucks buys for her. I didn't have anything like that.

I told Mother and her face sank. We drove a hundred miles round-trip, searching every secondhand shop along the way, but found nothing. Sitting in the parking lot of the last shop, Mother pursed her lips, then said, 'There's one more place we can try.'

We drove to my aunt Angie's and parked in front of the white picket fence she shared with Grandma. Mother knocked, then stood back from the door and smoothed her hair. Angie looked surprised to see us — Mother rarely visited her sister — but she smiled warmly and invited us in. Her front room reminded me of fancy hotel lobbies from the movies, there was so much silk and lace. Mother and I sat on a pleated sofa of pale pink while Mother explained why we'd come. Angie said her daughter had a few dresses that might do.

Mother waited on the pink sofa while Angie led me upstairs to her daughter's room and laid out an armful of dresses, each so fine, with such intricate lace patterns and delicately tied bows, that at first I was afraid to touch them. Angie helped me into each one, knotting the sashes, fastening the buttons, plumping the bows. 'You should take this one,' she said, passing me a navy dress with white braided cords arranged across the bodice. 'Grandma sewed this detailing.' I took the dress, along with another made of red velvet collared with white lace, and Mother and I drove home.

The play opened a week later. Dad was in the front row. When the performance ended, he marched right to the box office and bought tickets for the next night. It was all he talked about that Sunday in church. Not doctors, or the Illuminati, or Y2K. Just the play over in town, where his youngest daughter was singing the lead.

Dad didn't stop me from auditioning for the next play, or the one after that, even though he worried about me spending so much time away from home. 'There's no telling what kind of cavorting takes place in that theater,' he said. 'It's probably a den of adulterers and fornicators.'

When the director of the next play got divorced, it confirmed Dad's suspicions. He said he hadn't kept me out of the public school for all these years just to see me corrupted on a stage. Then he drove me to the rehearsal. Nearly every night he said he was going to put a stop to my going, that one evening he'd just show up at Worm Creek and haul me home. But each time a play opened he was there, in the front row.

Sometimes he played the part of an agent or manager, correcting my technique or suggesting songs for my repertoire, even advising me about my health. That winter I caught a procession of sore throats and couldn't sing, and one night

Dad called me to him and pried my mouth open to look at my tonsils.

'They're swollen, all right,' he said. 'Big as apricots.' When Mother couldn't get the swelling down with echinacea and calendula, Dad suggested his own remedy. 'People don't know it, but the sun is the most powerful medicine we have. That's why people don't get sore throats in summer.' He nodded, as if approving of his own logic, then said, 'If I had tonsils like yours, I'd go outside every morning and stand in the sun with my mouth open — let those rays seep in for a half hour or so. They'll shrink in no time.' He called it a treatment.

I did it for a month.

It was uncomfortable, standing with my jaw dropped and my head tilted back so the sun could shine into my throat. I never lasted a whole half hour. My jaw would ache after ten minutes, and I'd half-freeze standing motionless in the Idaho winter. I kept catching more sore throats, and anytime Dad noticed I was a bit croaky, he'd say, 'Well, what do you expect? I ain't seen you getting treatment all week!'

* * *

It was at the Worm Creek Opera House that I first saw him: a boy I didn't know, laughing with a group of public school kids, wearing big white shoes, khaki shorts and a wide grin. He wasn't in the play, but there wasn't much to do in town, and I saw him several more times that week when he turned up to visit his friends. Then one night, when I was wandering alone in the dark wings backstage, I turned a corner and found him sitting on the wooden crate that was a favorite haunt of mine. The crate was isolated — that was why I liked it.

He shifted to the right, making room for me. I sat slowly, tensely, as if the seat were made of needles.

'I'm Charles,' he said. There was a pause while he waited for me to give my name, but I didn't. 'I saw you in the last play,' he said after a moment. 'I wanted to tell you something.' I braced myself, for what I wasn't sure, then he said, 'I wanted to tell you that your singing is about the best I ever heard.'

★ ★ ★

I came home one afternoon from packing macadamias to find Dad and Richard gathered around a large metal box, which they'd hefted onto the kitchen table. While Mother and I cooked meatloaf, they assembled the contents. It took more than an hour, and when they'd finished they stood back, revealing what looked like an enormous military-green telescope, with its long barrel set firmly atop a short, broad tripod. Richard was so excited he was hopping from one foot to the other, reciting what it could do. 'Got a range more than a mile! Can bring down a helicopter!'

Dad stood quietly, his eyes shining.

'What is it?' I asked.

'It's a fifty-caliber rifle,' he said. 'Wanna try it?'

I peered through the scope, searching the mountainside, fixing distant stalks of wheat between its crosshairs.

The meatloaf was forgotten. We charged outside. It was past sunset; the horizon was dark. I watched as Dad lowered himself to the frozen ground, positioned his eye at the scope and, after what felt like an hour, pulled the trigger. The blast was thunderous. I had both palms pressed to my ears, but after the initial boom I dropped them, listening as the shot echoed through the ravines. He fired again and again, so that by the time we went inside my ears were ringing. I could barely hear Dad's reply when I asked what the gun was for.

'Defense,' he said.

The next night I had a rehearsal at Worm Creek. I was perched on my crate, listening to the monologue being performed onstage, when Charles appeared and sat next to me.

'You don't go to school,' he said.

It wasn't a question.

'You should come to choir. You'd like choir.'

'Maybe,' I said, and he smiled. A few of his friends stepped into the wing and called to him. He stood and said goodbye, and I watched him join them, taking in the easy way they joked together and imagining an alternate reality in which I was one of them. I imagined Charles inviting me to his house, to play a game or watch a movie, and felt a rush of pleasure. But when I pictured Charles visiting Buck's Peak, I felt something else, something like panic. What if he found the root cellar? What if he discovered the fuel tank? Then I understood, finally, what the rifle was for. That mighty barrel, with its special range that could reach from the mountain to the valley, was a defensive perimeter for the house, for our supplies, because Dad said we would be driving when everyone else was hotfooting it. We would have food, too, when everyone else was starving, looting. Again I imagined Charles climbing the hill to our house. But in my imagination I was on the ridge, and I was watching his approach through crosshairs.

★   ★   ★

Christmas was sparse that year. We weren't poor — Mother's business was doing well and Dad was still scrapping — but we'd spent everything on supplies.

Before Christmas, we continued our preparations as if every action, every minor addition to our stores might make the difference between surviving, and not; after Christmas, we waited. 'When the hour of need arises,' Dad said, 'the time of preparation has passed.'

The days dragged on, and then it was December 31. Dad was calm at breakfast but under his tranquillity I sensed excitement, and something like longing. He'd been waiting for so many years, burying guns and stockpiling food and warning others to do the same. Everyone at church had read the prophecies; they knew the Days of Abomination were coming. But still they'd teased Dad, they'd laughed at him. Tonight he would be vindicated.

After dinner, Dad studied Isaiah for hours. At around ten he closed his Bible and turned on the TV. The television was new. Aunt Angie's husband worked for a satellite-TV company, and he'd offered Dad a deal on a subscription. No one had believed it when Dad said yes, but in retrospect it was entirely characteristic for my father to move, in the space of a day, from no TV or radio to full-blown cable. I sometimes wondered if Dad allowed the television *that* year, specifically, because he knew it would all disappear on January 1. Perhaps he did it to give us a little taste of the world, before it was swept away.

Dad's favorite program was *The Honeymooners*, and that night there was a special, with episodes playing back to back. We watched, waiting for The End. I checked the clock every few minutes from ten until eleven, then every few seconds until midnight. Even Dad, who was rarely stirred by anything outside himself, glanced often at the clock.

11:59.

I held my breath. One more minute, I thought, before everything is gone.

Then it was 12:00. The TV was still buzzing, its lights dancing across the carpet. I wondered if our clock was fast. I went to the kitchen and turned on the tap. We had water. Dad stayed still, his eyes on the screen. I returned to the couch.

12:05.

How long would it take for the electricity to fail? Was there a reserve somewhere that was keeping it going these few extra minutes?

The black-and-white specters of Ralph and Alice Kramden argued over a meatloaf.

12:10.

I waited for the screen to flicker and die. I was trying to take it all in, this last, luxurious moment — of sharp yellow light, of warm air flowing from the heater. I was experiencing nostalgia for the life I'd had before, which I would lose at any second, when the world turned and began to devour itself.

The longer I sat motionless, breathing deeply, trying to inhale the last scent of the fallen world, the more I resented its continuing solidity. Nostalgia turned to fatigue.

Sometime after 1:30 I went to bed. I glimpsed Dad as I left, his face frozen in the dark, the light from the TV leaping across his square glasses. He sat as if posed, with no agitation, no embarrassment, as if there were a perfectly mundane explanation for why he was sitting up, alone, at near two in the morning, watching Ralph and Alice Kramden prepare for a Christmas party.

He seemed smaller to me than he had that morning. The disappointment in his features was so childlike, for a moment I wondered how God could deny him this. He, a faithful servant, who suffered willingly just as Noah had willingly suffered to build the ark.

But God withheld the flood.

10

Shield of Feathers

When January 1 dawned like any other morning, it broke Dad's spirit. He never again mentioned Y2K. He slipped into despondency, dragging himself in from the junkyard each night, silent and heavy. He'd sit in front of the TV for hours, a black cloud hovering.

Mother said it was time for another trip to Arizona. Luke was serving a mission for the church, so it was just me, Richard and Audrey who piled into the old Chevy Astro van Dad had fixed up. Dad removed the seats, except the two in front, and in their place he put a queen mattress; then he heaved himself onto it and didn't move for the rest of the drive.

As it had years before, the Arizona sun revived Dad. He lay out on the porch on the hard cement, soaking it up, while the rest of us read or watched TV. After a few days he began to improve, and we braced ourselves for the nightly arguments between him and Grandma. Grandma was seeing a lot of doctors these days, because she had cancer in her bone marrow.

'Those doctors will just kill you quicker,' Dad said one evening when Grandma returned from a consultation. Grandma refused to quit chemotherapy, but she did ask Mother about herbal treatments. Mother had brought some with her, hoping Grandma would ask, and Grandma tried them — foot soaks in red clay, cups of bitter parsley tea, tinctures of horsetail and hydrangea.

'Those herbs won't do a damned thing,' Dad said. 'Herbals operate by faith. You can't put your trust in a doctor, then ask the Lord to heal you.'

Grandma didn't say a word. She just drank her parsley tea.

I remember watching Grandma, searching for signs that her body was giving way. I didn't see any. She was the same taut, undefeated woman.

The rest of the trip blurs in my memory, leaving me with only snapshots — of Mother muscle-testing remedies for Grandma, of Grandma listening silently to Dad, of Dad sprawled out in the dry heat.

Then I'm in a hammock on the back porch, rocking lazily in the orange light of the desert sunset, and Audrey appears and says Dad wants us to get our stuff, we're leaving. Grandma is incredulous. 'After what happened last time?' she shouts. 'You're going to drive through the night *again?* What about the storm?' Dad says we'll beat the storm. While we load the van Grandma paces, cussing. She says Dad hasn't learned a damned thing.

Richard drives the first six hours. I lie in the back on the mattress with Dad and Audrey.

It's three in the morning, and we are making our way from southern to northern Utah, when the weather changes from the dry chill of the desert to the freezing gales of an alpine winter. Ice claims the road. Snowflakes flick against the windshield like tiny insects, a few at first, then so many the road disappears. We push forward into the heart of the storm. The van skids and jerks. The wind is furious, the view out the window pure white. Richard pulls over. He says we can't go any further.

Dad takes the wheel, Richard moves to the passenger seat, and Mother lies next to me and Audrey on the mattress. Dad pulls onto the highway and accelerates, rapidly, as if to make a point, until he has doubled Richard's speed.

'Shouldn't we drive slower?' Mother asks.

Dad grins. 'I'm not driving faster than our angels can fly.' The van is still accelerating. To fifty, then to sixty.

Richard sits tensely, his hand clutching the armrest, his knuckles bleaching each time the tires slip. Mother lies on her side, her face next to mine, taking small sips of air each time the van fishtails, then holding her breath as Dad corrects and it snakes back into the lane. She is so rigid, I think she might shatter. My body tenses with hers; together we brace a hundred times for impact.

It is a relief when the van finally leaves the road.

* * *

I awoke to blackness. Something ice-cold was running down my back. *We're in a lake!* I thought. Something heavy was on top of me. The mattress. I tried to kick it off but couldn't, so I crawled beneath it, my hands and knees pressing into the ceiling of the van, which was upside down. I came to a broken window. It was full of snow. Then I understood: we were in a field, not a lake. I crawled through the broken glass and stood, unsteadily. I couldn't seem to gain my balance. I looked around but saw no one. The van was empty. My family was gone.

I circled the wreck twice before I spied Dad's hunched silhouette on a hillock in the distance. I called to him, and he called to the others, who were spread out through the field. Dad waded toward me through the snowdrifts, and as he stepped into a beam from the broken headlights I saw a six-inch gash in his forearm and blood slashing into the snow.

I was told later that I'd been unconscious, hidden under the mattress, for several minutes. They'd shouted my name. When I didn't answer, they thought I must have been thrown from the van, through the broken window, so they'd left to search for me.

Everyone returned to the wreck and stood around it awkwardly, shaking, either from the cold or from shock. We didn't look at Dad, didn't want to accuse.

The police arrived, then an ambulance. I don't know who called them. I didn't tell them I'd blacked out — I was afraid they'd take me to a hospital. I just sat in the police car next to Richard, wrapped in a reflective blanket like the one I had in my 'head for the hills' bag. We listened to the radio while the cops asked Dad why the van wasn't insured, and why he'd removed the seats and seatbelts.

We were far from Buck's Peak, so the cops took us to the nearest police station. Dad called Tony, but Tony was trucking long-haul. He tried Shawn next. No answer. We would later learn that Shawn was in jail that night, having been in some kind of brawl.

Unable to reach his sons, Dad called Rob and Diane Hardy, because Mother had midwifed five of their eight children. Rob arrived a few hours later, cackling. 'Didn't you folks damned near kill yerselves last time?'

* * *

A few days after the crash, my neck froze.

I awoke one morning and it wouldn't move. It didn't hurt, not at first, but no matter how hard I concentrated on turning my head, it wouldn't give more than an inch. The paralysis spread lower, until it felt like I had a metal rod running the length of my back and into my skull. When I couldn't bend forward or turn my head, the soreness set in. I had a constant, crippling headache, and I couldn't stand without holding on to something.

Mother called an energy specialist named Rosie. I was lying on my bed, where I'd been for two weeks, when she appeared in the doorway, wavy and distorted, as if I were looking at her through a pool of water. Her voice was high in pitch, cheerful. It told me to imagine myself, whole and healthy, protected by a white bubble. Inside the bubble I was to place all the objects I loved, all the colors that made me feel at peace. I envisioned the bubble; I imagined myself at its center, able to stand, to run. Behind me was a Mormon temple, and Kamikaze, Luke's old goat, long dead. A green glow lighted everything.

'Imagine the bubble for a few hours every day,' she said, 'and you will heal.' She patted my arm and I heard the door close behind her.

I imagined the bubble every morning, afternoon and night, but my neck remained immobile. Slowly, over the course of a month, I got used to the headaches. I learned how to stand, then how to walk. I used my eyes to stay upright; if I closed them even for a moment, the world would shift and I would fall. I went back to work — to Randy's and occasionally to the junkyard. And every night I fell asleep imagining that green bubble.

★ ★ ★

During the month I was in bed I heard another voice. I remembered it but it was no longer familiar to me. It had been six years since that impish laugh had echoed down the hall.

It belonged to my brother Shawn, who'd quarreled with my father at seventeen and run off to work odd jobs, mostly trucking and welding. He'd come home because Dad had asked for his help. From my bed, I'd heard Shawn say that he would only stay until Dad could put together a real crew. This was just a favor, he said, until Dad could get back on his feet.

It was odd finding him in the house, this brother who was nearly a stranger to me. People

138

in town seemed to know him better than I did. I'd heard rumors about him at Worm Creek. People said he was trouble, a bully, a bad egg, that he was always hunting or being hunted by hooligans from Utah or even further afield. People said he carried a gun, either concealed on his body or strapped to his big black motorcycle. Once someone said that Shawn wasn't really bad, that he only got into brawls because he had a reputation for being unbeatable — for knowing all there was to know about martial arts, for fighting like a man who feels no pain — so every strung-out wannabe in the valley thought he could make a name for himself by besting him. It wasn't Shawn's fault, really. As I listened to these rumors, he came alive in my mind as more legend than flesh.

My own memory of Shawn begins in the kitchen, perhaps two months after the second accident.

I am making corn chowder. The door squeaks and I twist at the waist to see who's come in, then twist back to chop an onion.

'You gonna be a walking Popsicle stick forever?' Shawn says.

'Nope.'

'You need a chiropractor,' he says.

'Mom'll fix it.'

'You need a chiropractor,' he says again.

The family eats, then disperses. I start the dishes. My hands are in the hot, soapy water when I hear a step behind me and feel thick, callused hands wrap around my skull. Before I can react, he jerks my head with a swift, savage motion. *CRACK!* It's so loud, I'm sure my head has come off and he's holding it. My body folds, I collapse. Everything is black but somehow spinning. When I open my eyes moments later, his hands are under my arms and he's holding me upright.

'Might be a while before you can stand,' he says. 'But when you can, I need to do the other side.'

I was too dizzy, too nauseous, for the effect to be immediate. But throughout the evening I observed small changes. I could look at the ceiling. I could cock my head to tease Richard. Seated on the couch, I could turn to smile at the person next to me.

That person was Shawn, and I was looking at him but I wasn't seeing him. I don't know what I saw — what creature I conjured from that violent, compassionate act — but I think it was my father, or perhaps my father as I wished he were, some longed-for defender, some fanciful champion, one who wouldn't fling me into a storm, and who, if I was hurt, would make me whole.

11

Instinct

When Grandpa-down-the-hill was a young man, there'd been herds of livestock spread across the mountain, and they were tended on horseback. Grandpa's ranching horses were the stuff of legend. Seasoned as old leather, they moved their burly bodies delicately, as if guided by the rider's thoughts.

At least, that's what I was told. I never saw them. As Grandpa got older he ranched less and farmed more, until one day he stopped farming. He had no need for horses, so he sold the ones that had value and set the rest loose. They multiplied, and by the time I was born there was a whole herd of wild horses on the mountain.

Richard called them dog-food horses. Once a year, Luke, Richard and I would help Grandpa round up a dozen or so to take to the auction in town, where they'd be sold for slaughter. Some years Grandpa would look out over the small, frightened herd bound for the meat grinder, at the young stallions pacing, coming to terms with their first captivity, and a hunger would appear in his eyes. Then he'd point to one and say, 'Don't load that 'un. That 'un we'll break.'

But feral horses don't yield easily, not even to a man like Grandpa. My brothers and I would spend days, even weeks, earning the horse's trust, just so we could touch it. Then we would stroke its long face and gradually, over more weeks, work our hands around its wide neck and down its muscular body. After a month of this we'd bring out the saddle, and the horse would toss its head suddenly and with such violence that the halter would snap or the rope break. Once a large copper stallion busted the corral fence, smashed through it as if it weren't there, and came out the other side bloody and bruised.

We tried not to name them, these beasts we hoped to tame, but we had to refer to them somehow. The names we chose were descriptive, not sentimental: Big Red, Black Mare, White Giant. I was thrown from dozens of these horses as they bucked, reared, rolled or leapt. I hit the dirt in a hundred sprawling postures, each time righting myself in an instant and skittering to the safety of a tree, tractor or fence, in case the horse was feeling vengeful.

We never triumphed; our strength of will faltered long before theirs. We got some so they wouldn't buck when they saw the saddle, and a few who'd tolerate a human on their back for jaunts around the corral, but not even Grandpa dared ride them on the mountain. Their natures hadn't changed. They were pitiless, powerful avatars from another world. To mount them was to surrender your footing, to move into their domain. To risk being borne away.

The first domesticated horse I ever saw was a bay gelding, and it was standing next to the corral, nibbling sugar cubes from Shawn's hand. It was spring, and I was fourteen. It had been many years since I'd touched a horse.

The gelding was mine, a gift from a great-uncle on my mother's side. I approached warily, certain that as I moved closer the horse would buck, or rear, or charge. Instead it sniffed my shirt, leaving a long, wet stain. Shawn tossed me a cube. The horse smelled the sugar, and the prickles from his chin tickled my fingers until I opened my palm.

'Wanna break him?' Shawn said.

I did *not*. I was terrified of horses, or I was terrified of what I thought horses were — that is, thousand-pound devils whose ambition was to dash brains against rock. I told Shawn he could break the horse. I would watch from the fence.

I refused to name the horse, so we called him the Yearling. The Yearling was already broke to a halter and lead, so Shawn brought out the saddle that first day. The Yearling pawed the dirt nervously when he saw it; Shawn moved slowly, letting him smell the stirrups and nibble curiously at the horn. Then Shawn rubbed the smooth leather across his broad chest, moving steadily but without hurry.

'Horses don't like things where they can't see 'em,' Shawn said. 'Best to get him used to the saddle in front. Then when he's real comfortable with it, with the way it smells and feels, we can move it around back.'

An hour later the saddle was cinched. Shawn said it was time to mount, and I climbed onto the barn roof, sure the corral would descend into violence. But when Shawn hoisted himself into the saddle, the Yearling merely skittered. His

143

front hooves raised a few inches off the dirt, as if he'd pondered rearing but thought better of it, then he dropped his head and his paws stilled. In the space of a moment, he had accepted our claim to ride him, to his being ridden. He had accepted the world as it was, in which he was an owned thing. He had never been feral, so he could not hear the maddening call of that *other* world, on the mountain, in which he could not be owned, could not be ridden.

I named him Bud. Every night for a week I watched Shawn and Bud gallop through the corral in the gray haze of dusk. Then, on a soft summer evening, I stood next to Bud, grasping the reins while Shawn held the halter steady, and stepped into the saddle.

★ ★ ★

Shawn said he wanted out of his old life, and that the first step was to stay away from his friends. Suddenly he was home every evening, looking for something to do. He began to drive me to my rehearsals at Worm Creek. When it was just the two of us floating down the highway, he was mellow, lighthearted. He joked and teased, and he sometimes gave me advice, which was mostly 'Don't do what I did.' But when we arrived at the theater, he would change.

At first he watched the younger boys with wary concentration, then he began to bait them. It wasn't obvious aggression, just small provocations. He might flick off a boy's hat or knock a soda can from his hand and laugh as the stain

144

spread over the boy's jeans. If he was challenged — and he usually wasn't — he would play the part of the ruffian, a hardened 'Whatcha gonna do about it?' expression disguising his face. But after, when it was just the two of us, the mask lowered, the bravado peeled off like a breast-plate, and he was my brother.

It was his smile I loved best. His upper canines had never grown in, and the string of holistic dentists my parents had taken him to as a child had failed to notice until it was too late. By the time he was twenty-three, and he got himself to an oral surgeon, they had rotated sideways inside his gums and were ejecting themselves through the tissue under his nose. The surgeon who removed them told Shawn to preserve his baby teeth for as long as possible, then when they rotted out, he'd be given posts. But they never rotted out. They stayed, stubborn relics of a misplaced childhood, reminding anyone who witnessed his pointless, endless, feckless belliger-ence, that this man was once a boy.

* * *

It was a hazy summer evening, a month before I turned fifteen. The sun had dipped below Buck's Peak but the sky still held a few hours of light. Shawn and I were in the corral. After breaking Bud that spring, Shawn had taken up horses in a serious way. All summer he'd been buying horses, Thoroughbreds and Paso Finos, most of them unbroken because he could pick them up cheap. We were still working with Bud. We'd

145

taken him on a dozen rides through the open pasture, but he was inexperienced, skittish, unpredictable.

That evening, Shawn saddled a new horse, a copper-coated mare, for the first time. She was ready for a short ride, Shawn said, so we mounted, him on the mare, me on Bud. We made it about half a mile up the mountain, moving deliberately so as not to frighten the horses, winding our way through the wheat fields. Then I did something foolish. I got too close to the mare. She didn't like having the gelding behind her, and with no warning she leapt forward, thrusting her weight onto her front legs, and with her hind legs kicked Bud full in the chest.

Bud went berserk.

I'd been tying a knot in my reins to make them more secure and didn't have a firm hold. Bud gave a tremendous jolt, then began to buck, throwing his body in tight circles. The reins flew over his head. I gripped the saddle horn and squeezed my thighs together, curving my legs around his bulging belly. Before I could get my bearings, Bud took off at a dead run straight up a ravine, bucking now and then but running, always running. My foot slipped through a stirrup up to my calf.

All those summers breaking horses with Grandpa, and the only advice I remembered him giving was, 'Whate'er you do, don't git your foot caught in the stirrup.' I didn't need him to explain. I knew that as long as I came off clean, I'd likely be fine. At least I'd be on the ground.

But if my foot got caught, I'd be dragged until my head split on a rock.

Shawn couldn't help me, not on that unbroken mare. Hysteria in one horse causes hysteria in others, especially in the young and spirited. Of all Shawn's horses, there was only one — a seven-year-old buckskin named Apollo — who might have been old enough, and calm enough, to do it: to explode in furious speed, a nostril-flapping gallop, then coolly navigate while the rider detached his body, lifting one leg out of the stirrup and reaching to the ground to catch the reins of another horse wild with fright. But Apollo was in the corral, half a mile down the mountain.

My instincts told me to let go of the saddle horn — the only thing keeping me on the horse. If I let go I'd fall, but I'd have a precious moment to reach for the flapping reins or try to yank my calf from the stirrup. *Make a play for it*, my instincts screamed.

Those instincts were my guardians. They had saved me before, guiding my movements on a dozen bucking horses, telling me when to cling to the saddle and when to pitch myself clear of pounding hooves. They were the same instincts that, years before, had prompted me to hoist myself from the scrap bin when Dad was dumping it, because they had understood, even if I had not, that it was better to fall from that great height rather than hope Dad would intervene. All my life those instincts had been instructing me in this single doctrine — that the odds are better if you rely only on yourself.

Bud reared, thrusting his head so high I thought he might tumble backward. He landed hard and bucked. I tightened my grip on the horn, making a decision, based on another kind of instinct, not to surrender my hold.

Shawn would catch up, even on that unbroken mare. He'd pull off a miracle. The mare wouldn't even understand the command when he shouted, 'Giddy-yap!'; at the jab of his boot in her gut, which she'd never felt before, she would rear, twisting wildly. But he would yank her head down, and as soon as her hooves touched the dirt, kick her a second time, harder, knowing she would rear again. He would do this until she leapt into a run, then he would drive her forward, welcoming her wild acceleration, somehow guiding her even though she'd not yet learned the strange dance of movements that, over time, becomes a kind of language between horse and rider. All this would happen in seconds, a year of training reduced to a single, desperate moment.

I knew it was impossible. I knew it even as I imagined it. But I kept hold of the saddle horn.

Bud had worked himself into a frenzy. He leapt wildly, arching his back as he shot upward, then tossing his head as he smashed his hooves to the ground. My eyes could barely unscramble what they saw. Golden wheat flew in every direction, while the blue sky and the mountain lurched absurdly.

I was so disoriented that I felt, rather than saw, the powerful penny-toned mare moving into place beside me. Shawn lifted his body from the saddle and tilted himself toward the ground, holding his reins tightly in one hand while, with the other, he snatched Bud's reins from the weeds. The leather straps pulled taut; the bit forced Bud's head up and forward. With his head raised, Bud could no longer buck and he entered a smooth, rhythmic gallop. Shawn yanked hard on his own reins, pulling the mare's head toward his knee, forcing her to run in a circle. He pulled her head tighter on every pass, wrapping the strap around his forearm, shrinking the circle until it was so small, the pounding hooves stood still. I slid from the saddle and lay in the wheat, the itchy stalks poking through my shirt. Above my head the horses panted, their bellies swelling and collapsing, their hooves pawing at the dirt.

12

Fish Eyes

My brother Tony had taken out a loan to buy his
own rig — a semi and trailer — but in order to
make the payments, he had to keep the truck on
the road, so that's where he was living, on the
road. Until his wife got sick and the doctor she
consulted (she had consulted a doctor) put her
on bed rest. Tony called Shawn and asked if he
could run the rig for a week or two.

Shawn hated trucking long-haul, but he said
he'd do it if I came along. Dad didn't need me in
the junkyard, and Randy could spare me for a
few days, so we set off, heading down to Las
Vegas, then east to Albuquerque, west to Los
Angeles, then up to Washington State. I'd
thought I would see the cities, but mostly I saw
truck stops and interstate. The windshield was
enormous and elevated like a cockpit, which
made the cars below seem like toys. The sleeper
cab, where the bunks were, was musty and dark
as a cave, littered with bags of Doritos and trail
mix.

Shawn drove for days with little sleep,
navigating our fifty-foot trailer as if it were his
own arm. He doctored the books whenever we
crossed a checkpoint, to make it seem he was
getting more sleep than he was. Every other day
we stopped to shower and eat a meal that wasn't

dried fruit and granola.

Near Albuquerque, the Walmart warehouse was backed up and couldn't unload us for two days. We were outside the city — there was nothing but a truck stop and red sand stretching out in all directions — so we ate Cheetos and played Mario Kart in the sleeper. By sunset on the second day, our bodies ached from sitting, and Shawn said he should teach me martial arts. We had our first lesson at dusk in the parking lot.

'If you know what you're doing,' he said, 'you can incapacitate a man with minimal effort. You can control someone's whole body with two fingers. It's about knowing where the weak points are, and how to exploit them.' He grabbed my wrist and folded it, bending my fingers downward so they reached uncomfortably toward the inside of my forearm. He continued to add pressure until I twisted slightly, wrapping my arm behind my back to relieve the strain.

'See? This is a weak point,' he said. 'If I fold it any more, you'll be immobilized.' He grinned his angel grin. 'I won't, though, because it'd hurt like hell.'

He let go and said, 'Now you try.'

I folded his wrist onto itself and squeezed hard, trying to get his upper body to collapse the way mine had. He didn't move.

'Maybe another strategy for you,' he said.

He gripped my wrist a different way — the way an attacker might, he said. He taught me how to break the hold, where the fingers were weakest and the bones in my arm strongest, so that after a few minutes I could cut through even his thick fingers. He taught me how to throw my weight behind a punch, and where to aim to crush the windpipe.

The next morning, the trailer was unloaded. We climbed into the truck, picked up a new load and drove for another two days, watching the white lines disappear hypnotically beneath the hood, which was the color of bone. We had few forms of entertainment, so we made a game of talking. The game had only two rules. The first was that every statement had to have at least two words in which the first letters were switched.

'You're not my little sister,' Shawn said. 'You're my sittle lister.' He pronounced the words lazily, blunting the *t*'s to *d*'s so that it sounded like 'siddle lister.'

The second rule was that every word that sounded like a number, or like it had a number in it, had to be changed so that the number was one higher. The word 'to' for example, because it sounds like the number 'two,' would become 'three.'

'Siddle Lister,' Shawn might say, 'we should pay a-elevention. There's a checkpoint ahead and I can't a-five-d a ticket. Time three put on your seatbelt.'

When we tired of this, we'd turn on the CB and listen to the lonely banter of truckers stretched out across the interstate.

'Look out for a green four-wheeler,' a gruff voice said, when we were somewhere between Sacramento and Portland. 'Been picnicking in my blind spot for a half hour.'

A four-wheeler, Shawn explained, is what big

152

rigs call cars and pickups.

Another voice came over the CB to complain about a red Ferrari that was weaving through traffic at 120 miles per hour. 'Bastard damned near hit a little blue Chevy,' the deep voice bellowed through the static. 'Shit, there's kids in that Chevy. Anybody up ahead wanna cool this hothead down?' The voice gave its location.

Shawn checked the mile marker. We were ahead. 'I'm a white Pete pulling a fridge,' he said. There was silence while everybody checked their mirrors for a Peterbilt with a reefer. Then a third voice, gruffer than the first, answered: 'I'm the blue KW hauling a dry box.'

'I see you,' Shawn said, and for my benefit pointed to a navy-colored Kenworth a few cars ahead.

When the Ferrari appeared, multiplied in our many mirrors, Shawn shifted into high gear, revving the engine and pulling beside the Kenworth so that the two fifty-foot trailers were running side by side, blocking both lanes. The Ferrari honked, weaved back and forth, braked, honked again.

'How long should we keep him back there?' the husky voice said, with a deep laugh.

'Until he calms down,' Shawn answered.

Five miles later, they let him pass.

The trip lasted about a week, then we told Tony to find us a load to Idaho.

'Well, Siddle Lister,' Shawn said when we pulled into the junkyard, 'back three work.'

* * *

The Worm Creek Opera House announced a new play: *Carousel*. Shawn drove me to the audition, then surprised me by auditioning himself. Charles was also there, talking to a girl named Sadie, who was seventeen. She nodded at what Charles was saying, but her eyes were fixed on Shawn.

At the first rehearsal she came and sat next to him, laying her hand on his arm, laughing and tossing her hair. She was very pretty, with soft, full lips and large dark eyes, but when I asked Shawn if he liked her, he said he didn't.

'She's got fish eyes,' he said.

'Fish eyes?'

'Yup, fish eyes. They're dead stupid, fish. They're beautiful, but their heads're as empty as a tire.'

Sadie started dropping by the junkyard around quitting time, usually with a milkshake for Shawn, or cookies or cake. Shawn hardly even spoke to her, just grabbed whatever she'd brought him and kept walking toward the corral. She would follow and try to talk to him while he fussed over his horses, until one evening she asked if he would teach her to ride. I tried to explain that our horses weren't broke all the way, but she was determined, so Shawn put her on Apollo and the three of us headed up the mountain. Shawn ignored her and Apollo. He offered none of the help he'd given me, teaching me how to stand in the stirrups while going down steep ravines or how to squeeze my thighs when the horse leapt over a branch. Sadie trembled for the entire ride, but she pretended to

154

be enjoying herself, restoring her lipsticked smile every time he glanced in her direction.

At the next rehearsal, Charles asked Sadie about a scene, and Shawn saw them talking. Sadie came over a few minutes later but Shawn wouldn't speak to her. He turned his back and she left crying.

'What's that about?' I said.

'Nothing,' he said.

By the next rehearsal, a few days later, Shawn seemed to have forgotten it. Sadie approached him warily, but he smiled at her, and a few minutes later they were talking and laughing. Shawn asked her to cross the street and buy him a Snickers at the dime store. She seemed pleased that he would ask and hurried out the door, but when she returned a few minutes later and gave him the bar, he said, 'What is this shit? I asked for a Milky Way.'

'You didn't,' she said. 'You said Snickers.'

'I want a Milky Way.'

Sadie left again and fetched the Milky Way. She handed it to him with a nervous laugh, and Shawn said, 'Where's my Snickers? What, you forgot again?'

'You didn't want it!' she said, her eyes shining like glass. 'I gave it to Charles!'

'Go get it.'

'I'll buy you another.'

'No,' Shawn said, his eyes cold. His baby teeth, which usually gave him an impish, playful appearance, now made him seem unpredictable, volatile. 'I want *that* one. Get it, or don't come back.'

A tear slid down Sadie's cheek, smearing her mascara. She paused for a moment to wipe it away and pull up her smile. Then she walked over to Charles and, laughing as if it were nothing, asked if she could have the Snickers. He reached into his pocket and pulled it out, then watched her walk back to Shawn. Sadie placed the Snickers in his palm like a peace offering and waited, staring at the carpet. Shawn pulled her onto his lap and ate the bar in three bites.

'You have lovely eyes,' he said. 'Just like a fish.'

★ ★ ★

Sadie's parents were divorcing and the town was awash in rumors about her father. When Mother heard the rumors, she said now it made sense why Shawn had taken an interest in Sadie. 'He's always protected angels with broken wings,' she said.

Shawn found out Sadie's class schedule and memorized it. He made a point of driving to the high school several times a day, particularly at those times when he knew she'd be moving between buildings. He'd pull over on the highway and watch her from a distance, too far for her to come over, but not so far that she wouldn't see him. It was something we did together, he and I, nearly every time we went to town, and some-times when we didn't need to go to town at all. Until one day, when Sadie appeared on the steps of the high school with Charles. They were laughing together; Sadie hadn't noticed Shawn's truck.

I watched his face harden, then relax. He

smiled at me. 'I have the perfect punishment,' he said. 'I simply won't see her. All I have to do is not see her, and she will suffer.'

He was right. When he didn't return her calls, Sadie became desperate. She told the boys at school not to walk with her, for fear Shawn would see, and when Shawn said he disliked one of her friends, she stopped seeing them.

Sadie came to our house every day after school, and I watched the Snickers incident play out over and over, in different forms, with different objects. Shawn would ask for a glass of water. When Sadie brought it, he'd want ice. When she brought that he'd ask for milk, then water again, ice, no ice, then juice. This could go on for thirty minutes before, in a final test, he would ask for something we didn't have. Then Sadie would drive to town to buy it — vanilla ice cream, fries, a burrito — only to have him demand something else the moment she got back. The nights they went out, I was grateful.

One night, he came home late and in a strange mood. Everyone was asleep except me, and I was on the sofa, reading a chapter of scripture before bed. Shawn plopped down next to me. 'Get me a glass of water.'

'You break your leg?' I said.

'Get it, or I won't drive you to town tomorrow.'

I fetched the water. As I handed it over, I saw the smile on his face and without thinking dumped the whole thing on his head. I made it down the hall and was nearly to my room when he caught me.

'Apologize,' he said. Water dripped from his nose onto his T-shirt.

'No.'

He grabbed a fistful of my hair, a large clump, his grip fixed near the root to give him greater leverage, and dragged me into the bathroom. I groped at the door, catching hold of the frame, but he lifted me off the ground, flattened my arms against my body, then dropped my head into the toilet. 'Apologize,' he said again. I said nothing. He stuck my head in further, so my nose scraped the stained porcelain. I closed my eyes, but the smell wouldn't let me forget where I was.

I tried to imagine something else, something that would take me out of myself, but the image that came to mind was of Sadie, crouching, compliant. It pumped me full of bile. He held me there, my nose touching the bowl, for perhaps a minute, then he let me up. The tips of my hair were wet; my scalp was raw.

I thought it was over. I'd begun to back away when he seized my wrist and folded it, curling my fingers and palm into a spiral. He continued folding until my body began to coil, then he added more pressure, so that without thinking, without realizing, I twisted myself into a dramatic bow, my back bent, my head nearly touching the floor, my arm behind my back.

In the parking lot, when Shawn had shown me this hold, I'd moved only a little, responding more to his description than to any physical necessity. It hadn't seemed particularly effective at the time, but now I understood the maneuver

158

for what it was: control. I could scarcely move, scarcely breathe, without breaking my own wrist. Shawn held me in position with one hand; the other he dangled loosely at his side, to show me how easy it was.

Still harder than if I were Sadie, I thought.

As if he could read my mind, he twisted my wrist further; my body was coiled tightly, my face scraping the floor. I'd done all I could do to relieve the pressure in my wrist. If he kept twisting, it would break.

'Apologize,' he said.

There was a long moment in which fire burned up my arm and into my brain. 'I'm sorry,' I said.

He dropped my wrist and I fell to the floor. I could hear his steps moving down the hall. I stood and quietly locked the bathroom door, then I stared into the mirror at the girl clutching her wrist. Her eyes were glassy and drops slid down her cheeks. I hated her for her weakness, for having a heart to break. That he could hurt her, that anyone could hurt her like *that*, was inexcusable.

I'm only crying from the pain, I told myself. *From the pain in my wrist. Not from anything else.*

This moment would define my memory of that night, and of the many nights like it, for a decade. In it I saw myself as unbreakable, as tender as stone. At first I merely believed this, until one day it became the truth. Then I was able to tell myself, without lying, that it didn't affect me, that *he* didn't affect me, because nothing affected me. I didn't understand how morbidly right I was. How I had hollowed myself out. For all my obsessing over the consequences of that night, I had misunderstood the vital truth: that its not affecting me, that *was* its effect.

13

Silence in the Churches

In September the twin towers fell. I'd never heard of them until they were gone. Then I watched as planes sank into them, and I stared, bewildered, at the TV as the unimaginably tall structures swayed, then buckled. Dad stood next to me. He'd come in from the junkyard to watch. He said nothing. That evening he read aloud from the Bible, familiar passages from Isaiah, Luke, and the Book of Revelation, about wars and rumors of wars.

Three days later, when she was nineteen, Audrey was married — to Benjamin, a blond-haired farm boy she'd met waitressing in town. The wedding was solemn. Dad had prayed and received a revelation: 'There will be a conflict, a final struggle for the Holy Land,' he'd said. 'My sons will be sent to war. Some of them will not come home.'

I'd been avoiding Shawn since the night in the bathroom. He'd apologized. He'd come into my room an hour later, his eyes glassy, his voice croaking, and asked me to forgive him. I'd said that I would, that I already had. But I hadn't.

At Audrey's wedding, seeing my brothers in their suits, those black uniforms, my rage turned to fear, of some predetermined loss, and I forgave Shawn. It was easy to forgive: after all, it

161

was the End of the World.

For a month I lived as if holding my breath. Then there was no draft, no further attacks. The skies didn't darken, the moon didn't turn to blood. There were distant rumblings of war but life on the mountain remained unchanged. Dad said we should stay vigilant, but by winter my attention had shifted back to the trifling dramas of my own life.

I was fifteen and I felt it, felt the race I was running with time. My body was changing, bloating, swelling, stretching, bulging. I wished it would stop, but it seemed my body was no longer mine. It belonged to itself now, and cared not at all how I felt about these strange alterations, about whether I *wanted* to stop being a child, and become something else.

That something else thrilled and frightened me. I'd always known that I would grow differently than my brothers, but I'd never thought about what that might mean. Now it was all I thought about. I began to look for cues to understand this difference, and once I started looking, I found them everywhere.

One Sunday afternoon, I helped Mother prepare a roast for dinner. Dad was kicking off his shoes and loosening his tie. He'd been talking since we left the church.

'That hemline was three inches above Lori's knee,' Dad said. 'What's a woman thinking when she puts on a dress like that?' Mother nodded absently while chopping a carrot. She was used to this particular lecture.

'And Jeanette Barney,' Dad said. 'If a woman

162

wears a blouse that low-cut, she ought not bend over.' Mother agreed. I pictured the turquoise blouse Jeanette had worn that day. The neckline was only an inch below her collarbone, but it was loose-fitting, and I imagined that if she bent it would give a full view. As I thought this I felt anxious, because although a tighter blouse would have made Jeanette's bending more modest, the tightness itself would have been less modest. Righteous women do not wear tight clothing. *Other* women do that.

I was trying to figure out exactly how much tightness would be the right amount when Dad said, 'Jeanette waited to bend for that hymnal until I was looking. She *wanted* me to see.' Mother made a disapproving *tsk* sound with her teeth, then quartered a potato.

This speech would stay with me in a way that a hundred of its precursors had not. I would remember the words very often in the years that followed, and the more I considered them, the more I worried that I might be growing into the wrong sort of woman. Sometimes I could scarcely move through a room, I was so preoccupied with not walking or bending or crouching like *them*. But no one had ever taught me the modest way to bend over, so I knew I was probably doing it the bad way.

* * *

Shawn and I auditioned for a melodrama at Worm Creek. I saw Charles at the first rehearsal and spent half the evening working up the

163

courage to talk to him. When I did, finally, he confided in me that he was in love with Sadie. This wasn't ideal, but it did give us something to talk about.

Shawn and I drove home together. He sat behind the wheel, glaring at the road as if it had wronged him.

'I saw you talking to Charles,' he said. 'You don't want people thinking you're that kind of girl.'

'The kind that talks?'

'You know what I mean,' he said.

The next night, Shawn came into my room unexpectedly and found me smudging my eyelashes with Audrey's old mascara.

'You wear *makeup* now?' he said.

'I guess.'

He spun around to leave but paused in the doorframe. 'I thought you were better,' he said. 'But you're just like the rest.'

He stopped calling me Siddle Lister. 'Let's go, Fish Eyes!' he shouted from across the theater one night. Charles looked around curiously. Shawn began to explain the name, so I started laughing — loud enough, I hoped, to drown him out. I laughed as if I loved the name.

The first time I wore lip gloss, Shawn said I was a whore. I was in my bedroom, standing in front of my mirror, trying it out, when Shawn appeared in the doorway. He said it like a joke but I wiped the color from my lips anyway. Later that night, at the theater, when I noticed Charles staring at Sadie, I reapplied it and saw Shawn's expression twist. The drive home that night was

164

tense. The temperature outside had fallen well below zero. I said I was cold and Shawn moved to turn up the heat. Then he paused, laughed to himself, and rolled all the windows down. The January wind hit me like a bucket of ice. I tried to roll up my window, but he'd put on the child lock. I asked him to roll it up. 'I'm cold,' I kept saying, 'I'm really, really cold.' He just laughed. He drove all twelve miles like that, cackling as if it were a game, as if we were both in on it, as if my teeth weren't clattering.

I thought things would get better when Shawn dumped Sadie — I suppose I'd convinced myself that it was *her* fault, the things he did, and that without her he would be different. After Sadie, he took up with an old girlfriend, Erin. She was older, less willing to play his games, and at first it seemed I was right, that he was doing better.

Then Charles asked Sadie to dinner, Sadie said yes, and Shawn heard about it. I was working late at Randy's that night when Shawn turned up, frothing at the mouth. I left with him, thinking I could calm him, but I couldn't. He drove around town for two hours, searching for Charles's Jeep, cursing and swearing that when he found that bastard he was 'gonna give him a new face.' I sat in the passenger seat of his truck, listening to the engine rev as it guzzled diesel, watching the yellow lines disappear beneath the hood. I thought of my brother as he had been, as I remembered him, as I wanted to remember him. I thought of Albuquerque and Los Angeles, and of the miles of lost interstate in between.

A pistol lay on the seat between us, and when

165

he wasn't shifting gears, Shawn picked it up and caressed it, sometimes spinning it over his index like a gunslinger before laying it back on the seat, where light from passing cars glinted off the steel barrel.

★ ★ ★

I awoke with needles in my brain. Thousands of them, biting, blocking out everything. Then they disappeared for one dizzying moment and I got my bearings.

It was morning, early; amber sunlight poured in through my bedroom window. I was standing but not on my own strength. Two hands were gripping my throat, and they'd been shaking me. The needles, that was my brain crashing into my skull. I had only a few seconds to wonder why before the needles returned, shredding my thoughts. My eyes were open but I saw only white flashes. A few sounds made it through to me.

'SLUT!
'WHORE!'

Then another sound. Mother. She was crying. 'Stop! You're killing her! Stop!'

She must have grabbed him because I felt his body twist. I fell to the floor. When I opened my eyes, Mother and Shawn were facing each other, Mother wearing only a tattered bathrobe.

I was yanked to my feet. Shawn grasped a fistful of my hair — using the same method as before, catching the clump near my scalp so he could maneuver me — and dragged me into the

166

hallway. My head was pressed into his chest. All I could see were bits of carpet flying past my tripping feet. My head pounded, I had trouble breathing, but I was starting to understand what was happening. Then there were tears in my eyes.

From the pain, I thought.

'Now the bitch cries,' Shawn said. 'Why? Because someone sees you for the slut you are?'

I tried to look at him, to search his face for my brother, but he shoved my head toward the ground and I fell. I scrambled away, then pulled myself upright. The kitchen was spinning; strange flecks of pink and yellow drifted before my eyes.

Mother was sobbing, clawing at her hair.

'I see you for what you are,' Shawn said. His eyes were wild. 'You pretend to be saintly and churchish. But I see you. I see how you prance around with Charles like a prostitute.' He turned to Mother to observe the effect of his words on her. She had collapsed at the kitchen table.

'She does *not*,' Mother whispered.

Shawn was still turned toward her. He said she had no idea of the lies I told, how I'd fooled her, how I played the good girl at home but in town I was a lying whore. I inched toward the back door.

Mother told me to take her car and go. Shawn turned to me. 'You'll be needing these,' he said, holding up Mother's keys.

'She's not going anywhere until she admits she's a whore,' Shawn said.

He grabbed my wrist and my body slipped

into the familiar posture, head thrust forward, arm coiled around my lower back, wrist folded absurdly onto itself. Like a dance step, my muscles remembered and raced to get ahead of the music. The air poured from my lungs as I tried to bend deeper, to give my wrist bone every possible inch of relief.

'Say it,' he said.

But I was somewhere else. I was in the future. In a few hours, Shawn would be kneeling by my bed, and he'd be so very sorry. I knew it even as I hunched there.

'What's going on?' A man's voice floated up from the stairwell in the hall.

I turned my head and saw a face hovering between two wooden railings. It was Tyler.

I was hallucinating. Tyler never came home. As I thought that, I laughed out loud, a high-pitched cackle. What kind of lunatic would come back here once they'd escaped? There were now so many pink and yellow specks in my vision, it was as if I were inside a snow globe. That was good. It meant I was close to passing out. I was looking forward to it.

Shawn dropped my wrist and again I fell. I looked up and saw that his gaze was fixed on the stairwell. Only then did it occur to me that Tyler was real.

Shawn took a step back. He had waited until Dad and Luke were out of the house, away on a job, so his physicality could go unchallenged. Confronting his younger brother — less vicious but powerful in his own way — was more than he'd bargained for.

'What's going on?' Tyler repeated. He eyed Shawn, inching forward as if approaching a rattlesnake.

Mother stopped crying. She was embarrassed. Tyler was an outsider now. He'd been gone for so long, he'd been shifted to that category of people who we kept secrets from. Who we kept *this* from.

Tyler moved up the stairs, advancing on his brother. His face was taut, his breath shallow, but his expression held no hint of surprise. It seemed to me that Tyler knew exactly what he was doing, that he had done this before, when they were younger and less evenly matched. Tyler halted his forward march but he didn't blink. He glared at Shawn as if to say, *Whatever is happening here, it's done.*

Shawn began to murmur about my clothes and what I did in town. Tyler cut him off with a wave of his hand. 'I don't want to know,' he said. Then, turning to me: 'Go, get out of here.'

'She's not going anywhere,' Shawn repeated, flashing the key rings.

Tyler tossed me his own keys. 'Just go,' he said.

I ran to Tyler's car, which was wedged between Shawn's truck and the chicken coop. I tried to back out, but I stomped too hard on the gas and the tires spun out, sending gravel flying. On my second attempt I succeeded. The car shot backward and circled around. I shifted into drive and was ready to shoot down the hill when Tyler appeared on the porch. I lowered the window. 'Don't go to work,' he said. 'He'll find you there.'

That night, when I came home, Shawn was gone. Mother was in the kitchen blending oils. She said nothing about that morning, and I knew I shouldn't mention it. I went to bed, but I was still awake hours later when I heard a pickup roar up the hill. A few minutes later, my bedroom door creaked open. I heard the click of the lamp, saw the light leaping over the walls, and felt his weight drop onto my bed. I turned over and faced him. He'd put a black velvet box next to me. When I didn't touch it, he opened the box and withdrew a string of milky pearls.

He said he could see the path I was going down and it was not good. I was losing myself, becoming like other girls, frivolous, manipulative, using how I looked to get things.

I thought about my body, all the ways it had changed. I hardly knew what I felt toward it: sometimes I *did* want it to be noticed, to be admired, but then afterward I'd think of Jeanette Barney, and I'd feel disgusted.

'You're special, Tara,' Shawn said.

Was I? I wanted to believe I was. Tyler had said I was special once, years before. He'd read me a passage of scripture from the Book of Mormon, about *a sober child, quick to observe*. 'This reminds me of you,' Tyler had said.

The passage described the great prophet Mormon, a fact I'd found confusing. A woman could never be a prophet, yet here was Tyler, telling me I reminded him of one of the greatest prophets of all. I still don't know what he meant by it, but what I understood at the time was that I could trust myself: that there was something in me, something like what was in the prophets, and that it was not male or female, not old or young; a kind of worth that was inherent and unshakable.

But now, as I gazed at the shadow Shawn cast on my wall, aware of my maturing body, of its evils and of my desire to do evil with it, the meaning of that memory shifted. Suddenly that worth felt conditional, like it could be taken or squandered. It was not inherent; it was bestowed. What was of worth was not *me*, but the veneer of constraints and observances that obscured me.

I looked at my brother. He seemed old in that moment, wise. He knew about the world. He knew about worldly women, so I asked him to keep me from becoming one.

'Okay, Fish Eyes,' he said. 'I will.'

★ ★ ★

When I awoke the next morning, my neck was bruised and my wrist swollen. I had a headache — not an ache *in* my brain but an actual aching *of* my brain, as if the organ itself was tender. I went to work but came home early and lay in a dark corner of the basement, waiting it out. I was lying on the carpet, feeling the pounding in my brain, when Tyler found me and folded himself onto the sofa near my head. I was not pleased to see him. The only thing worse than being dragged through the house by my hair was

Tyler's having seen it. Given the choice between letting it play out, and having Tyler there to stop it, I'd have chosen to let it play out. Obviously I would have chosen that. I'd been close to passing out anyway, and then I could have forgotten about it. In a day or two it wouldn't even have been real. It would become a bad dream, and in a month, a mere echo of a bad dream. But Tyler had seen it, had made it real.

'Have you thought about leaving?' Tyler asked.

'And go where?'

'School,' he said.

I brightened. 'I'm going to enroll in high school in September,' I said. 'Dad won't like it, but I'm gonna go.' I thought Tyler would be pleased; instead, he grimaced.

'You've said that before.'

'I'm going to.'

'Maybe,' Tyler said. 'But as long as you live under Dad's roof, it's hard to go when he asks you not to, easy to delay just one more year, until there aren't any years left. If you start as a sophomore, can you even graduate?'

We both knew I couldn't.

'It's time to go, Tara,' Tyler said. 'The longer you stay, the less likely you will ever leave.'

'You think I need to leave?'

Tyler didn't blink, didn't hesitate. 'I think this is the worst possible place for you.' He'd spoken softly, but it felt as though he'd shouted the words.

'Where could I go?'

'Go where I went,' Tyler said. 'Go to college.'

I snorted.

'BYU takes homeschoolers,' he said.

'Is that what we are?' I said. 'Homeschoolers?' I tried to remember the last time I'd read a textbook.

'The admissions board won't know anything except what we tell them,' Tyler said. 'If we say you were homeschooled, they'll believe it.'

'I won't get in.'

'You will,' he said. 'Just pass the ACT. One lousy test.'

Tyler stood to go. 'There's a world out there, Tara,' he said. 'And it will look a lot different once Dad is no longer whispering his view of it in your ear.'

★　★　★

The next day I drove to the hardware store in town and bought a slide-bolt lock for my bedroom door. I dropped it on my bed, then fetched a drill from the shop and started fitting screws. I thought Shawn was out — his truck wasn't in the driveway — but when I turned around with the drill, he was standing in my doorframe.

'What are you doing?' he said.

'Doorknob's broke,' I lied. 'Door blows open. This lock was cheap but it'll do the trick.'

Shawn fingered the thick steel, which I was sure he could tell was not cheap at all. I stood silently, paralyzed by dread but also by pity. In that moment I hated him, and I wanted to scream it in his face. I imagined the way he would crumple, crushed under the weight of my

173

words and his own self-loathing. Even then I understood the truth of it: that Shawn hated himself far more than I ever could.

'You're using the wrong screws,' he said. 'You need long ones for the wall and grabbers for the door. Otherwise, it'll bust right off.'

We walked to the shop. Shawn shuffled around for a few minutes, then emerged with a handful of steel screws. We walked back to the house and he installed the lock, humming to himself and smiling, flashing his baby teeth.

14

My Feet No Longer Touch Earth

In October Dad won a contract to build industrial granaries in Malad City, the dusty farmtown on the other side of Buck's Peak. It was a big job for a small outfit — the crew was just Dad, Shawn, Luke, and Audrey's husband, Benjamin — but Shawn was a good foreman, and with him in charge Dad had acquired a reputation for fast, reliable work.

Shawn wouldn't let Dad take shortcuts. Half the time I passed the shop, I'd hear the two of them shouting at each other, Dad saying Shawn was wasting time, Shawn screaming that Dad had damned near taken someone's head off.

Shawn worked long days cleaning, cutting and welding the raw materials for the granaries, and once construction began he was usually on-site in Malad. When he and Dad came home, hours after sunset, they were nearly always cussing. Shawn wanted to professionalize the operation, to invest the profits from the Malad job in new equipment; Dad wanted things to stay the same. Shawn said Dad didn't understand that construction was more competitive than scrapping, and that if they wanted to land real contracts, they needed to spend real money on real equipment — specifically, a new welder and a man lift with a basket.

'We can't keep using a forklift and an old cheese pallet,' Shawn said. 'It looks like shit, and it's dangerous besides.'

Dad laughed out loud at the idea of a man basket. He'd been using a forklift and pallet for twenty years.

* * *

I worked late most nights. Randy planned to take a big road trip to find new accounts, and he'd asked me to manage the business while he was gone. He taught me how to use his computer to keep the books, process orders, maintain inventory. It was from Randy that I first heard of the Internet. He showed me how to get online, how to visit a webpage, how to write an email. The day he left, he gave me a cellphone so he could reach me at all hours.

Tyler called one night just as I was getting home from work. He asked if I was studying for the ACT. 'I can't take the test,' I said. 'I don't know any math.'

'You've got money,' Tyler said. 'Buy books and learn it.'

I said nothing. College was irrelevant to me. I knew how my life would play out: when I was eighteen or nineteen, I would get married. Dad would give me a corner of the farm, and my husband would put a house on it. Mother would teach me about herbs, and also about midwifery, which she'd gone back to now the migraines were less frequent. When I had children, Mother would deliver them, and one day, I supposed, *I*

176

would be the Midwife. I didn't see where college fit in.

Tyler seemed to read my thoughts. 'You know Sister Sears?' he said. Sister Sears was the church choir director. 'How do you think she knows how to lead a choir?'

I'd always admired Sister Sears, and been jealous of her knowledge of music. I'd never thought about how she'd learned it.

'She studied,' Tyler said. 'Did you know you can get a degree in music? If you had one, you could give lessons, you could direct the church choir. Even Dad won't argue with that, not much anyway.'

Mother had recently purchased a trial version of AOL. I'd only ever used the Internet at Randy's, for work, but after Tyler hung up I turned on our computer and waited for the modem to dial. Tyler had said something about BYU's web-page. It only took a few minutes to find it. Then the screen was full of pictures — of neat brick buildings the color of sun-stone surrounded by emerald trees, of beautiful people walking and laughing, with books tucked under their arms and backpacks slung over their shoulders. It looked like something from a movie. A happy movie.

The next day, I drove forty miles to the nearest bookstore and bought a glossy ACT study guide. I sat on my bed and turned to the mathematics practice test. I scanned the first page. It wasn't that I didn't know how to solve the equations; I didn't recognize the symbols. It was the same on the second page, and the third.

I took the test to Mother. 'What's this?' I asked.

'Math,' she said.

'Then where are the numbers?'

'It's algebra. The letters stand in for numbers.'

'How do I do it?'

Mother fiddled with a pen and paper for several minutes, but she wasn't able to solve any of the first five equations.

The next day I drove the same forty miles, eighty round-trip, and returned home with a large algebra textbook.

★ ★ ★

Every evening, as the crew was leaving Malad, Dad would phone the house so Mother could have dinner waiting when the truck bumped up the hill. I listened for that call, and when it came I would get in Mother's car and drive away. I didn't know why. I would go to Worm Creek, where I'd sit in the balcony and watch rehearsals, my feet on the ledge, a math book open in front of me. I hadn't studied math since long division, and the concepts were unfamiliar. I understood the theory of fractions but struggled to manipulate them, and seeing a decimal on the page made my heart race. Every night for a month I sat in the opera house, in a chair of red velvet, and practiced the most basic operations — how to multiply fractions, how to use a reciprocal, how to add and multiply and divide with decimals — while on the stage, characters recited their lines.

178

I began to study trigonometry. There was solace in its strange formulas and equations. I was drawn to the Pythagorean theorem and its promise of a universal — the ability to predict the nature of any three points containing a right angle, anywhere, always. What I knew of physics I had learned in the junkyard, where the physical world often seemed unstable, capricious. But here was a principle through which the dimensions of life could be defined, captured. Perhaps reality was not wholly volatile. Perhaps it could be explained, predicted. Perhaps it could be made to make sense.

The misery began when I moved beyond the Pythagorean theorem to sine, cosine and tangent. I couldn't grasp such abstractions. I could feel the logic in them, could sense their power to bestow order and symmetry, but I couldn't unlock it. They kept their secrets, becoming a kind of gateway beyond which I believed there was a world of law and reason. But I could not pass through the gate.

Mother said that if I wanted to learn trigonometry, it was her responsibility to teach me. She set aside an evening, and the two of us sat at the kitchen table, scratching at bits of paper and tugging our hair. We spent three hours on a single problem, and every answer we produced was wrong.

'I wasn't any good at trig in high school,' Mother moaned, slamming the book shut. 'And I've forgotten what little I knew.'

Dad was in the living room, shuffling through blueprints for the granaries and mumbling to himself. I'd watched him sketch those blueprints, watched him perform the calculations, altering this angle or lengthening that beam. Dad had little formal education in mathematics but it was impossible to doubt his aptitude: somehow I knew that if I put the equation before my father, he would be able to solve it.

When I'd told Dad that I planned to go to college, he'd said a woman's place was in the home, that I should be learning about herbs — 'God's pharmacy' he'd called it, smiling to himself — so I could take over for Mother. He'd said a lot more, of course, about how I was whoring after man's knowledge instead of God's, but still I decided to ask him about trigonometry. Here was a sliver of man's knowledge I was certain he possessed.

I scribbled the problem on a fresh sheet of paper. Dad didn't look up as I approached, so gently, slowly, I slid the paper over the blueprints. 'Dad, can you solve this?'

He looked at me harshly, then his eyes softened. He rotated the paper, gazed at it for a moment, and began to scrawl, numbers and circles and great, arcing lines that doubled back on themselves. His solution didn't look like anything in my textbook. It didn't look like anything I had ever seen. His mustache twitched; he mumbled. Then he stopped scribbling, looked up and gave the correct answer.

I asked how he'd solved it. 'I don't know how to *solve* it,' he said, handing me the paper. 'All I know is, that's the answer.'

I walked back to the kitchen, comparing the

clean, balanced equation to the mayhem of unfinished computations and dizzying sketches. I was struck by the strangeness of that page: Dad could command this science, could decipher its language, decrypt its logic, could bend and twist and squeeze from it the truth. But as it passed through him, it turned to chaos.

★ ★ ★

I studied trigonometry for a month. I sometimes dreamed about sine, cosine and tangent, about mysterious angles and concussed computations, but for all this I made no real progress. I could not self-teach trigonometry. But I knew someone who had.

Tyler told me to meet him at our aunt Debbie's house, because she lived near Brigham Young University. The drive was three hours. I felt uncomfortable knocking on my aunt's door. She was Mother's sister, and Tyler had lived with her during his first year at BYU, but that was all I knew of her.

Tyler answered the door. We settled in the living room while Debbie prepared a casserole. Tyler solved the equations easily, writing out orderly explanations for every step. He was studying mechanical engineering, set to graduate near the top of his class, and soon after would start a PhD at Purdue. My trig equations were far beneath his abilities, but if he was bored he didn't show it; he just explained the principles patiently, over and over. The gate opened a little, and I peeked through it.

Tyler had gone, and Debbie was pushing a plate of casserole into my hands, when the phone rang. It was Mother.

'There's been an accident in Malad,' she said.

★　★　★

Mother had little information. Shawn had fallen. He'd landed on his head. Someone had called 9–11, and he'd been airlifted to a hospital in Pocatello. The doctors weren't sure if he would live. That was all she knew.

I wanted more, some statement of the odds, even if it was just so I could reason against them. I wanted her to say, 'They think he'll be fine' or even 'They expect we'll lose him.' Anything but what she was saying, which was, 'They don't know.'

Mother said I should come to the hospital. I imagined Shawn on a white gurney, the life leaking out of him. I felt such a wave of loss that my knees nearly buckled, but in the next moment I felt something else. Relief.

There was a storm coming, set to lay three feet of snow over Sardine Canyon, which guarded the entrance to our valley. Mother's car, which I had driven to Debbie's, had bald tires. I told Mother I couldn't get through.

★　★　★

The story of how Shawn fell would come to me in bits and pieces, thin lines of narrative from Luke and Benjamin, who were there. It was a

182

frigid afternoon and the wind was fierce, whipping the fine dust up in soft clouds. Shawn was standing on a wooden pallet, twenty feet in the air. Twelve feet below him was a half-finished concrete wall, with rebar jutting outward like blunt skewers. I don't know for certain what Shawn was doing on the pallet, but he was probably fitting posts or welding, because that was the kind of work he did. Dad was driving the forklift.

I've heard conflicting accounts of why Shawn fell.[4] Someone said Dad moved the boom unexpectedly and Shawn pitched over the edge. But the general consensus is that Shawn was standing near the brink, and for no reason at all stepped backward and lost his footing. He plunged twelve feet, his body revolving slowly in the air, so that when he struck the concrete wall with its outcropping of rebar, he hit headfirst, then tumbled the last eight feet to the dirt.

This is how the fall was described to me, but my mind sketches it differently — on a white page with evenly spaced lines. He ascends, falls at a slope, strikes the rebar and returns to the ground. I perceive a triangle. The event makes sense when I think of it in these terms. Then the logic of the page yields to my father.

Dad looked Shawn over. Shawn was disoriented. One of his pupils was dilated and the other wasn't, but no one knew what that meant. No one knew it meant there was a bleed inside his brain.

Dad told Shawn to take a break. Luke and Benjamin helped him prop himself against the pickup, then went back to work.

The facts after this point are even more hazy.

The story I heard was that fifteen minutes later Shawn wandered onto the site. Dad thought he was ready to work and told him to climb onto the pallet, and Shawn, who never liked being told what to do, started screaming at Dad about everything — the equipment, the granary designs, his pay. He screamed himself hoarse, then just when Dad thought he had calmed down, he gripped Dad around the waist and flung him like a sack of grain. Before Dad could scramble to his feet Shawn took off, leaping and howling and laughing, and Luke and Benjamin, now sure something was very wrong, chased after him. Luke reached him first but couldn't hold him; then Benjamin added his weight and Shawn slowed a little. But it wasn't until all three men tackled him — throwing his body to the ground, where, because he was resisting, his head hit hard — that he finally lay still.

No one has ever described to me what happened when Shawn's head struck that second time. Whether he had a seizure, or vomited, or lost consciousness, I'm not sure. But it was so chilling that someone — maybe Dad, probably Benjamin — dialed 9-11, which no member of my family had ever done before.

They were told a helicopter would arrive in minutes. Later the doctors would speculate that when Dad, Luke and Benjamin had wrestled Shawn to the ground — and he'd sustained a concussion — he was already in critical

184

condition. They said it was a miracle he hadn't died the moment his head hit the ground.

I struggle to imagine the scene while they waited for the chopper. Dad said that when the paramedics arrived, Shawn was sobbing, begging for Mother. By the time he reached the hospital, his state of mind had shifted. He stood naked on the gurney, eyes bulging, bloodshot, screaming that he would rip out the eyes of the next bastard who came near him. Then he collapsed into sobs and finally lost consciousness.

★ ★ ★

Shawn lived through the night.

In the morning I drove to Buck's Peak. I couldn't explain why I wasn't rushing to my brother's bedside. I told Mother I had to work.

'He's asking for you,' she said.

'You said he doesn't recognize anyone.'

'He doesn't,' she said. 'But the nurse just asked me if he knows someone named Tara. He said your name over and over this morning, when he was asleep and when he was awake. I told them Tara is his sister, and now they're saying it would be good if you came. He might recognize you, and that would be something. Yours is the only name he's said since he got to the hospital.'

I was silent.

'I'll pay for the gas,' Mother said. She thought I wouldn't come because of the thirty dollars it would cost in fuel. I was embarrassed that she thought that, but then, if it wasn't the money, I

185

had no reason at all.

'I'm leaving now,' I said.

I remember strangely little of the hospital, or of how my brother looked. I vaguely recall that his head was wrapped in gauze, and that when I asked why, Mother said the doctors had performed a surgery, cutting into his skull to relieve some pressure, or stop a bleed, or repair something — actually, I can't remember what she said. Shawn was tossing and turning like a child with a fever. I sat with him for an hour. A few times his eyes opened, but if he was conscious, he didn't recognize me.

When I came the next day, he was awake. I walked into the room and he blinked and looked at Mother, as if to check that she was seeing me, too.

'You came,' he said. 'I didn't think you would.' He took my hand and fell asleep.

I stared at his face, at the bandages wrapped around his forehead and over his ears, and was bled of my bitterness. Then I understood why I hadn't come sooner. I'd been afraid of how I would feel, afraid that if he died, I might be glad.

I'm sure the doctors wanted to keep him in the hospital, but we didn't have insurance, and the bill was already so large that Shawn would be making payments a decade later. The moment he was stable enough to travel, we took him home.

He lived on the sofa in the front room for two months. He was physically weak — it was all he had in him to make it to the bathroom and back. He'd lost his hearing completely in one ear and had trouble hearing with the other, so he often turned his head when people spoke to him, orienting his better ear toward them, rather than his eyes. Except for this strange movement and the bandages from the surgery, he looked normal, no swelling, no bruises. According to the doctors, this was because the damage was very serious: a lack of external injuries meant the damage was all internal.

It took some time for me to realize that although Shawn looked the same, he wasn't. He seemed lucid, but if you listened carefully his stories didn't make sense. They weren't really stories at all, just one tangent after another.

I felt guilty that I hadn't visited him immediately in the hospital, so to make it up to him I quit my job and tended him day and night. When he wanted water, I fetched it; if he was hungry, I cooked.

Sadie started coming around, and Shawn welcomed her. I looked forward to her visits because they gave me time to study. Mother thought it was important that I stay with Shawn, so no one interrupted me. For the first time in my life I had long stretches in which to learn — without having to scrap, or strain tinctures, or check inventory for Randy. I examined Tyler's notes, read and reread his careful explanations. After a few weeks of this, by magic or miracle, the concepts took hold. I retook the practice test. The advanced algebra was still indecipherable — it came from a world beyond my ability to perceive — but the trigonometry had become intelligible, messages written in a language I could understand, from a world of logic and order that only existed in black ink and on white paper.

The real world, meanwhile, plunged into chaos. The doctors told Mother that Shawn's injury might have altered his personality — that in the hospital, he had shown tendencies toward volatility, even violence, and that such changes might be permanent.

He did succumb to rages, moments of blind anger when all he wanted was to hurt someone. He had an intuition for nastiness, for saying the single most devastating thing, that left Mother in tears more nights than not. These rages changed, and worsened, as his physical strength improved, and I found myself cleaning the toilet every morning, knowing my head might be inside it before lunch. Mother said I was the only one who could calm him, and I persuaded myself that that was true. *Who better?* I thought. *He doesn't affect me.*

Reflecting on it now, I'm not sure the injury changed him that much, but I convinced myself that it had, and that any cruelty on his part was entirely new. I can read my journals from this period and trace the evolution — of a young girl rewriting her history. In the reality she constructed for herself nothing had been wrong before her brother fell off that pallet. *I wish I had my best friend back*, she wrote. *Before his injury, I never got hurt at all.*

15

No More a Child

There was a moment that winter. I was kneeling on the carpet, listening to Dad testify of Mother's calling as a healer, when my breath caught in my chest and I felt taken out of myself. I no longer saw my parents or our living room. What I saw was a woman grown, with her own mind, her own prayers, who no longer sat, childlike, at her father's feet.

I saw the woman's swollen belly and it was my belly. Next to her sat her mother, the midwife. She took her mother's hand and said she wanted the baby delivered in a hospital, by a doctor. I'll drive you, her mother said. The women moved toward the door, but the door was blocked — by loyalty, by obedience. By her father. He stood, immovable. But the woman was *his* daughter, and she had drawn to herself all his conviction, all his weightiness. She set him aside and moved through the door.

I tried to imagine what future such a woman might claim for herself. I tried to conjure other scenes in which she and her father were of two minds. When she ignored his counsel and kept her own. But my father had taught me that there are not two reasonable opinions to be had on any subject: there is Truth and there are Lies. So as I knelt on the carpet, listening to my father but studying this stranger, and felt suspended between them, drawn to each, repelled by both, I understood that no future could hold them; no destiny could tolerate him *and* her. I would remain a child, in perpetuity, always, or I would lose him.

★ ★ ★

I was lying on my bed, watching the shadows my feeble lamp cast on the ceiling, when I heard my father's voice at the door. Instinctively I jerked to my feet in a kind of salute, but once I was standing I wasn't sure what to do. There was no precedent for this: my father had never visited my room before.

He strode past me and sat on my bed, then patted the mattress next to him. I took my seat, nervously, my feet barely touching the floor. I waited for him to speak, but the moments passed silently. His eyes were closed, his jaw slackened, as if he were listening to seraphic voices. 'I've been praying,' he said. His voice was soft, a loving voice. 'I've been praying about your decision to go to college.'

His eyes opened. His pupils had dilated in the lamplight, absorbing the hazel of the iris. I'd never seen eyes so given over to blackness; they seemed unearthly, tokens of spiritual power.

'The Lord has called me to testify,' he said. 'He is displeased. You have cast aside His blessings to whore after man's knowledge. His wrath is stirred against you. It will not be long in coming.'

I don't remember my father standing to leave but he must have, while I sat, gripped by fear. God's wrath had laid waste to cities, it had flooded the whole earth. I felt weak, then wholly powerless. I remembered that my life was not mine. I could be taken out of my body at any moment, dragged heavenward to reckon with a furious Father.

The next morning I found Mother mixing oils in the kitchen. 'I've decided not to go to BYU,' I said.

She looked up, fixing her eyes on the wall behind me, and whispered, 'Don't say that. I don't want to hear that.'

I didn't understand. I'd thought she would be glad to see me yield to God.

Her gaze shifted to me. I hadn't felt its strength in years and I was stunned by it. 'Of all my children,' she said, 'you were the one I thought would burst out of here in a blaze. I didn't expect it from Tyler — that was a surprise — but *you*. Don't you stay. Go. Don't let anything stop you from going.'

I heard Dad's step on the stairwell. Mother sighed and her eyes fluttered, as if she were coming out of a trance.

Dad took his seat at the kitchen table and Mother stood to fix his breakfast. He began a lecture about liberal professors, and Mother mixed batter for pancakes, periodically murmuring in agreement.

★   ★   ★

191

Without Shawn as foreman, Dad's construction business dwindled. I'd quit my job at Randy's to look after Shawn. Now I needed money, so when Dad went back to scrapping that winter, so did I.

It was an icy morning, much like the first, when I returned to the junkyard. It had changed. There were still pillars of mangled cars but they no longer dominated the landscape. A few years before, Dad had been hired by Utah Power to dismantle hundreds of utility towers. He had been allowed to keep the angle iron, and it was now stacked — four hundred thousand pounds of it — in tangled mountains all over the yard.

I woke up every morning at six to study — because it was easier to focus in the mornings, before I was worn out from scrapping. Although I was still fearful of God's wrath, I reasoned with myself that my passing the ACT was so unlikely, it would take an act of God. And if God acted, then surely my going to school was His will.

The ACT was composed of four sections: math, English, science and reading. My math skills were improving but they were not strong. While I could answer most of the questions on the practice exam, I was slow, needing double or triple the allotted time. I lacked even a basic knowledge of grammar, though I was learning, beginning with nouns and moving on to prepositions and gerunds. Science was a mystery, perhaps because the only science book I'd ever read had had detachable pages for coloring. Of the four sections, reading was the only one about which I felt confident.

BYU was a competitive school. I'd need a high score — a twenty-seven at least, which meant the top fifteen percent of my cohort. I was sixteen, had never taken an exam, and had only recently undertaken anything like a systematic education; still I registered for the test. It felt like throwing dice, like the roll was out of my hands. God would score the toss.

I didn't sleep the night before. My brain conjured so many scenes of disaster, it burned as if with a fever. At five I got out of bed, ate breakfast, and drove the forty miles to Utah State University. I was led into a white classroom with thirty other students, who took their seats and placed their pencils on their desks. A middle-aged woman handed out strange pink sheets I'd never seen before.

'Excuse me,' I said when she gave me mine. 'What is this?'

'It's a bubble sheet. To mark your answers.'

'How does it work?' I said.

'It's the same as any other bubble sheet.' She began to move away from me, visibly irritated, as if I were playing a prank.

'I've never used one before.'

She appraised me for a moment. 'Fill in the bubble of the correct answer,' she said. 'Blacken it completely. Understand?'

The test began. I'd never sat at a desk for four hours in a room full of people. The noise was unbelievable, yet I seemed to be the only person who heard it, who couldn't divert her attention from the rustle of turning pages and the scratch of pencils on paper.

When it was over I suspected that I'd failed the math, and I was positive that I'd failed the science. My answers for the science portion couldn't even be called guesses. They were random, just patterns of dots on that strange pink sheet.

I drove home. I felt stupid, but more than stupid I felt ridiculous. Now that I'd seen the other students — watched them march into the classroom in neat rows, claim their seats and calmly fill in their answers, as if they were performing a practiced routine — it seemed absurd that I had thought I could score in the top fifteen percent.

That was their world. I stepped into overalls and returned to mine.

* * *

There was an unusually hot day that spring, and Luke and I spent it hauling purlins — the iron beams that run horizontally along the length of a roof. The purlins were heavy and the sun relentless. Sweat dripped from our noses and onto the painted iron. Luke slipped out of his shirt, grabbed hold of the sleeves and tore them, leaving huge gashes a breeze could pass through. I wouldn't have dreamed of doing anything so radical, but after the twentieth purlin my back was sticky with sweat, and I flapped my T-shirt to make a fan, then rolled up my sleeves until an inch of my shoulders was visible. When Dad saw me a few minutes later, he strode over and yanked the sleeves down. 'This ain't a whorehouse,' he said.

I watched him walk away and, mechanically, as

194

if I weren't making the decision, rerolled them. He returned an hour later, and when he caught sight of me he paused mid-step, confused. He'd told me what to do, and I hadn't done it. He stood uncertainly for a moment, then crossed over to me, took hold of both sleeves and jerked them down. He didn't make it ten steps before I'd rolled them up again.

I wanted to obey. I meant to. But the afternoon was so hot, the breeze on my arms so welcome. It was just a few inches. I was covered from my temples to my toes in grime. It would take me half an hour that night to dig the black dirt out of my nostrils and ears. I didn't feel much like an object of desire or temptation. I felt like a human forklift. How could an inch of skin matter?

★ ★ ★

I was hoarding my paychecks, in case I needed the money for tuition. Dad noticed and started charging me for small things. Mother had gone back to buying insurance after the second car accident, and Dad said I should pay my share. So I did. Then he wanted more, for registration. 'These Government fees will break you,' he said as I handed him the cash.

That satisfied Dad until my test results arrived. I returned from the junkyard to find a white envelope. I tore it open, staining the page with grease, and looked past the individual scores to the composite. Twenty-two. My heart was beating loud, happy beats. It wasn't a twenty-seven, but it opened up possibilities. Maybe Idaho State.

I showed Mother the score and she told Dad. He became agitated, then he shouted that it was time I moved out.

'If she's old enough to pull a paycheck, she's old enough to pay rent,' Dad yelled. 'And she can pay it somewhere else.' At first Mother argued with him, but within minutes he'd convinced her.

I'd been standing in the kitchen, weighing my options, thinking about how I'd just given Dad four hundred dollars, a third of my savings, when Mother turned to me and said, 'Do you think you could move out by Friday?'

Something broke in me, a dam or a levee. I felt tossed about, unable to hold myself in place. I screamed but the screams were strangled; I was drowning. I had nowhere to go. I couldn't afford to rent an apartment, and even if I could the only apartments for rent were in town. Then I'd need a car. I only had eight hundred dollars. I sputtered all this at Mother, then ran to my room and slammed the door.

She knocked moments later. 'I know you think we're being unfair,' she said, 'but when I was your age I was living on my own, getting ready to marry your father.'

'You were married at sixteen?' I said.

'Don't be silly,' she said. 'You are not sixteen.'

I stared at her. She stared at me. 'Yes, I am. I'm sixteen.'

She looked me over. 'You're at least twenty.' She cocked her head. 'Aren't you?'

We were silent. My heart pounded in my chest. 'I turned sixteen in September,' I said.

'Oh.' Mother bit her lip, then she stood and smiled. 'Well, don't worry about it then. You can stay. Don't know what your dad was thinking, really. I guess we forgot. Hard to keep track of how old you kids are.'

★ ★ ★

Shawn returned to work, hobbling unsteadily. He wore an Aussie outback hat, which was large, wide-brimmed, and made of chocolate-brown oiled leather. Before the accident, he had worn the hat only when riding horses, but now he kept it on all the time, even in the house, which Dad said was disrespectful. Disrespecting Dad might have been the reason Shawn wore it, but I suspect another reason was that it was large and comfortable and covered the scars from his surgery.

He worked short days at first. Dad had a contract to build a milking barn in Oneida County, about twenty miles from Buck's Peak, so Shawn puttered around the yard, adjusting schematics and measuring I-beams.

Luke, Benjamin and I were scrapping. Dad had decided it was time to salvage the angle iron stacked all around the farm. To be sold, each piece had to measure less than four feet. Shawn suggested we use torches to cut the iron, but Dad said it would be too slow and cost too much in fuel.

A few days later Dad came home with the

197

most frightening machine I've ever seen. He called it the Shear. At first glance it appeared to be a three-ton pair of scissors, and this turned out to be exactly what it was. The blades were made of dense iron, twelve inches thick and five feet across. They cut not by sharpness but by force and mass. They bit down, their great jaws propelled by a heavy piston attached to a large iron wheel. The wheel was animated by a belt and motor, which meant that if something got caught in the machine, it would take anywhere from thirty seconds to a minute to stop the wheel and halt the blades. Up and down they roared, louder than a passing train as they chewed through iron as thick as a man's arm. The iron wasn't being cut so much as snapped. Sometimes it would buck, propelling whoever was holding it toward the dull, chomping blades.

Dad had dreamed up many dangerous schemes over the years, but this was the first that really shocked me. Perhaps it was the obvious lethality of it, the certainty that a wrong move would cost a limb. Or maybe that it was utterly unnecessary. It was indulgent. Like a toy, if a toy could take your head off.

Shawn called it a death machine and said Dad had lost what little sense he'd ever had. 'Are you *trying* to kill someone?' he said. 'Because I got a gun in my truck that will make a lot less mess.' Dad couldn't suppress his grin. I'd never seen him so enraptured.

Shawn lurched back to the shop, shaking his head. Dad began feeding iron through the Shear. Each length bucked him forward and twice he nearly pitched headfirst into the blades. I jammed my eyes shut, knowing that if Dad's head got caught, the blades wouldn't even slow, just hack through his neck and keep chomping.

Now that he was sure the machine worked, Dad motioned for Luke to take over, and Luke, ever eager to please, stepped forward. Five minutes later Luke's arm was gashed to the bone and he was running toward the house, blood spurting.

Dad scanned his crew. He motioned to Benjamin, but Benjamin shook his head, saying he liked his fingers attached, thanks anyway. Dad looked longingly at the house, and I imagined him wondering how long it would take Mother to stop the bleeding. Then his eyes settled on me.

'Come here, Tara.'

I didn't move.

'Get over here,' he said.

I stepped forward slowly, not blinking, watching the Shear as if it might attack. Luke's blood was still on the blade. Dad picked up a six-foot length of angle iron and handed me the end. 'Keep a good hold on it,' he said. 'But if it bucks, let go.'

The blades chomped, growling as they snapped up and down — a warning, I thought, like a dog's snarl, to get the hell away. But Dad's mania for the machine had carried him beyond the reach of reason.

'It's easy,' he said.

I prayed when I fed the first piece to the blades. Not to avoid injury — there was no possibility of that — but that the injury would be like Luke's, a wedge of flesh, so I could go to the house, too. I chose smaller pieces, hoping my weight could control the lurch. Then I ran out of small pieces. I picked up the smallest of what was left, but the metal was still thick. I shoved it through and waited for the jaws to crash shut. The sound of solid iron fracturing was thunderous. The iron bucked, tossing me forward so both my feet left the ground. I let go and collapsed in the dirt, and the iron, now free, and being chewed violently by the blades, launched into the air then crashed down next to me.

'WHAT THE HELL IS GOING ON?' Shawn appeared in the corner of my vision. He strode over and pulled me to my feet, then spun around to face Dad.

'Five minutes ago, this monster nearly ripped Luke's arm off! So you've put Tara on it?'

'She's made of strong stuff,' Dad said, winking at me.

Shawn's eyes bulged. He was supposed to be taking it easy, but he looked apoplectic.

'It's going to take her head off!' he screamed. He turned to me and waved toward the iron-worker in the shop. 'Go make clips to fit those purlins. I don't want you coming near this thing again.'

Dad moved forward. 'This is *my* crew. You work for me and so does Tara. I told her to run the Shear, and she will run it.'

They shouted at each other for fifteen minutes. It was different from the fights they'd had before — this was unrestrained somehow, hateful. I'd never seen anyone yell at my father like that, and I was astonished by, then afraid of, the change it wrought in his features. His face transformed, becoming rigid, desperate. Shawn had awoken something in Dad, some primal need. Dad could not lose this argument and save face. If I didn't run the Shear, Dad would no longer be Dad.

Shawn leapt forward and shoved Dad hard in the chest. Dad stumbled backward, tripped and fell. He lay in the mud, shocked, for a moment, then he climbed to his feet and lunged toward his son. Shawn raised his arms to block the punch, but when Dad saw this he lowered his fists, perhaps remembering that Shawn had only recently regained the ability to walk.

'I told her to do it, and she *will* do it,' Dad said, low and angry. 'Or she won't live under my roof.'

Shawn looked at me. For a moment, he seemed to consider helping me pack — after all, he had run away from Dad at my age — but I shook my head. I wasn't leaving, not like that. I would work the Shear first, and Shawn knew it. He looked at the Shear, then at the pile next to it, about fifty thousand pounds of iron. 'She'll do it,' he said.

Dad seemed to grow five inches. Shawn bent unsteadily and lifted a piece of heavy iron, then heaved it toward the Shear.

'Don't be stupid,' Dad said.

'If she's doing it, I'm doing it,' Shawn said. The fight had left his voice. I'd never seen Shawn give way to Dad, not once, but he'd decided to lose this argument. He understood that if *he* didn't submit, I surely would.

'You're my foreman!' Dad shouted. 'I need you in Oneida, not mucking with scrap!'

'Then shut down the Shear.'

Dad walked away cursing, exasperated, but probably thinking that Shawn would get tired and go back to being foreman before supper. Shawn watched Dad leave, then he turned to me and said, 'Okay, Siddle Liss. You bring the pieces and I'll feed them through. If the iron is thick, say a half inch, I'll need your weight on the back to keep me from getting tossed into the blades. Okay?'

Shawn and I ran the Shear for a month. Dad was too stubborn to shut it down, even though it cost him more to have his foreman salvaging than it would have cost him to cut the iron with torches. When we finished, I had some bruises but I wasn't hurt. Shawn seemed bled of life. It had only been a few months since his fall from the pallet, and his body couldn't take the wear. He was cracked in the head many times when a length of iron bucked at an unexpected angle. When that happened he'd sit for a minute in the dirt, his hands over his eyes, then he'd stand and reach for the next length. In the evenings he lay on the kitchen floor in his stained shirt and dusty jeans, too weary even to shower.

I fetched all the food and water he asked for. Sadie came most evenings, and the two of us would run side by side when he sent us for ice, then to remove the ice, then to put the ice back in. We were both Fish Eyes.

The next morning Shawn and I would return to the Shear, and he would feed iron through its jaws, which chewed with such force that it pulled him off his feet, easily, playfully, as if it were a game, as if he were a child.

16

Disloyal Man, Disobedient Heaven

Construction began on the milking barn in Oneida. Shawn designed and welded the main frame — the massive beams that formed the skeleton of the building. They were too heavy for the loader; only a crane could lift them. It was a delicate procedure, requiring the welders to balance on opposite ends of a beam while it was lowered onto columns, then welded in place. Shawn surprised everyone when he announced that he wanted me to operate the crane.

'Tara can't drive the crane,' Dad said. 'It'll take half the morning to teach her the controls, and she still won't know what the hell she's doing.'

'But she'll be careful,' Shawn said, 'and I'm done falling off shit.'

An hour later I was in the man box, and Shawn and Luke were standing on either end of a beam, twenty feet in the air. I brushed the lever lightly, listening as the hydraulic cylinders hissed softly to protract. 'Hold!' Shawn shouted when the beam was in place, then they nodded their helmets down and began to weld.

My operating the crane was one of a hundred disputes between Dad and Shawn that Shawn won that summer. Most were not resolved so peacefully. They argued nearly every day

— about a flaw in the schematics or a tool that had been left at home. Dad seemed eager to fight, to prove who was in charge.

One afternoon Dad walked over and stood right next to Shawn, watching him weld. A minute later, for no reason, he started shouting: that Shawn had taken too long at lunch, that he wasn't getting the crew up early enough or working us hard enough. Dad yelled for several minutes, then Shawn took off his welding helmet, looked at him calmly and said, 'You gonna shut up so I can work?'

Dad kept yelling. He said Shawn was lazy, that he didn't know how to run a crew, didn't understand the value of hard work. Shawn stepped down from his welding and ambled over to the flatbed pickup. Dad followed, still hollering. Shawn pulled off his gloves, slowly, delicately, one finger at a time, as if there weren't a man screaming six inches from his face. For several moments he stood still, letting the abuse wash over him, then he stepped into the pickup and drove off, leaving Dad to shout at the dust.

I remember the awe I felt as I watched that pickup roll down the dirt road. Shawn was the only person I had ever seen stand up to Dad, the only one whose force of mind, whose sheer tonnage of conviction, could make Dad give way. I had seen Dad lose his temper and shout at every one of my brothers. Shawn was the only one I ever saw walk away.

* * *

205

It was a Saturday night. I was at Grandma-over-in-town's, my math book propped open on the kitchen table, a plate of cookies next to me. I was studying to retake the ACT. I often studied at Grandma's so Dad wouldn't lecture me.

The phone rang. It was Shawn. Did I want to watch a movie? I said I did, and a few minutes later I heard a loud rumble and looked out the window. With his booming black motorcycle and his wide-brimmed Aussie hat, he seemed entirely out of place parking parallel to Grandma's white picket fence. Grandma started making brownies, and Shawn and I went upstairs to choose a movie.

We paused the movie when Grandma delivered the brownies. We ate them in silence, our spoons clicking loudly against Grandma's porcelain plates. 'You'll get your twenty-seven,' Shawn said suddenly when we'd finished.

'It doesn't matter,' I said. 'I don't think I'll go either way. What if Dad's right? What if I get brainwashed?'

Shawn shrugged. 'You're as smart as Dad. If Dad's right, you'll know when you get there.'

The movie ended. We told Grandma good night. It was a balmy summer evening, perfect for the motorcycle, and Shawn said I should ride home with him, we'd get the car tomorrow. He revved the engine, waiting for me to climb on. I took a step toward him, then remembered the math book on Grandma's table.

'You go,' I said. 'I'll be right behind you.'

Shawn yanked his hat down on his head, spun the bike around and charged down the empty street.

I drove in a happy stupor. The night was black — that thick darkness that belongs only in backcountry, where the houses are few and the streetlights fewer, where starlight goes unchallenged. I navigated the winding highway as I'd done numberless times before, racing down the Bear River Hill, coasting through the flat stretch parallel to Fivemile Creek. Up ahead the road climbed and bent to the right. I knew the curve was there without looking for it, and wondered at the still headlights I saw shining in the blackness.

I began the ascent. There was a pasture to my left, a ditch to my right. As the incline began in earnest I saw three cars pulled off near the ditch. The doors were open, the cab lights on. Seven or eight people huddled around something on the gravel. I changed lanes to drive around them, but stopped when I saw a small object lying in the middle of the highway.

It was a wide-brimmed Aussie hat.

I pulled over and ran toward the people clustered by the ditch. 'Shawn!' I shouted.

The crowd parted to let me through. Shawn was facedown on the gravel, lying in a pool of blood that looked pink in the glare from the headlights. He wasn't moving. 'He hit a cow coming around the corner,' a man said. 'It's so dark tonight, he didn't even see it. We've called an ambulance. We don't dare move him.'

Shawn's body was contorted, his back twisted. I had no idea how long an ambulance might take, and there was so much blood. I decided to stop the bleeding. I dug my hands under his shoulder and heaved but I couldn't lift him. I looked up at the crowd and recognized a face. Dwain.[5] He was one of *us*. Mother had midwifed four of his eight children.

'Dwain! Help me turn him.'

Dwain hefted Shawn onto his back. For a second that contained an hour, I stared at my brother, watching the blood trickle out of his temple and down his right cheek, pouring over his ear and onto his white T-shirt. His eyes were closed, his mouth open. The blood was oozing from a hole the size of a golf ball in his forehead. It looked as though his temple had been dragged on the asphalt, scraping away skin, then bone. I leaned close and peered inside the wound. Something soft and spongy glistened back at me. I slipped out of my jacket and pressed it to Shawn's head.

When I touched the abrasion, Shawn released a long sigh and his eyes opened.

'Sidlister,' he mumbled. Then he seemed to lose consciousness.

My cellphone was in my pocket. I dialed. Dad answered.

I must have been frantic, sputtering. I said Shawn had crashed his bike, that he had a hole in his head.

'Slow down. What happened?'

I said it all a second time. 'What should I do?'

'Bring him home,' Dad said. 'Your mother will deal with it.'

I opened my mouth but no words came out. Finally, I said, 'I'm not joking. His brain, I can see it!'

208

'Bring him home,' Dad said. 'Your mother can handle it.' Then: the dull drone of a dial tone. He'd hung up.

Dwain had overheard. 'I live just through this field,' he said. 'Your mother can treat him there.'

'No,' I said. 'Dad wants him home. Help me get him in the car.'

Shawn groaned when we lifted him but he didn't speak again. Someone said we should wait for the ambulance. Someone else said we should drive him to the hospital ourselves. I don't think anyone believed we would take him home, not with his brain dribbling out of his forehead.

We folded Shawn into the backseat. I got behind the wheel, and Dwain climbed in on the passenger side. I checked my rearview mirror to pull onto the highway, then reached up and shoved the mirror downward so it reflected Shawn's face, blank and bloodied. My foot hovered over the gas.

Three seconds passed, maybe four. That's all it was.

Dwain was shouting, 'Let's go!' but I barely heard him. I was lost to panic. My thoughts wandered wildly, feverishly, through a fog of resentment. The state was dreamlike, as if the hysteria had freed me from a fiction that, five minutes before, I had needed to believe.

I had never thought about the day Shawn had fallen from the pallet. There was nothing to think about. He had fallen because God wanted him to fall; there was no deeper meaning in it than that. I had never imagined what it would have been like to be there. To see Shawn plunge, grasping at air. To watch him collide, then fold, then lie still. I had never allowed myself to imagine what happened *after* — Dad's decision to leave him by the pickup, or the worried looks that must have passed between Luke and Ben.

Now, staring at the creases in my brother's face, each a little river of blood, I remembered. I remembered that Shawn had sat by the pickup for a quarter of an hour, his brain bleeding. Then he'd had that fit and the boys had wrestled him to the ground, so that he'd fallen, sustained a second injury, the injury the doctors said should have killed him. It was the reason Shawn would never quite be Shawn again.

If the first fall was God's will, whose was the second?

★ ★ ★

I'd never been to the hospital in town, but it was easy to find.

Dwain had asked me what the hell I was doing when I flipped a U-turn and accelerated down the hillside. I'd listened to Shawn's shallow breathing as I raced through the valley, along Fivemile Creek, then shot up the Bear River Hill. At the hospital, I parked in the emergency lane, and Dwain and I carried Shawn through the glass doors. I shouted for help. A nurse appeared, running, then another. Shawn was conscious by then. They took him away and someone shoved me into the waiting room.

There was no avoiding what had to be done next. I called Dad.

'You nearly home?' he said.

'I'm at the hospital.'

There was silence, then he said, 'We're coming.'

Fifteen minutes later they were there, and the three of us waited awkwardly together, me chewing my fingernails on a pastel-blue sofa, Mother pacing and clicking her fingers, and Dad sitting motionless beneath a loud wall clock.

The doctor gave Shawn a CAT scan. He said the wound was nasty but the damage was minimal, and then I remembered what the last doctors had told me — that with head injuries, often the ones that look the worst are actually less severe — and I felt stupid for panicking and bringing him here. The hole in the bone was small, the doctor said. It might grow over on its own, or a surgeon could put in a metal plate. Shawn said he'd like to see how it healed, so the doctor folded the skin over the hole and stitched it.

We took Shawn home around three in the morning. Dad drove, with Mother next to him, and I rode in the backseat with Shawn. No one spoke. Dad didn't yell or lecture; in fact, he never mentioned that night again. But there was something in the way he fixed his gaze, never looking directly at me, that made me think a fork had come along in the road, and I'd gone one way and he the other. After that night, there was never any question of whether I would go or stay. It was as if we were living in the future, and I was already gone.

When I think of that night now, I don't think

of the dark highway, or of my brother lying in a pool of his own blood. I think of the waiting room, with its ice-blue sofa and pale walls. I smell its sterilized air. I hear the ticking of a plastic clock.

Sitting across from me is my father, and as I look into his worn face it hits me, a truth so powerful I don't know why I've never understood it before. The truth is this: that I am not a good daughter. I am a traitor, a wolf among sheep; there is something different about me and that difference is not good. I want to bellow, to weep into my father's knees and promise never to do it again. But wolf that I am, I am still above lying, and anyway he would sniff the lie. We both know that if I ever again find Shawn on the highway, soaked in crimson, I will do exactly what I have just done.

I am not sorry, merely ashamed.

★ ★ ★

The envelope arrived three weeks later, just as Shawn was getting back on his feet. I tore it open, feeling numb, as if I were reading my sentence after the guilty verdict had already been handed down. I scanned down to the composite score. Twenty-eight. I checked it again. I checked my name. There was no mistake. Somehow — and a miracle was the only way I could account for it — I'd done it.

My first thought was a resolution: I resolved to never again work for my father. I drove to the only grocery store in town, called Stokes, and applied for a job bagging groceries. I was only sixteen, but I didn't tell the manager that and he hired me for forty hours a week. My first shift started at four o'clock the next morning.

When I got home, Dad was driving the loader through the junkyard. I stepped onto the ladder and grabbed hold of the rail. Over the roar of the engine, I told him I'd found a job but that I would drive the crane in the afternoons, until he could hire someone. He dropped the boom and stared ahead.

'You've already decided,' he said without glancing at me. 'No point dragging it out.'

I applied to BYU a week later. I had no idea how to write the application, so Tyler wrote it for me. He said I'd been educated according to a rigorous program designed by my mother, who'd made sure I met all the requirements to graduate.

My feelings about the application changed from day to day, almost from minute to minute. Sometimes I was sure God wanted me to go to college, because He'd given me that twenty-eight. Other times I was sure I'd be rejected, and that God would punish me for applying, for trying to abandon my own family. But whatever the outcome, I knew I would leave. I would go somewhere, even if it wasn't to school. Home had changed the moment I'd taken Shawn to that hospital instead of to Mother. I had rejected some part of it; now it was rejecting me.

The admissions committee was efficient; I didn't wait long. The letter arrived in a normal envelope. My heart sank when I saw it. Rejection

213

letters are small, I thought. I opened it and read 'Congratulations.' I'd been admitted for the semester beginning January 5.

Mother hugged me. Dad tried to be cheerful. 'It proves one thing at least,' he said. 'Our home school is as good as any public education.'

* * *

Three days before I turned seventeen, Mother drove me to Utah to find an apartment. The search took all day, and we arrived home late to find Dad eating a frozen supper. He hadn't cooked it well and it was mush. The mood around him was charged, combustible. It felt like he might detonate at any moment. Mother didn't even kick off her shoes, just rushed to the kitchen and began shuffling pans to fix a real dinner. Dad moved to the living room and started cursing at the VCR. I could see from the hallway that the cables weren't connected. When I pointed this out, he exploded. He cussed and waved his arms, shouting that in a man's house the cables should *always* be hooked up, that a man should never have to come into a room and find the cables to his VCR unhooked. Why the hell had I unhooked them anyway?

Mother rushed in from the kitchen. '*I* disconnected the cables,' she said.

Dad rounded on her, sputtering. 'Why do you always take her side! A man should be able to expect support from his wife!'

I fumbled with the cables while Dad stood over me, shouting. I kept dropping them. My

214

mind pulsed with panic, which overpowered every thought, so that I could not even remember how to connect red to red, white to white.

Then it was gone. I looked up at my father, at his purple face, at the vein pulsing in his neck. I still hadn't managed to attach the cables. I stood, and once on my feet, didn't care whether the cables were attached. I walked out of the room. Dad was still shouting when I reached the kitchen. As I moved down the hall I looked back. Mother had taken my place, crouching over the VCR, groping for the wires, as Dad towered over her.

★ ★ ★

Waiting for Christmas that year felt like waiting to walk off the edge of a cliff. Not since Y2K had I felt so certain that something terrible was coming, something that would obliterate everything I'd known before. And what would replace it? I tried to imagine the future, to populate it with professors, homework, classrooms, but my mind couldn't conjure them. There was no future in my imagination. There was New Year's Eve, then there was nothing.

I knew I should prepare, try to acquire the high school education Tyler had told the university I had. But I didn't know how, and I didn't want to ask Tyler for help. He was starting a new life at Purdue — he was even getting married — and I doubted he wanted responsibility for mine.

I noticed, though, when he came home for Christmas, that he was reading a book called Les

Misérables, and I decided that it must be the kind of a book a college student reads. I bought my own copy, hoping it would teach me about history or literature, but it didn't. It couldn't, because I was unable to distinguish between the fictional story and the factual backdrop. Napoleon felt no more real to me than Jean Valjean. I had never heard of either.

PART TWO

PART TWO

17

To Keep It Holy

On New Year's Day, Mother drove me to my new life. I didn't take much with me: a dozen jars of home-canned peaches, bedding, and a garbage bag full of clothes. As we sped down the interstate I watched the landscape splinter and barb, the rolling black summits of the Bear River Mountains giving way to the razor-edged Rockies. The university was nestled in the heart of the Wasatch Mountains, whose white massifs jutted mightily out of the earth. They were beautiful, but to me their beauty seemed aggressive, menacing.

My apartment was a mile south of campus. It had a kitchen, living room and three small bedrooms. The other women who lived there — I knew they would be women because at BYU all housing was segregated by gender — had not yet returned from the Christmas holiday. It took only a few minutes to bring in my stuff from the car. Mother and I stood awkwardly in the kitchen for a moment, then she hugged me and drove away.

I lived alone in the quiet apartment for three days. Except it wasn't quiet. *Nowhere* was quiet. I'd never spent more than a few hours in a city and found it impossible to defend myself from the strange noises that constantly invaded. The chirrup of crosswalk signals, the shrieking of sirens, the hissing of air brakes, even the hushed chatter of people strolling on the sidewalk — I heard every sound individually. My ears, accustomed to the silence of the peak, felt battered by them.

I was starved for sleep by the time my first roommate arrived. Her name was Shannon, and she studied at the cosmetology school across the street. She was wearing plush pink pajama bottoms and a tight white tank with spaghetti straps. I stared at her bare shoulders. I'd seen women dressed this way before — Dad called them gentiles — and I'd always avoided getting too near them, as if their immorality might be catching. Now there was one in my house.

Shannon surveyed me with frank disappointment, taking in my baggy flannel coat and oversized men's jeans. 'How old are you?' she said.

'I'm a freshman,' I said. I didn't want to admit I was only seventeen, and that I should be in high school, finishing my junior year.

Shannon moved to the sink and I saw the word 'Juicy' written across her rear. That was more than I could take. I backed away toward my room, mumbling that I was going to bed.

'Good call,' she said. 'Church is early. I'm usually late.'

'You go to church?'

'Sure,' she said. 'Don't you?'

'Of course I do. But you, you really go?'

She stared at me, chewing her lip, then said, 'Church is at eight. Good night!'

My mind was spinning as I shut my bedroom

220

door. How could *she* be a Mormon?

Dad said there were gentiles everywhere — that most Mormons were gentiles, they just didn't know it. I thought about Shannon's tank and pajamas, and suddenly realized that probably everyone at BYU was a gentile.

My other roommate arrived the next day. Her name was Mary and she was a junior studying early childhood education. She dressed like I expected a Mormon to dress on Sunday, in a floral skirt that reached to the floor. Her clothes were a kind of shibboleth to me; they signaled that she was not a gentile, and for a few hours I felt less alone.

Until that evening. Mary stood suddenly from the sofa and said, 'Classes start tomorrow. Time to stock up on groceries.' She left and returned an hour later with two paper bags. Shopping was forbidden on the Sabbath — I'd never purchased so much as a stick of gum on a Sunday — but Mary casually unpacked eggs, milk and pasta without acknowledging that every item she was placing in our communal fridge was a violation of the Lord's Commandments. When she withdrew a can of Diet Coke, which my father said was a violation of the Lord's counsel for health, I again fled to my room.

★ ★ ★

The next morning, I got on the bus going the wrong direction. By the time I'd corrected my mistake, the lecture was nearly finished. I stood awkwardly in the back until the professor, a thin

221

woman with delicate features, motioned for me to take the only available seat, which was near the front. I sat down, feeling the weight of everyone's eyes. The course was on Shakespeare, and I'd chosen it because I'd heard of Shakespeare and thought that was a good sign. But now I was here I realized I knew nothing about him. It was a word I'd heard, that was all.

When the bell rang, the professor approached my desk. 'You don't belong here,' she said.

I stared at her, confused. Of course I didn't belong, but how did she know? I was on the verge of confessing the whole thing — that I'd never gone to school, that I hadn't really met the requirements to graduate — when she added, 'This class is for seniors.'

'There are classes for seniors?' I said.

She rolled her eyes as if I were trying to be funny. 'This is 382. You should be in 110.'

It took most of the walk across campus before I understood what she'd said, then I checked my course schedule and, for the first time, noticed the numbers next to the course names.

I went to the registrar's office, where I was told that every freshman-level course was full. What I should do, they said, was check online every few hours and join if someone dropped. By the end of the week I'd managed to squeeze into introductory courses in English, American history, music and religion, but I was stuck in a junior-level course on art in Western civilization.

Freshman English was taught by a cheerful woman in her late twenties who kept talking about something called the 'essay form,' which, she assured us, we had learned in high school.

My next class, American history, was held in an auditorium named for the prophet Joseph Smith. I'd thought American history would be easy because Dad had taught us about the Founding Fathers — I knew all about Washington, Jefferson, Madison. But the professor barely mentioned them at all, and instead talked about 'philosophical underpinnings' and the writings of Cicero and Hume, names I'd never heard.

In the first lecture, we were told that the next class would begin with a quiz on the readings. For two days I tried to wrestle meaning from the textbook's dense passages, but terms like 'civic humanism' and 'the Scottish Enlightenment' dotted the page like black holes, sucking all the other words into them. I took the quiz and missed every question.

That failure sat uneasily in my mind. It was the first indication of whether I would be okay, whether whatever I had in my head by way of *education* was enough. After the quiz, the answer seemed clear: it was not enough. On realizing this, I might have resented my upbringing but I didn't. My loyalty to my father had increased in proportion to the miles between us. On the mountain, I could rebel. But here, in this loud, bright place, surrounded by gentiles disguised as saints, I clung to every truth, every doctrine he had given me. Doctors were Sons of Perdition. Homeschooling was a commandment from the Lord.

Failing a quiz did nothing to undermine my new devotion to an old creed, but a lecture on Western art did.

The classroom was bright when I arrived, the morning sun pouring in warmly through a high wall of windows. I chose a seat next to a girl in a high-necked blouse. Her name was Vanessa. 'We should stick together,' she said. 'I think we're the only freshmen in the whole class.'

The lecture began when an old man with small eyes and a sharp nose shuttered the windows. He flipped a switch and a slide projector filled the room with white light. The image was of a painting. The professor discussed the composition, the brushstrokes, the history. Then he moved to the next painting, and the next and the next.

Then the projector showed a peculiar image, of a man in a faded hat and overcoat. Behind him loomed a concrete wall. He held a small paper near his face but he wasn't looking at it. He was looking at us.

I opened the picture book I'd purchased for the class so I could take a closer look. Something was written under the image in italics but I couldn't understand it. It had one of those black-hole words, right in the middle, devouring the rest. I'd seen other students ask questions, so I raised my hand.

The professor called on me, and I read the sentence aloud. When I came to the word, I paused. 'I don't know this word,' I said. 'What does it mean?'

There was silence. Not a hush, not a muting of the noise, but utter, almost violent silence. No papers shuffled, no pencils scratched.

The professor's lips tightened. 'Thanks for *that*,' he said, then returned to his notes.

I scarcely moved for the rest of the lecture. I stared at my shoes, wondering what had happened, and why, whenever I looked up, there was always someone staring at me as if I was a freak. Of course I *was* a freak, and I knew it, but I didn't understand how *they* knew it.

When the bell rang, Vanessa shoved her notebook into her pack. Then she paused and said, 'You shouldn't make fun of that. It's not a joke.' She walked away before I could reply.

I stayed in my seat until everyone had gone, pretending the zipper on my coat was stuck so I could avoid looking anyone in the eye. Then I went straight to the computer lab to look up the word 'Holocaust.'

I don't know how long I sat there reading about it, but at some point I'd read enough. I leaned back and stared at the ceiling. I suppose I was in shock, but whether it was the shock of learning about something horrific, or the shock of learning about my own ignorance, I'm not sure. I do remember imagining for a moment, not the camps, not the pits or chambers of gas, but my mother's face. A wave of emotion took me, a feeling so intense, so unfamiliar, I wasn't sure what it was. It made me want to shout at her, at my own mother, and that frightened me.

I searched my memories. In some ways the word 'Holocaust' wasn't wholly unfamiliar. Perhaps Mother *had* taught me about it, when we were picking rosehips or tincturing hawthorn. I did seem to have a vague knowledge that Jews had been killed somewhere, long ago. But I'd thought it was a small conflict, like the Boston

Massacre, which Dad talked about a lot, in which half a dozen people had been martyred by a tyrannical government. To have misunderstood it on this scale — five versus six million — seemed impossible.

I found Vanessa before the next lecture and apologized for the joke. I didn't explain, because I couldn't explain. I just said I was sorry and that I wouldn't do it again. To keep that promise, I didn't raise my hand for the rest of the semester.

* * *

That Saturday, I sat at my desk with a stack of homework. Everything had to be finished that day because I could not violate the Sabbath.

I spent the morning and afternoon trying to decipher the history textbook, without much success. In the evening, I tried to write a personal essay for English, but I'd never written an essay before — except for the ones on sin and repentance, which no one had ever read — and I didn't know how. I had no idea what the teacher meant by the 'essay form.' I scribbled a few sentences, crossed them out, then began again. I repeated this until it was past midnight.

I knew I should stop — this was the Lord's time — but I hadn't even started the assignment for music theory, which was due at seven A.M. on Monday. The Sabbath begins when I wake up, I reasoned, and kept working.

I awoke with my face pressed to the desk. The room was bright. I could hear Shannon and Mary in the kitchen. I put on my Sunday dress and the three of us walked to church. Because it was a congregation of students, everyone was sitting with their roommates, so I settled into a pew with mine. Shannon immediately began chatting with the girl behind us. I looked around the chapel and was again struck by how many women were wearing skirts cut above the knee.

The girl talking to Shannon said we should come over that afternoon to see a movie. Mary and Shannon agreed but I shook my head. I didn't watch movies on Sunday.

Shannon rolled her eyes. 'She's *very* devout,' she whispered.

I'd always known that my father believed in a different God. As a child, I'd been aware that although my family attended the same church as everyone in our town, our religion was not the same. They *believed* in modesty; we practiced it. They believed in God's power to heal; we left our injuries in God's hands. They believed in preparing for the Second Coming; we were actually prepared. For as long as I could remember, I'd known that the members of my own family were the only true Mormons I had ever known, and yet for some reason, here at this university, in this chapel, for the first time I felt the immensity of the gap. I understood now: I could stand with my family, or with the gentiles, on the one side or the other, but there was no foothold in between.

The service ended and we filed into Sunday school. Shannon and Mary chose seats near the front. They saved me one but I hesitated, thinking of how I'd broken the Sabbath. I'd been here less than a week, and already I had robbed the Lord of an hour. Perhaps *that* was why Dad hadn't wanted me to come: because he knew that by living with them, with people whose faith was *less*, I risked becoming like them.

Shannon waved to me and her V-neck plunged. I walked past her and folded myself into a corner, as far from Shannon and Mary as I could get. I was pleased by the familiarity of the arrangement: me, pressed into the corner, away from the other children, a precise reproduction of every Sunday school lesson from my childhood. It was the only sensation of familiarity I'd felt since coming to this place, and I relished it.

18

Blood and Feathers

After that, I rarely spoke to Shannon or Mary and they rarely spoke to me, except to remind me to do my share of the chores, which I never did. The apartment looked fine to me. So what if there were rotting peaches in the fridge and dirty dishes in the sink? So what if the smell slapped you in the face when you came through the door? To my mind if the stench was bearable, the house was clean, and I extended this philosophy to my person. I never used soap except when I showered, usually once or twice a week, and sometimes I didn't use it even then. When I left the bathroom in the morning, I marched right past the hallway sink where Shannon and Mary always — *always* — washed their hands. I saw their raised eyebrows and thought of Grandma-over-in-town. *Frivolous*, I told myself. *I don't pee on my hands.*

The atmosphere in the apartment was tense. Shannon looked at me like I was a rabid dog, and I did nothing to reassure her.

★ ★ ★

My bank account decreased steadily. I had been worried that I might not pass my classes, but a month into the semester, after I'd paid tuition and rent and bought food and books, I began to think that even if I did pass I wouldn't be coming back to school for one obvious reason: I couldn't afford it. I looked up the requirements for a scholarship online. A full-tuition waiver would require a near-perfect GPA.

I was only a month into the semester, but even so I knew a scholarship was comically out of reach. American history was getting easier, but only in that I was no longer failing the quizzes outright. I was doing well in music theory, but I struggled in English. My teacher said I had a knack for writing but that my language was oddly formal and stilted. I didn't tell her that I'd learned to read and write by reading only the Bible, the Book of Mormon, and speeches by Joseph Smith and Brigham Young.

The real trouble, however, was Western Civ. To me, the lectures were gibberish, probably because for most of January, I thought Europe was a country, not a continent, so very little of what the professor said made sense. And after the Holocaust incident, I wasn't about to ask for clarification.

Even so, it was my favorite class, because of Vanessa. We sat together for every lecture. I liked her because she seemed like the same kind of Mormon I was: she wore high-necked, loose-fitting clothing, and she'd told me that she never drank Coke or did homework on Sunday. She was the only person I'd met at the university who didn't seem like a gentile.

In February, the professor announced that instead of a single midterm he would be giving monthly exams, the first of which would be the following week. I didn't know how to prepare. There wasn't a textbook for the class, just the picture book of paintings and a few CDs of classical compositions. I listened to the music while flipping through the paintings. I made a vague effort to remember who had painted or composed what, but I didn't memorize spelling. The ACT was the only exam I'd ever taken, and it had been multiple choice, so I assumed all exams were multiple choice.

The morning of the exam, the professor instructed everyone to take out their blue books. I barely had time to wonder what a blue book was before everyone produced one from their bags. The motion was fluid, synchronized, as if they had practiced it. I was the only dancer on the stage who seemed to have missed rehearsal. I asked Vanessa if she had a spare, and she did. I opened it, expecting a multiple-choice exam, but it was blank.

The windows were shuttered; the projector flickered on, displaying a painting. We had sixty seconds to write the work's title and the artist's full name. My mind produced only a dull buzz. This continued through several questions: I sat completely still, giving no answers at all.

A Caravaggio flickered onto the screen — *Judith Beheading Holofernes*. I stared at the image, that of a young girl calmly drawing a sword toward her body, pulling the blade through a man's neck as she might have pulled a string through cheese. I'd beheaded chickens with Dad, clutching their scabby legs while he raised the ax and brought it down with a loud *thwack*, then tightening my grip, holding on with all I had, when the chicken convulsed with death, scattering feathers and spattering my jeans with blood. Remembering the chickens, I wondered at the plausibility of Caravaggio's scene: no one had *that* look on their face — that tranquil, disinterested expression — when taking off something's head.

I knew the painting was by Caravaggio but I remembered only the surname and even that I couldn't spell. I was certain the title was *Judith Beheading Someone* but could not have produced *Holofernes* even if it had been my neck behind the blade.

Thirty seconds left. Perhaps I could score a few points if I could just get something — anything — on the page, so I sounded out the name phonetically: 'Carevajio.' That didn't look right. One of the letters was doubled up, I remembered, so I scratched that out and wrote 'Carrevagio.' Wrong again. I auditioned different spellings, each worse than the last. Twenty seconds.

Next to me, Vanessa was scribbling steadily. Of course she was. She belonged here. Her handwriting was neat, and I could read what she'd written: Michelangelo Merisi da Caravaggio. And next to it, in equally pristine print, *Judith Beheading Holofernes*. Ten seconds. I copied the text, not including Caravaggio's full name because, in a selective display of integrity, I decided that would be cheating. The projector flashed to the next slide.

I glanced at Vanessa's paper a few more times

232

during the exam but it was hopeless. I couldn't copy her essays, and I lacked the factual and stylistic know-how to compose my own. In the absence of skill or knowledge, I must have scribbled down whatever occurred to me. I don't recall whether we were asked to evaluate *Judith Beheading Holofernes*, but if we were I'm sure I would have given my impressions: that the calm on the girl's face didn't sit well with my experience slaughtering chickens. Dressed in the right language this might have made a fantastic answer — something about the woman's serenity standing in powerful counterpoint to the general realism of the piece. But I doubt the professor was much impressed by my observation that, 'When you chop a chicken's head off, you shouldn't smile because you might get blood and feathers in your mouth.'

The exam ended. The shutters were opened. I walked outside and stood in the winter chill, gazing up at the pinnacles of the Wasatch Mountains. I wanted to stay. The mountains were as unfamiliar and menacing as ever, but I wanted to stay.

I waited a week for the exam results, and twice during that time I dreamed of Shawn, of finding him lifeless on the asphalt, of turning his body and seeing his face alight in crimson. Suspended between fear of the past and fear of the future, I recorded the dream in my journal. Then, without any explanation, as if the connection between the two were obvious, I wrote, *I don't understand why I wasn't allowed to get a decent education as a child.*

The results were handed back a few days later. I had failed.

* * *

One winter, when I was very young, Luke found a great horned owl in the pasture, unconscious and half frozen. It was the color of soot, and seemed as big as me to my child eyes. Luke carried it into the house, where we marveled at its soft plumage and pitiless talons. I remember stroking its striped feathers, so smooth they were waterlike, as my father held its limp body. I knew that if it were conscious, I would never get this close. I was in defiance of nature just by touching it.

Its feathers were soaked in blood. A thorn had lanced its wing. 'I'm not a vet,' Mother said. 'I treat *people*.' But she removed the thorn and cleaned the wound. Dad said the wing would take weeks to mend, and that the owl would wake up long before then. Finding itself trapped, surrounded by predators, it would beat itself to death trying to get free. It was wild, he said, and in the wild that wound was fatal.

We laid the owl on the linoleum by the back door and, when it awoke, told Mother to stay out of the kitchen. Mother said hell would freeze over before she surrendered her kitchen to an owl, then marched in and began slamming pots to make breakfast. The owl flopped about pathetically, its talons scratching the door, bashing its head in a panic. We cried, and Mother retreated. Two hours later Dad had blocked off half the kitchen with plywood sheets. The owl convalesced there for several weeks. We trapped mice to feed it, but sometimes it didn't eat them, and we couldn't clear away the carcasses. The smell of death was strong and foul, a punch to the gut.

The owl grew restless. When it began to refuse food, we opened the back door and let it escape. It wasn't fully healed, but Dad said its chances were better with the mountain than with us. It didn't belong. It couldn't be taught to belong.

★ ★ ★

I wanted to tell someone I'd failed the exam, but something stopped me from calling Tyler. It might have been shame. Or it might have been that Tyler was preparing to be a father. He'd met his wife, Stefanie, at Purdue, and they'd married quickly. She didn't know anything about our family. To me, it felt as though he preferred his new life — his new family — to his old one.

I called home. Dad answered. Mother was delivering a baby, which she was doing more and more now the migraines had stopped.

'When will Mother be home?' I said.

'Don't know,' said Dad. 'Might as well ask the Lord as me, as He's the one deciding.' He chuckled, then asked, 'How's school?'

Dad and I hadn't spoken since he'd screamed at me about the VCR. I could tell he was trying to be supportive, but I didn't think I could admit to him that I was failing. I wanted to tell him it was going well. *So easy,* I imagined myself saying.

'Not great,' I said instead. 'I had no idea it would be this hard.'

The line was silent, and I imagined Dad's stern face hardening. I waited for the jab I imagined he was preparing, but instead a quiet voice said, 'It'll be okay, honey.'

'It won't,' I said. 'There will be no scholarship. I'm not even going to pass.' My voice was shaky now.

'If there's no scholarship, there's no scholarship,' he said. 'Maybe I can help with the money. We'll figure it out. Just be happy, okay?'

'Okay,' I said.

'Come on home if you need.'

I hung up, not sure what I'd just heard. I knew it wouldn't last, that the next time we spoke everything would be different, the tenderness of this moment forgotten, the endless struggle between us again in the foreground. But tonight he wanted to help. And that was something.

★   ★   ★

In March, there was another exam in Western Civ. This time I made flash cards. I spent hours memorizing odd spellings, many of them French (France, I now understood, was a part of Europe). Jacques-Louis David and François Boucher: I couldn't say them but I could spell them.

My lecture notes were nonsensical, so I asked Vanessa if I could look at hers. She looked at me skeptically, and for a moment I wondered if she'd noticed me cheating off her exam. She said she wouldn't give me her notes but that we could

236

study together, so after class I followed her to her dorm room. We sat on the floor with our legs crossed and our notebooks open in front of us.

I tried to read from my notes but the sentences were incomplete, scrambled. 'Don't worry about your notes,' Vanessa said. 'They aren't as important as the textbook.'

'What textbook?' I said.

'*The* textbook,' Vanessa said. She laughed as if I were being funny. I tensed because I wasn't.

'I don't have a textbook,' I said.

'Sure you do!' She held up the thick picture book I'd used to memorize titles and artists.

'Oh that,' I said. 'I looked at that.'

'You *looked* at it? You didn't read it?'

I stared at her. I didn't understand. This was a class on music and art. We'd been given CDs with music to listen to, and a book with pictures of art to look at. It hadn't occurred to me to read the art book any more than it had to read the CDs.

'I thought we were just supposed to look at the pictures.' This sounded stupid when said aloud.

'So when the syllabus assigned pages fifty through eighty-five, you didn't think you had to *read* anything?'

'I looked at the pictures,' I said again. It sounded worse the second time.

Vanessa began thumbing through the book, which suddenly looked very much like a text-book.

'That's your problem then,' she said. 'You have to read the textbook.' As she said this, her voice lilted with sarcasm, as if this blunder, after everything else — after joking about the Holocaust and glancing at her test — was too much and she was done with me. She said it was time for me to go; she had to study for another class. I picked up my notebook and left.

'Read the textbook' turned out to be excellent advice. On the next exam I scored a B, and by the end of the semester I was pulling A's. It was a miracle and I interpreted it as such. I continued to study until two or three A.M. each night, believing it was the price I had to pay to earn God's support. I did well in my history class, better in English, and best of all in music theory. A full-tuition scholarship was unlikely, but I could maybe get half.

During the final lecture in Western Civ, the professor announced that so many students had failed the first exam, he'd decided to drop it altogether. And *poof*. My failing grade was gone. I wanted to punch the air, give Vanessa a high five. Then I remembered that she didn't sit with me anymore.

19

In the Beginning

When the semester ended I returned to Buck's Peak. In a few weeks BYU would post grades; then I'd know if I could return in the fall.

I filled my journals with promises that I would stay out of the junkyard. I needed money — Dad would have said I was broker than the Ten Commandments — so I went to get my old job back at Stokes. I turned up at the busiest hour in the afternoon, when I knew they'd be understaffed, and sure enough, the manager was bagging groceries when I found him. I asked if he'd like me to do that, and he looked at me for all of three seconds, then lifted his apron over his head and handed it to me. The assistant manager gave me a wink: she was the one who'd suggested I ask during the rush. There was something about Stokes — about its straight, clean aisles and the warm people who worked there — that made me feel calm and happy. It's a strange thing to say about a grocery store, but it felt like home.

Dad was waiting for me when I came through the back door. He saw the apron and said, 'You're working for me this summer.'

'I'm working at Stokes,' I said.

'Think you're too good to scrap?' His voice was raised. '*This* is your family. You belong here.'

Dad's face was haggard, his eyes bloodshot.

He'd had a spectacularly bad winter. In the fall, he'd invested a large sum of money in new construction equipment — an excavator, a man lift and a welding trailer. By spring it was all gone. Luke had accidentally lit the welding trailer on fire, burning it to the ground; the man lift had come off a trailer because someone — I never asked who — hadn't secured it properly; and the excavator had joined the scrap heap when Shawn, pulling it on an enormous trailer, had taken a corner too fast and rolled the truck and trailer both. With the luck of the damned, Shawn had crawled from the wreckage, although he'd hit his head and couldn't remember the days before the accident. Truck, trailer and excavator were totaled.

Dad's determination was etched into his face. It was in his voice, in the harshness of it. He *had* to win this standoff. He'd convinced himself that if I was on the crew, there'd be fewer accidents, fewer setbacks. 'You're slower than tar running uphill,' he'd told me a dozen times. 'But you get the job done without smashing anything.'

But I couldn't do the job, because to do it would be to slide backward. I had moved home, to my old room, to my old life. If I went back to working for Dad, to waking up every morning and pulling on steel-toed boots and trudging out to the junkyard, it would be as if the last four months had never happened, as if I had never left.

I pushed past Dad and shut myself in my room. Mother knocked a moment later. She stepped into the room quietly and sat so lightly on the bed, I barely felt her weight next to me. I thought she would say what she'd said last time. Then I'd remind her I was only seventeen, and she'd tell me I could stay.

'You have an opportunity to help your father,' she said. 'He needs you. He'll never say it but he does. It's your choice what to do.' There was silence, then she added, 'But if you don't help, you can't stay here. You'll have to live somewhere else.'

The next morning, at four A.M., I drove to Stokes and worked a ten-hour shift. It was early afternoon, and raining heavily, when I came home and found my clothes on the front lawn. I carried them into the house. Mother was mixing oils in the kitchen, and she said nothing as I passed by with my dripping shirts and jeans.

I sat on my bed while the water from my clothes soaked into the carpet. I'd taken a phone with me, and I stared at it, unsure what it could do. There was no one to call. There was nowhere to go and no one to call.

I dialed Tyler in Indiana. 'I don't want to work in the junkyard,' I said when he answered. My voice was hoarse.

'What happened?' he said. He sounded worried; he thought there'd been another accident. 'Is everyone okay?'

'Everyone's fine,' I said. 'But Dad says I can't stay here unless I work in the junkyard, and I can't do that anymore.' My voice was pitched unnaturally high, and it quivered.

Tyler said, 'What do you want me to do?'

In retrospect I'm sure he meant this literally,

241

that he was asking how he could help, but my ears, solitary and suspicious, heard something else: *What do you expect me to do?* I began to shake; I felt light-headed. Tyler had been my lifeline. For years he'd lived in my mind as a last resort, a lever I could pull when my back was against the wall. But now that I had pulled it, I understood its futility. It did nothing after all.

'What happened?' Tyler said again.

'Nothing. Everything's fine.'

I hung up and dialed Stokes. The assistant manager answered. 'You done working today?' she said brightly. I told her I quit, said I was sorry, then put down the phone. I opened my closet and there they were, where I'd left them four months before: my scrapping boots. I put them on. It felt as though I'd never taken them off.

Dad was in the forklift, scooping up a stack of corrugated tin. He would need someone to place wooden blocks on the trailer so he could offload the stack. When he saw me, he lowered the tin so I could step onto it, and I rode the stack up and onto the trailer.

★　★　★

My memories of the university faded quickly. The scratch of pencils on paper, the *clack* of a projector moving to the next slide, the peal of the bells signaling the end of class — all were drowned out by the clatter of iron and the roar of diesel engines. After a month in the junkyard, BYU seemed like a dream, something I'd

242

conjured. Now I was awake.

My daily routine was exactly what it had been: after breakfast I sorted scrap or pulled copper from radiators. If the boys were working on-site, sometimes I'd go along to drive the loader or forklift or crane. At lunch I'd help Mother cook and do the dishes, then I'd return, either to the junkyard or to the forklift.

The only difference was Shawn. He was not what I remembered. He never said a harsh word, seemed at peace with himself. He was studying for his GED, and one night when we were driving back from a job, he told me he was going to try a semester at a community college. He wanted to study law.

There was a play that summer at the Worm Creek Opera House, and Shawn and I bought tickets. Charles was also there, a few rows ahead of us, and at intermission when Shawn moved away to chat up a girl, he shuffled over. For the first time I was not utterly tongue-tied. I thought of Shannon and how she'd talked to people at church, the friendly merriment of her, the way she laughed and smiled. *Just be Shannon*, I thought to myself. And for five minutes, I was.

Charles was looking at me strangely, the way I'd seen men look at Shannon. He asked if I'd like to see a movie on Saturday. The movie he suggested was vulgar, worldly, one I would never want to see, but I was being Shannon, so I said I'd love to.

I tried to be Shannon on Saturday night. The movie was terrible, worse than I'd expected, the kind of movie only a gentile would see. But it was hard for me to see Charles as a gentile. He was just Charles. I thought about telling him the movie was immoral, that he shouldn't be seeing such things, but — still being Shannon — I said nothing, just smiled when he asked if I'd like to get ice cream.

Shawn was the only one still awake when I got home. I was smiling when I came through the door. Shawn joked that I had a boyfriend, and it was a real joke — he wanted me to laugh. He said Charles had good taste, that I was the most decent person he knew, then he went to bed.

In my room, I stared at myself in the mirror for a long time. The first thing I noticed was my men's jeans and how they were nothing like the jeans other girls wore. The second thing I noticed was that my shirt was too large and made me seem more square than I was.

Charles called a few days later. I was standing in my room after a day of roofing. I smelled of paint thinner and was covered in dust the color of ash, but he didn't know that. We talked for two hours. He called the next night, and the one after. He said we should get a burger on Friday.

★ ★ ★

On Thursday, after I'd finished scrapping, I drove forty miles to the nearest Walmart and bought a pair of women's jeans and two shirts, both blue. When I put them on, I barely recognized my own body, the way it narrowed and curved. I took them off immediately, feeling that somehow they were immodest. They weren't, not technically, but I knew why I wanted them — for my body, so it would be noticed — and that seemed immodest even if the clothes were not.

The next afternoon, when the crew had finished for the day, I ran to the house. I showered, blasting away the dirt, then I laid the new clothes on my bed and stared at them. After several minutes, I put them on and was again shocked by the sight of myself. There wasn't time to change so I wore a jacket even though it was a warm evening, and at some point, though I can't say when or why, I decided that I didn't need the jacket after all. For the rest of the night, I didn't have to remember to be Shannon; I talked and laughed without pretending at all.

Charles and I spent every evening together that week. We haunted public parks and ice cream shops, burger joints and gas stations. I took him to Stokes, because I loved it there, and because the assistant manager would always give me the unsold doughnuts from the bakery. We talked about music — about bands I'd never heard of and about how he wanted to be a musician and travel the world. We never talked about us — about whether we were friends or something else. I wished he would bring it up but he didn't. I wished he would let me know some other way — by gently taking my hand or putting an arm around me — but he didn't do that, either.

On Friday we stayed out late, and when I came home the house was dark. Mother's computer was on, the screen saver casting a green light over the living room. I sat down and mechanically checked BYU's website. Grades had been posted. I'd passed. More than passed. I'd earned A's in every subject except Western Civ. I would get a scholarship for half of my tuition. I could go back.

Charles and I spent the next afternoon in the park, rocking lazily in tire swings. I told him about the scholarship. I'd meant it as a brag, but for some reason my fears came out with it. I said I shouldn't even be in college, that I should be made to finish high school first. Or to at least start it.

Charles sat quietly while I talked and didn't say anything for a long time after. Then he said, 'Are you angry your parents didn't put you in school?'

'It was an advantage!' I said, half-shouting. My response was instinctive. It was like hearing a phrase from a catchy song: I couldn't stop myself from reciting the next line. Charles looked at me skeptically, as if asking me to reconcile that with what I'd said only moments before.

'Well, I'm angry,' he said. 'Even if you aren't.'

I said nothing. I'd never heard anyone criticize my father except Shawn, and I wasn't able to respond to it. I wanted to tell Charles about the Illuminati, but the words belonged to my father, and even in my mind they sounded awkward, rehearsed. I was ashamed at my inability to take possession of them. I believed then — and part of me will always believe — that my father's words ought to be my own.

Every night for a month, when I came in from the junkyard, I'd spend an hour scrubbing grime from my fingernails and dirt from my ears. I'd brush the tangles from my hair and clumsily apply makeup. I'd rub handfuls of lotion into the pads of my fingers to soften the calluses, just in case that was the night Charles touched them.

When he finally did, it was early evening and we were in his jeep, driving to his house to watch a movie. We were just coming parallel to Fivemile Creek when he reached across the gearshift and rested his hand on mine. His hand was warm and I wanted to take it, but instead I jerked away as if I'd been burned. The response was involuntary, and I wished immediately that I could take it back. It happened again when he tried a second time. My body convulsed, yielding to a strange, potent instinct.

The instinct passed through me in the form of a word, a bold lyric, strong, declarative. The word was not new. It had been with me for a while now, hushed, motionless, as if asleep, in some remote corner of memory. By touching me Charles had awakened it, and it throbbed with life.

I shoved my hands under my knees and leaned into the window. I couldn't let him near me — not that night, and not any night for months — without shuddering as that word, my word, ripped its way into remembrance. *Whore*.

We arrived at his house. Charles turned on the TV and settled onto the sofa; I perched lightly on one side. The lights dimmed, the opening credits rolled. Charles inched toward me, slowly at first, then more confidently, until his leg brushed mine. In my mind I bolted, I ran a thousand miles in a single heartbeat. In reality I merely flinched. Charles flinched, too — I'd startled him. I repositioned myself, driving my body into the sofa arm, gathering my limbs and pressing them away from him. I held that unnatural pose for perhaps twenty seconds, until he understood, hearing the words I couldn't say, and moved to the floor.

20

Recitals of the Fathers

Charles was my first friend from that other world, the one my father had tried to protect me from. He was conventional in all the ways and for all the reasons my father despised conventionality: he talked about football and popular bands more than the End of Days; he loved everything about high school; he went to church, but like most Mormons, if he was ill, he was as likely to call a doctor as a Mormon priest.

I couldn't reconcile his world with mine so I separated them. Every evening I watched for his red jeep from my window, and when it appeared on the highway I ran for the door. By the time he'd bumped up the hill I'd be waiting on the lawn, and before he could get out I'd be in the jeep, arguing with him about my seatbelt. (He refused to drive unless I wore one.)

Once, he arrived early and made it to the front door. I stammered nervously as I introduced him to Mother, who was blending bergamot and ylang-ylang, clicking her fingers to test the proportions. She said hello but her fingers kept pulsing. When Charles looked at me as if to ask why, Mother explained that God was speaking through her fingers. 'Yesterday I tested that I'd get a migraine today if I didn't have a bath in lavender,' she said. 'I took the bath and guess what? No headache!'

'Doctors can't cure a migraine before it happens,' Dad chimed in, 'but the Lord can!'

As we walked to his jeep, Charles said, 'Does your house always smell like that?'

'Like what?'

'Like rotted plants.'

I shrugged.

'You must have smelled it,' he said. 'It was *strong*. I've smelled it before. On you. You always smell of it. Hell, I probably do, too, now.' He sniffed his shirt. I was quiet. I hadn't smelled anything.

★ ★ ★

Dad said I was becoming 'uppity.' He didn't like that I rushed home from the junkyard the moment the work was finished, or that I removed every trace of grease before going out with Charles. He knew I'd rather be bagging groceries at Stokes than driving the loader in Blackfoot, the dusty town an hour north where Dad was building a milking barn. It bothered him, knowing I wanted to be in another place, dressed like someone else.

On the site in Blackfoot, he dreamed up strange tasks for me to do, as if he thought my doing them would remind me who I was. Once, when we were thirty feet in the air, scrambling on the purlins of the unfinished roof, not wearing harnesses because we never wore them, Dad realized that he'd left his chalk line on the other side of the building. 'Fetch me that chalk line, Tara,' he said. I mapped the trip. I'd need to jump from purlin to purlin, about fifteen of them, spaced four feet apart, to get the chalk, then the same number back. It was exactly the sort of order from Dad that was usually met with Shawn saying, 'She's not doing that.'

'Shawn, will you run me over in the forklift?'

'You can fetch it,' Shawn said. 'Unless your fancy school and fancy boyfriend have made you too good for it.' His features hardened in a way that was both new and familiar.

I shimmied the length of a purlin, which took me to the framing beam at the barn's edge. This was more dangerous in one sense — if I fell to the right, there would be no purlins to catch me — but the framing beam was thicker, and I could walk it like a tightrope.

That was how Dad and Shawn became comrades, even if they only agreed on one thing: that my brush with education had made me uppity, and that what I needed was to be dragged through time. Fixed, anchored to a former version of myself.

Shawn had a gift for language, for using it to define others. He began searching through his repertoire of nicknames. 'Wench' was his favorite for a few weeks. 'Wench, fetch me a grinding wheel,' he'd shout, or 'Raise the boom, Wench!' Then he'd search my face for a reaction. He never found one. Next he tried 'Wilbur.' Because I ate so much, he said. 'That's *some* pig,' he'd shout with a whistle when I bent over to fit a screw or check a measurement.

Shawn took to lingering outside after the crew

had finished for the day. I suspect he wanted to be near the driveway when Charles drove up it. He seemed to be forever changing the oil in his truck. The first night he was out there, I ran out and jumped into the jeep before he could say a word. The next night he was quicker on the draw. 'Isn't Tara beautiful?' he shouted to Charles. 'Eyes like a fish and she's nearly as smart as one.' It was an old taunt, blunted by overuse. He must have known I wouldn't react on the site so he'd saved it, hoping that in front of Charles it might still have sting.

The next night: 'You going to dinner? Don't get between Wilbur and her food. Won't be nothin' left of you but a splat on the pavement.'

Charles never responded. We entered into an unspoken agreement to begin our evenings the moment the mountain disappeared in the rear-view mirror. In the universe we explored together there were gas stations and movie theaters; there were cars dotting the highway like trinkets, full of people laughing or honking, always waving, because this was a small town and everybody knew Charles; there were dirt roads dusted white with chalk, canals the color of beef stew, and endless wheat fields glowing bronze. But there was no Buck's Peak.

During the day, Buck's Peak was all there was — that and the site in Blackfoot. Shawn and I spent the better part of a week making purlins to finish the barn roof. We used a machine the size of a mobile home to press them into a Z shape, then we attached wire brushes to grinders and blasted away the rust so they could be painted.

When the paint was dry we stacked them next to the shop, but within a day or two the wind from the peak had covered them in black dust, which turned to grime when it mixed with the oils on the iron. Shawn said they had to be washed before they could be loaded, so I fetched a rag and a bucket of water.

It was a hot day, and I wiped beads of sweat from my forehead. My hairband broke. I didn't have a spare. The wind swept down the mountain, blowing strands in my eyes, and I reached across my face and brushed them away. My hands were black with grease, and each stroke left a dark smudge.

I shouted to Shawn when the purlins were clean. He appeared from behind an I-beam and raised his welding shield. When he saw me, his face broke into a wide smile. 'Our Nigger's back!' he said.

★ ★ ★

The summer Shawn and I had worked the Shear, there'd been an afternoon when I'd wiped the sweat from my face so many times that, by the time we quit for supper, my nose and cheeks had been black. That was the first time Shawn called me 'Nigger.' The word was surprising but not unfamiliar. I'd heard Dad use it, so in one sense I knew what it meant. But in another sense, I didn't understand it as meaning anything at all. I'd only ever seen one black person, a little girl, the adoptive daughter of a family at church. Dad obviously hadn't meant her.

Shawn had called me Nigger that entire summer: 'Nigger, run and fetch those C-clamps!' or 'It's time for lunch, Nigger!' It had never given me a moment's pause.

Then the world had turned upside down: I had entered a university, where I'd wandered into an auditorium and listened, eyes wide, mind buzzing, to lectures on American history. The professor was Dr. Richard Kimball, and he had a resonant, contemplative voice. I knew about slavery; I'd heard Dad talk about it, and I'd read about it in Dad's favorite book on the American founding. I had read that slaves in colonial times were happier and more free than their masters, because the masters were burdened with the cost of their care. That had made sense to me.

The day Dr. Kimball lectured on slavery, he filled the overhead screen with a charcoal sketch of a slave market. The screen was large; as in a movie theater it dominated the room. The sketch was chaotic. Women stood, naked or half naked, and chained, while men circled them. The projector clacked. The next image was a photograph, black and white and blurred with age. Faded and overexposed, the image is iconic. In it a man sits, stripped above the waist, exposing for the camera a map of raised, crisscrossing scars. The flesh hardly looks like flesh, from what has been done to it.

I saw many more images in the coming weeks. I'd heard of the Great Depression years before when I'd played Annie, but the slides of men in hats and long coats lined up in front of soup kitchens were new to me. When Dr. Kimball

254

lectured on World War II, the screen showed rows of fighter planes interspersed with the skeletal remains of bombed cities. There were faces mixed in — FDR, Hitler, Stalin. Then World War II faded with the lights of the projector.

The next time I entered the auditorium there were new faces on the screen and they were black. There hadn't been a black face on that screen — at least none that I remembered — since the lectures on slavery. I'd forgotten about them, these other Americans who were foreign to me. I had not tried to imagine the end of slavery: surely the call of justice had been heard by all, and the issue had been resolved.

This was my state of mind when Dr. Kimball began to lecture on something called the civil rights movement. A date appeared on the screen: 1963. I figured there'd been a mistake. I recalled that the Emancipation Proclamation had been issued in 1863. I couldn't account for that hundred years, so I assumed it was a typo. I copied the date into my notes with a question mark, but as more photographs flashed across the screen, it became clear which century the professor meant. The photos were black and white but their subjects were modern — vibrant, well defined. They were not dry stills from another era; they captured movement. Marches. Police. Firefighters turning hoses on young men.

Dr. Kimball recited names I'd never heard. He began with Rosa Parks. An image appeared of a policeman pressing a woman's finger into an ink sponge. Dr. Kimball said she'd taken a seat on a

255

bus. I understood him as saying she had stolen the seat, although it seemed an odd thing to steal.

Her image was replaced by another, of a black boy in a white shirt, tie and round-brimmed hat. I didn't hear his story. I was still wondering at Rosa Parks, and how someone could steal a bus seat. Then the image was of a corpse and I heard Dr. Kimball say, 'They pulled his body from the river.'

There was a date beneath the image: 1955. I realized that Mother had been four years old in 1955, and with that realization, the distance between me and Emmett Till collapsed. My proximity to this murdered boy could be measured in the lives of people I knew. The calculation was not made with reference to vast historical or geological shifts — the fall of civilizations, the erosion of mountains. It was measured in the wrinkling of human flesh. In the lines on my mother's face.

The next name was Martin Luther King Jr. I had never seen his face before, or heard his name, and it was several minutes before I understood that Dr. Kimball didn't mean Martin Luther, who I had heard of. It took several more minutes for me to connect the name with the image on the screen — of a dark-skinned man standing in front of a white marble temple and surrounded by a vast crowd. I had only just understood who he was and why he was speaking when I was told he had been murdered. I was still ignorant enough to be surprised.

'Our Nigger's back!'

I don't know what Shawn saw on my face — whether it was shock, anger or a vacant expression. Whatever it was, he was delighted by it. He'd found a vulnerability, a tender spot. It was too late to feign indifference.

'Don't call me that,' I said. 'You don't know what it means.'

'Sure I do,' he said. 'You've got black all over your face, like a nigger!'

For the rest of the afternoon — for the rest of the summer — I was Nigger. I'd answered to it a thousand times before with indifference. If anything, I'd been amused and thought Shawn was clever. Now it made me want to gag him. Or sit him down with a history book, as long as it wasn't the one Dad still kept in the living room, under the framed copy of the Constitution.

I couldn't articulate how the name made me feel. Shawn had meant it to humiliate me, to lock me in time, into an old idea of myself. But far from fixing me in place, that word transported me. Every time he said it — 'Hey Nigger, raise the boom' or 'Fetch me a level, Nigger' — I returned to the university, to that auditorium, where I had watched human history unfold and wondered at my place in it. The stories of Emmett Till, Rosa Parks and Martin Luther King were called to my mind every time Shawn shouted, 'Nigger, move to the next row.' I saw their faces superimposed on every purlin Shawn welded into place that summer, so that by the end of it, I had finally begun to grasp something that should have been immediately apparent: that someone had opposed the great march toward equality; someone had been the person from whom freedom had to be wrested.

I did not think of my brother as that person; I doubt I will ever think of him that way. But something had shifted nonetheless. I had started on a path of awareness, had perceived something elemental about my brother, my father, myself. I had discerned the ways in which we had been sculpted by a tradition given to us by others, a tradition of which we were either willfully or accidentally ignorant. I had begun to understand that we had lent our voices to a discourse whose sole purpose was to dehumanize and brutalize others — because nurturing that discourse was easier, because retaining power always *feels* like the way forward.

I could not have articulated this, not as I sweated through those searing afternoons in the forklift. I did not have the language I have now. But I understood this one fact: that a thousand times I had been called Nigger, and laughed, and now I could not laugh. The word and the way Shawn said it hadn't changed; only my ears were different. They no longer heard the jingle of a joke in it. What they heard was a signal, a call through time, which was answered with a mounting conviction: that never again would I allow myself to be made a foot soldier in a conflict I did not understand.

258

21

Skullcap

Dad paid me the day before I returned to BYU. He didn't have the money to give what he'd promised, but it was enough to cover the half tuition I owed. I spent my last day in Idaho with Charles. It was a Sunday, but I didn't go to church. I'd had an earache for two days, and during the night it had changed from a dull twinge to a constant sharp stab. I had a fever. My vision was distorted, sensitive to light. That's when Charles called. Did I want to come to his house? I said I couldn't see well enough to drive. He picked me up fifteen minutes later.

I cupped my ear and slouched in the passenger seat, then took off my jacket and put it over my head to block the light. Charles asked what medicine I'd taken.

'Lobelia,' I said. 'And skullcap.'

'I don't think they're working,' he said.

'They will. They take a few days.'

He raised his eyebrows but said nothing.

Charles's house was neat and spacious, with large, bright windows and shiny floors. It reminded me of Grandma-over-in-town's house. I sat on a stool, my head pressed against the cold counter. I heard the *creak* of a cabinet opening and the *pop* of a plastic lid. When I opened my eyes, two red pills were on the counter in front of me.

'This is what people take for pain,' Charles said.

'Not us.'

'Who is this *us?*' Charles said. 'You're leaving tomorrow. You're not one of them anymore.'

I closed my eyes, hoping he would drop it.

'What do you think will happen if you take the pills?' he said.

I didn't answer. I didn't know what would happen. Mother always said that medical drugs are a special kind of poison, one that never leaves your body but rots you slowly from the inside for the rest of your life. She told me if I took a drug now, even if I didn't have children for a decade, they would be deformed.

'People take drugs for pain,' he said. 'It's *normal.*'

I must have winced at the word 'normal,' because he went quiet. He filled a glass of water and set it in front of me, then gently pushed the pills forward until they touched my arm. I picked one up. I'd never seen a pill up close before. It was smaller than I'd expected.

I swallowed it, then the other.

For as long as I could remember, whenever I was in pain, whether from a cut or a toothache, Mother would make a tincture of lobelia and skullcap. It had never lessened the pain, not one degree. Because of this, I had come to respect pain, even revere it, as necessary and untouchable.

Twenty minutes after I swallowed the red pills, the earache was gone. I couldn't comprehend its absence. I spent the afternoon swinging my head from left to right, trying to jog the pain loose again. I thought if I could shout loudly enough, or move quickly enough, perhaps the earache would return and I would know the medicine had been a sham after all.

Charles watched in silence but he must have found my behavior absurd, especially when I began to pull on my ear, which still ached dully, so I could test the limits of this strange witchcraft.

★ ★ ★

Mother was supposed to drive me to BYU the next morning, but during the night, she was called to deliver a baby. There was a car sitting in the driveway — a Kia Sephia Dad had bought from Tony a few weeks before. The keys were in the ignition. I loaded my stuff into it and drove it to Utah, figuring the car would just about make up for the money Dad owed me. I guess he figured that, too, because he never said a word about it.

I moved into an apartment half a mile from the university. I had new roommates. Robin was tall and athletic, and the first time I saw her she was wearing running shorts that were much too short, but I didn't gape at her. When I met Jenni she was drinking a Diet Coke. I didn't stare at that, either, because I'd seen Charles drink dozens of them.

Robin was the oldest, and for some reason she was sympathetic to me. Somehow she understood that my missteps came from ignorance, not intention, and she corrected me gently but frankly. She told me exactly what I would need to do, or not do, to get along with the other girls in the apartment. No keeping rotten food in the cupboards or leaving rancid dishes in the sink.

Robin explained this at an apartment meeting. When she'd finished another roommate, Megan, cleared her throat.

'I'd like to remind everyone to wash their hands after they use the bathroom,' she said. 'And not just with water, but with soap.'

Robin rolled her eyes. 'I'm sure *everyone* here washes their hands.'

That night, after I left the bathroom, I stopped at the sink in the hall and washed my hands. With soap.

The next day was the first day of class. Charles had designed my course schedule. He'd signed me up for two music classes and a course on religion, all of which he said would be easy for me. Then he'd enrolled me in two more challenging courses — college algebra, which terrified me, and biology, which didn't but only because I didn't know what it was.

Algebra threatened to put an end to my scholarship. The professor spent every lecture muttering inaudibly as he paced in front of the chalkboard. I wasn't the only one who was lost, but I was more lost than anyone else. Charles tried to help, but he was starting his senior year of high school and had his own schoolwork. In October I took the midterm and failed it.

I stopped sleeping. I stayed up late, twisting my hair into knots as I tried to wrest meaning from the textbook, then lying in bed and brooding over my notes. I developed stomach ulcers. Once, Jenni found me curled up on a stranger's lawn, halfway between campus and our apartment. My stomach was on fire; I was shaking with the pain, but I wouldn't let her take me to a hospital. She sat with me for half an hour, then walked me home.

The pain in my stomach intensified, burning through the night, making it impossible to sleep. I needed money for rent, so I got a job as a janitor for the engineering building. My shift began every morning at four. Between the ulcers and the janitorial work, I barely slept. Jenni and Robin kept saying I should see a doctor but I didn't. I told them I was going home for Thanksgiving and that my mother would cure me. They exchanged nervous glances but didn't say anything.

Charles said my behavior was self-destructive, that I had an almost pathological inability to ask for help. He told me this on the phone, and he said it so quietly it was almost a whisper.

I told him he was crazy.

'Then go talk to your algebra professor,' he said. 'You're failing. Ask for help.'

It had never occurred to me to talk to a professor — I didn't realize we were allowed to talk to them — so I decided to try, if only to prove to Charles I could do it.

I knocked on his office door a few days before Thanksgiving. He looked smaller in his office than he did in the lecture hall, and more shiny: the light above his desk reflected off his head and glasses. He was shuffling through the papers on his desk, and he didn't look up when I sat down. 'If I fail this class,' I said, 'I'll lose my scholarship.' I didn't explain that without a scholarship, I couldn't come back.

'I'm sorry,' he said, barely looking at me. 'But this is a tough school. It might be better if you come back when you're older. Or transfer.'

I didn't know what he meant by 'transfer,' so I said nothing. I stood to go, and for some reason this softened him. 'Truthfully,' he said, 'a lot of people are failing.' He sat back in his chair. 'How about this: the final covers all the material from the semester. I'll announce in class that anyone who gets a perfect score on the final — not a ninety-eight but an actual one hundred — will get an A, no matter how they performed on the midterm. Sound good?'

I said it did. It was a long shot, but I was the queen of long shots. I called Charles. I told him I was coming to Idaho for Thanksgiving and I needed an algebra tutor. He said he would meet me at Buck's Peak.

22

What We Whispered and What We Screamed

When I arrived at the peak, Mother was making the Thanksgiving meal. The large oak table was covered with jars of tincture and vials of essential oil, which I cleared away. Charles was coming for dinner.

Shawn was in a mood. He sat on a bench at the table, watching me gather the bottles and hide them. I'd washed Mother's china, which had never been used, and I began laying it out, eyeing the distance between each plate and knife.

Shawn resented my making a fuss. 'It's just Charles,' he said. 'His standards aren't that high. He's with you, after all.'

I fetched glasses. When I put one in front of him, Shawn jabbed a finger into my ribs, digging hard. 'Don't touch me!' I shrieked. Then the room turned upside down. My feet were knocked out from under me and I was swept into the living room, just out of Mother's sight.

Shawn turned me onto my back and sat on my stomach, pinning my arms at my sides with his knees. The shock of his weight forced the breath from my chest. He pressed his forearm into my windpipe. I sputtered, trying to gulp enough air to shout, but the airway was blocked.

'When you act like a child, you force me to treat you like one.'

Shawn said this loudly, he almost shouted it. He was saying it *to* me, but he was not saying it *for* me. He was saying it for Mother, to define the moment: I was a misbehaving child; he was setting the child right. The pressure on my windpipe eased and I felt a delicious fullness in my lungs. He knew I would not call out.

'Knock it off,' Mother hollered from the kitchen, though I wasn't sure whether she meant Shawn or me.

'Yelling is rude,' Shawn said, again speaking to the kitchen. 'You'll stay down until you apologize.' I said I was sorry for yelling at him. A moment later I was standing.

I folded napkins from paper towels and put one at each setting. When I placed one at Shawn's plate, he again jabbed his finger into my ribs. I said nothing.

Charles arrived early — Dad hadn't even come in from the junkyard yet — and sat at the table across from Shawn, who glared at him, never blinking. I didn't want to leave them alone together, but Mother needed help with the cooking, so I returned to the stove but devised small errands to bring me back to the table. On one of those trips I heard Shawn telling Charles about his guns, and on another, about all the ways he could kill a man. I laughed loudly at both, hoping Charles would think they were jokes. The third time I returned to the table, Shawn pulled me onto his lap. I laughed at that, too.

266

The charade couldn't last, not even until supper. I passed Shawn carrying a large china plate of dinner rolls, and he stabbed my gut so hard it knocked the wind out of me. I dropped the plate. It shattered.

'Why did you do that?' I shouted.

It happened so quickly, I don't know how he got me to the floor, but again I was on my back and he was on top of me. He demanded that I apologize for breaking the plate. I whispered the apology, quietly, so Charles wouldn't hear, but this enraged Shawn. He grabbed a fistful of my hair, again near the scalp, for leverage, and yanked me upright, then dragged me toward the bathroom. The movement was so abrupt, Charles had no time to react. The last thing I saw as my head hurled down the hall was Charles leaping to his feet, eyes wide, face pale.

My wrist was folded, my arm twisted behind my back. My head was shoved into the toilet so that my nose hovered above the water. Shawn was yelling something but I didn't hear what. I was listening for the sound of footsteps in the hall, and when I heard them I became deranged. Charles could not see me like this. He could not know that for all my pretenses — my makeup, my new clothes, my china place settings — *this* is who I was.

I convulsed, arching my body and ripping my wrist away from Shawn. I'd caught him off guard; I was stronger than he'd expected, or maybe just more reckless, and he lost his hold. I sprang for the door. I'd made it through the frame and had taken a step into the hallway when my head shot backward. Shawn had caught me by the hair, and he yanked me toward him with such force that we both tumbled back and into the bathtub.

The next thing I remember, Charles was lifting me and I was laughing — a shrill, demented howl. I thought if I could just laugh loudly enough, the situation might still be saved, that Charles might yet be convinced it was all a joke. Tears streamed from my eyes — my big toe was broken — but I kept cackling. Shawn stood in the doorway looking awkward.

'Are you okay?' Charles kept saying.

'Of course I am! Shawn is so, so, so — *funny*.' My voice strangled on the last word as I put weight on my foot and a wave of pain swept through me. Charles tried to carry me but I pushed him off and walked on the break, grinding my teeth to stop myself from crying out, while I slapped playfully at my brother.

Charles didn't stay for supper. He fled to his jeep and I didn't hear from him for several hours, then he called and asked me to meet him at the church. He wouldn't come to Buck's Peak. We sat in his jeep in the dark, empty parking lot. He was crying.

'You didn't see what you thought you saw,' I said.

If someone had asked me, I'd have said Charles was the most important thing in the world to me. But he wasn't. And I would prove it to him. What *was* important to me wasn't love or friendship, but my ability to lie convincingly to myself: to believe I was strong. I could never forgive Charles for knowing I wasn't.

I became erratic, demanding, hostile. I devised a bizarre and ever-evolving rubric by which I measured his love for me, and when he failed to meet it, I became paranoid. I surrendered to rages, venting all my savage anger, every fearful resentment I'd ever felt toward Dad or Shawn, at him, this bewildered bystander who'd only ever helped me. When we argued, I screamed that I never wanted to see him again, and I screamed it so many times that one night, when I called to change my mind, like I always did, he wouldn't let me.

We met one final time, in a field off the highway. Buck's Peak loomed over us. He said he loved me but this was over his head. He couldn't save me. Only I could.

I had no idea what he was talking about.

* * *

Winter covered campus in thick snow. I stayed indoors, memorizing algebraic equations, trying to live as I had before — to imagine my life at the university as disconnected from my life on Buck's Peak. The wall separating the two had been impregnable. Charles was a hole in it.

The stomach ulcers returned, burning and aching through the night. Once, I awoke to Robin shaking me. She said I'd been shouting in my sleep. I touched my face and it was wet. She wrapped me in her arms so tight I felt cocooned.

The next morning, Robin asked me to go with her to a doctor — for the ulcers but also for an

X-ray of my foot, because my big toe had turned black. I said I didn't need a doctor. The ulcers would heal, and someone had already treated the toe.

Robin's eyebrow rose. 'Who? Who treated it?'

I shrugged. She assumed my mother had, and I let her believe it. The truth was, the morning after Thanksgiving, I had asked Shawn to tell me if it was broken. He'd knelt on the kitchen floor and I'd dropped my foot into his lap. In that posture he seemed to shrink. He examined the toe for a moment, then he looked up at me and I saw something in his blue eyes. I thought he was about to say he was sorry, but just when I expected his lips to part he grasped the tip of my toe and yanked. It felt as if my foot had exploded, so intense was the shock that shot through my leg. I was still trying to swallow spasms of pain when Shawn stood, put a hand on my shoulder and said, 'Sorry, Siddle Lister, but it hurts less if you don't see it coming.'

A week after Robin asked to take me to the doctor, I again awoke to her shaking me. She gathered me up and pressed me to her, as if her body could hold me together, could keep me from flying apart.

'I think you need to see the bishop,' she said the next morning.

'I'm fine,' I said, making a cliché of myself the way not-fine people do. 'I just need sleep.'

Soon after, I found a pamphlet for the university counseling service on my desk. I barely looked at it, just knocked it into the trash. I could *not* see a counselor. To see one would be to ask for help, and I believed myself invincible. It was an elegant deception, a mental pirouette. The toe was not broken because it was not breakable. Only an X-ray could prove otherwise. Thus, the X-ray would break my toe.

My algebra final was swept up in this superstition. In my mind, it acquired a kind of mystical power. I studied with the intensity of the insane, believing that if I could best *this* exam, win that impossible perfect score, even with my broken toe and without Charles to help me, it would prove that I was above it all. Untouchable.

The morning of the exam I limped to the testing center and sat in the drafty hall. The test was in front of me. The problems were compliant, pliable; they yielded to my manipulations, forming into solutions, one after the other. I handed in my answer sheet, then stood in the frigid hallway, staring up at the screen that would display my score. When it appeared, I blinked, and blinked again. One hundred. A perfect score.

I was filled with an exquisite numbness. I felt drunk with it and wanted to shout at the world: *Here's the proof:* nothing *touches me.*

★ ★ ★

Buck's Peak looked the way it always did at Christmas — a snowy spire, adorned with evergreens — and my eyes, increasingly accustomed to brick and concrete, were nearly blinded by the scale and clarity of it.

Richard was in the forklift as I drove up the hill, moving a stack of purlins for the shop Dad was building in Franklin, near town. Richard was twenty-two, and one of the smartest people I knew, but he lacked a high school diploma. As I passed him in the drive, it occurred to me that he'd probably be driving that forklift for the rest of his life.

I'd been home for only a few minutes when Tyler called. 'I'm just checking in,' he said. 'To see if Richard is studying for the ACT.'

'He's gonna take it?'

'I don't know,' Tyler said. 'Maybe. Dad and I have been working on him.'

'Dad?'

Tyler laughed. 'Yeah, Dad. He wants Richard to go to college.'

I thought Tyler was joking until an hour later when we sat down to dinner. We'd only just started eating when Dad, his mouth full of potatoes, said, 'Richard, I'll give you next week off, paid, if you'll use it to study them books.'

I waited for an explanation. It was not long in coming. 'Richard is a genius,' Dad told me a moment later, winking. 'He's five times smarter than that Einstein was. He can disprove all them socialist theories and godless speculations. He's gonna get down there and blow up the whole damn system.'

Dad continued with his raptures, oblivious to the effect he was having on his listeners. Shawn slumped on a bench, his back against the wall, his face tilted toward the floor. To look at him was to imagine a man cut from stone, so heavy did he seem, so void of motion. Richard was the miracle son, the gift from God, the Einstein to

272

disprove Einstein. Richard would move the world. Shawn would not. He'd lost too much of his mind when he'd fallen off that pallet. One of my father's sons would be driving the forklift for the rest of his life, but it wouldn't be Richard.

Richard looked even more miserable than Shawn. His shoulders hunched and his neck sank into them, as if he were compressing under the weight of Dad's praise. After Dad went to bed, Richard told me that he'd taken a practice test for the ACT. He'd scored so low, he wouldn't tell me the number.

'Apparently I'm Einstein,' Richard said, his head in his hands. 'What do I do? Dad is saying I'm going to blow this thing out of the water, and I'm not even sure I can pass.'

Every night was the same. Through dinner, Dad would list all the false theories of science that his genius son would disprove; then after dinner, I would tell Richard about college, about classes, books, professors, things I knew would appeal to his innate need to learn. I was worried: Dad's expectations were so high, and Richard's fear of disappointing him so intense, it seemed possible that Richard might not take the ACT at all.

★ ★ ★

The shop in Franklin was ready to roof, so two days after Christmas I forced my toe, still crooked and black, into a steel-toed boot, then spent the morning on a roof driving threading screws into galvanized tin. It was late afternoon

273

when Shawn dropped his screw gun and shimmied down the loader's extended boom. 'Time for a break, Siddle Liss,' he shouted up from the ground. 'Let's go into town.'

I hopped onto the pallet and Shawn dropped the boom to the ground. 'You drive,' he said, then he leaned his seat back and closed his eyes. I headed for Stokes.

I remember strange details about the moment we pulled into the parking lot — the smell of oil floating up from our leather gloves, the sandpaper feel of dust on my fingertips. And Shawn, grinning at me from the passenger seat. Through the city of cars I spy one, a red jeep. Charles. I pass through the main lot and turn into the open asphalt on the north side of the store, where employees park. I pull down the visor to evaluate myself, noting the tangle the windy roof has made of my hair, and the grease from the tin that has lodged in my pores, making them fat and brown. My clothes are heavy with dirt.

Shawn sees the red jeep. He watches me lick my thumb and scrub dirt from my face, and he becomes excited. 'Let's go!' he says.

'I'll wait in the car.'

'You're coming in,' Shawn says.

Shawn can smell shame. He knows that Charles has never seen me like this — that every day all last summer, I rushed home and removed every stain, every smudge, hiding cuts and calluses beneath new clothes and makeup. A hundred times Shawn has seen me emerge from the bathroom unrecognizable, having washed the junkyard down the shower drain.

'You're coming in,' Shawn says again. He walks around the car and opens my door. The movement is old-fashioned, vaguely chivalrous.

'I don't want to,' I say.

'Don't want your boyfriend to see you looking so glamorous?' He smiles and jabs me with his finger. He is looking at me strangely, as if to say, *This is who you are. You've been pretending that you're someone else. Someone better. But you are just this.*

He begins to laugh, loudly, wildly, as if something funny has happened but nothing has. Still laughing, he grabs my arm and draws it upward, as if he's going to throw me over his back and carry me in fireman-style. I don't want Charles to see that so I end the game. I say, flatly, 'Don't touch me.'

What happens next is a blur in my memory. I see only snapshots — of the sky flipping absurdly, of fists coming at me, of a strange, savage look in the eyes of a man I don't recognize. I see my hands grasping the wheel, and I feel strong arms wrenching my legs. Something shifts in my ankle, a crack or a pop. I lose my grip. I'm pulled from the car.

I feel icy pavement on my back; pebbles are grinding into my skin. My jeans have slid down past my hips. I'd felt them peeling off me, inch by inch, as Shawn yanked my legs. My shirt has risen up and I look at myself, at my body spread flat on the asphalt, at my bra and faded underwear. I want to cover myself but Shawn has pinned my hands above my head. I lie still, feeling the cold seep into me. I hear my voice begging him to let me go, but I don't sound like myself. I'm listening to the sobs of another girl.

I am dragged upward and set on my feet. I claw at my clothing. Then I'm doubled over and my wrist is being folded back, bending, bent as far as it will go and bending still. My nose is near the pavement when the bone begins to bow. I try to regain my balance, to use the strength in my legs to push back, but when my ankle takes weight, it buckles. I scream. Heads turn in our direction. People crane to see what the commotion is. Immediately I begin to laugh — a wild, hysterical cackle that despite all my efforts still sounds a little like a scream.

'You're going in,' Shawn says, and I feel the bone in my wrist crack.

I go with him into the bright lights. I laugh as we pass through aisle after aisle, gathering the things he wants to buy. I laugh at every word he says, trying to convince anyone who might have been in the parking lot that it was all a joke. I'm walking on a sprained ankle, but the pain barely registers.

We do not see Charles.

The drive back to the site is silent. It's only five miles but it feels like fifty. We arrive and I limp toward the shop. Dad and Richard are inside. I'd been limping before because of my toe, so my new hobble isn't so noticeable. Still, Richard takes one look at my face, streaked with grease and tears, and knows something is wrong; Dad sees nothing.

I pick up my screw gun and drive screws with my left hand, but the pressure is uneven, and with my weight gathered on one foot, my balance is poor. The screws bounce off the painted tin, leaving long, twisting marks like curled ribbons. Dad sends me home after I ruin two sheets.

That night, with a heavily wrapped wrist, I scratch out a journal entry. I ask myself questions. Why didn't he stop when I begged him? *It was like getting beaten by a zombie*, I write. *Like he couldn't hear me.*

Shawn knocks. I slide my journal under the pillow. His shoulders are rounded when he enters. He speaks quietly. It was a game, he says. He had no idea he'd hurt me until he saw me cradling my arm at the site. He checks the bones in my wrist, examines my ankle. He brings me ice wrapped in a dish towel and says that next time we're having fun, I should tell him if something is wrong. He leaves. I return to my journal. *Was it really fun and games?* I write. *Could he not tell he was hurting me? I don't know. I just don't know.*

I begin to reason with myself, to doubt whether I had spoken clearly: what had I whispered and what had I screamed? I decide that if I had asked differently, been more calm, he would have stopped. I write this until I believe it, which doesn't take long because I *want* to believe it. It's comforting to think the defect is mine, because that means it is under my power.

I put away my journal and lie in bed, reciting this narrative as if it is a poem I've decided to learn by heart. I've nearly committed it to memory when the recitation is interrupted. Images invade my mind — of me, pinned, arms pressed above my head. Then I'm back in the parking lot. I look down at my white stomach, then up at my brother. His expression is unforgettable: not anger or rage. There is no fury in it. Only pleasure, unperturbed. Then a part of me understands, even as I begin to argue against it, that my humiliation was the cause of that pleasure. It was not an accident or side effect. It was the objective.

This half-knowledge works in me like a kind of possession, and for a few minutes I'm taken over by it. I rise from my bed, retrieve my journal, and do something I have never done before: I write what happened. I do not use vague, shadowy language, as I have done in other entries; I do not hide behind hints and suggestion. I write what I remember: *There was one point when he was forcing me from the car, that he had both hands pinned above my head and my shirt rose up. I asked him to let me fix it but it was like he couldn't hear me. He just stared at it like a great big jerk. It's a good thing I'm as small as I am. If I was larger, at that moment, I would have torn him apart.*

★ ★ ★

'I don't know what you've done to your wrist,' Dad told me the next morning, 'but you're no good on the crew like that. You might as well head back to Utah.'

The drive to BYU was hypnotic; by the time I arrived, my memories of the previous day had blurred and faded.

They were brought into focus when I checked my email. There was a message from Shawn. An apology. But he'd apologized already, in my room. I had never known Shawn to apologize twice.

I retrieved my journal and I wrote another entry, opposite the first, in which I revised the memory. It was a misunderstanding, I wrote. If I'd asked him to stop, he would have.

But however I chose to remember it, that event would change everything. Reflecting on it now I'm amazed by it, not by what happened, but that I wrote what happened. That from somewhere inside that brittle shell — in that girl made vacant by the fiction of invincibility — there was a spark left.

The words of the second entry would not obscure the words of the first. Both would remain, *my* memories set down alongside *his*. There was a boldness in not editing for consistency, in not ripping out either the one page or the other. To admit uncertainty is to admit to weakness, to powerlessness, and to believe in yourself despite both. It is a frailty, but in this frailty there is a strength: the conviction to live in your own mind, and not in someone else's. I have often wondered if the most powerful words I wrote that night came not from anger or rage, but from doubt: *I don't know. I just don't know.*

Not knowing for certain, but refusing to give way to those who claim certainty, was a privilege I had never allowed myself. My life was narrated for me by others. Their voices were forceful, emphatic, absolute. It had never occurred to me that my voice might be as strong as theirs.

23

I'm from Idaho

On Sunday, a week later, a man at church asked me to dinner. I said no. It happened a second time a few days later with a different man. Again I said no. I couldn't say yes. I didn't want either of them anywhere near me.

Word reached the bishop that there was a woman in his flock who was set against marriage. His assistant approached me after the Sunday service and said I was wanted in the bishop's office.

My wrist was still tender when I shook the bishop's hand. He was a middle-aged man with a round face and dark, neatly parted hair. His voice was soft like satin. He seemed to know me before I even opened my mouth. (In a way he did; Robin had told him plenty.) He said I should enroll in the university counseling service so that one day I might enjoy an eternal marriage to a righteous man.

He talked and I sat, wordless as a brick.

He asked about my family. I didn't answer. I had already betrayed them by failing to love them as I should; the least I could do was stay silent.

'Marriage is God's plan,' the bishop said, then he stood. The meeting was over. He asked me to return the following Sunday. I said I would, but knew I wouldn't.

My body felt heavy as I walked to my apartment. All my life I had been taught that marriage was God's will, that to refuse it was a kind of sin. I was in defiance of God. And yet, I didn't want to be. I wanted children, my own family, but even as I longed for it I knew I would never have it. I was not capable. I could not be near any man without despising myself.

I had always scoffed at the word 'whore.' It sounded guttural and outmoded even to me. But even though I silently mocked Shawn for using it, I had come to identify with it. That it was old-fashioned only strengthened the association, because it meant I usually only heard the word in connection with myself.

Once, when I was fifteen, after I'd started wearing mascara and lip gloss, Shawn had told Dad that he'd heard rumors about me in town, that I had a reputation. Immediately Dad thought I was pregnant. He should never have allowed those plays in town, he screamed at Mother. Mother said I was trustworthy, modest. Shawn said no teenage girl was trustworthy, and that in his experience those who seemed pious were sometimes the worst of all.

I sat on my bed, knees pressed to my chest, and listened to them shout. Was I pregnant? I wasn't sure. I considered every interaction I'd had with a boy, every glance, every touch. I walked to the mirror and raised my shirt, then ran my fingers across my abdomen, examining it inch by inch and thought, *Maybe*.

I had never kissed a boy.

I had witnessed birth, but I'd been given none

of the facts of conception. While my father and brother shouted, ignorance kept me silent: I couldn't defend myself, because I didn't understand the accusation.

Days later, when it was confirmed that I was not pregnant, I evolved a new understanding of the word 'whore,' one that was less about actions and more about essence. It was not that I had *done* something wrong so much as that I *existed* in the wrong way. There was something impure in the fact of my being.

It's strange how you give the people you love so much power over you, I had written in my journal. But Shawn had more power over me than I could possibly have imagined. He had defined me to myself, and there's no greater power than that.

★ ★ ★

I stood outside the bishop's office on a cold night in February. I didn't know what had taken me there.

The bishop sat calmly behind his desk. He asked what he could do for me, and I said I didn't know. No one could give me what I wanted, because what I wanted was to be remade.

'I can help,' he said, 'but you'll need to tell me what's bothering you.' His voice was gentle, and that gentleness was cruel. I wished he would yell. If he yelled, it would make me angry, and when angry I felt powerful. I didn't know if I could do this without feeling powerful.

I cleared my throat, then talked for an hour.

The bishop and I met every Sunday until spring. To me he was a patriarch with authority over me, but he seemed to surrender that authority the moment I passed through his door. I talked and he listened, drawing the shame from me like a healer draws infection from a wound.

When the semester ended, I told him I was going home for the summer. I was out of money; I couldn't pay rent. He looked tired when I told him that. He said, 'Don't go home, Tara. The church will pay your rent.'

I didn't want the church's money. I'd made the decision. The bishop made me promise only one thing: that I wouldn't work for my father.

My first day in Idaho, I got my old job back at Stokes. Dad scoffed, said I'd never earn enough to return to school. He was right, but the bishop had said God would provide a way and I believed it. I spent the summer restocking shelves and walking elderly ladies to their cars.

I avoided Shawn. It was easy because he had a new girlfriend, Emily, and there was talk of a wedding. Shawn was twenty-eight; Emily was a senior in high school. Her temperament was compliant. Shawn played the same games with her he'd played with Sadie, testing his control. She never failed to follow his orders, quivering when he raised his voice, apologizing when he screamed at her. That their marriage would be manipulative and violent, I had no doubt — although those words were not mine. They had been given to me by the bishop, and I was still trying to wrest meaning from them.

When the summer ended, I returned to BYU with only two thousand dollars. On my first night back, I wrote in my journal: *I have so many bills I can't imagine how I'm going to pay them. But God will provide either trials for growth or the means to succeed.* The tone of that entry seems lofty, high-minded, but in it I detect a whiff of fatalism. Maybe I would have to leave school. That was fine. There were grocery stores in Utah. I would bag groceries, and one day I'd be manager.

I was shocked out of this resignation two weeks into the fall semester, when I awoke one night to a blinding pain in my jaw. I'd never felt anything so acute, so electrifying. I wanted to rip my jaw from my mouth, just to be rid of it. I stumbled to a mirror. The source was a tooth that had been chipped many years before, but now it had fractured again, and deeply. I visited a dentist, who said the tooth had been rotting for years. It would cost fourteen hundred dollars to repair. I couldn't afford to pay half that and stay in school.

I called home. Mother agreed to lend me the money, but Dad attached terms: I would have to work for him next summer. I didn't even consider it. I said I was finished with the junkyard, finished for life, and hung up.

I tried to ignore the ache and focus on my classes, but it felt as though I were being asked to sit through a lecture while a wolf gnawed on my jaw.

I'd never taken another ibuprofen since that day with Charles, but I began to swallow them

284

like breath mints. They helped only a little. The pain was in the nerves, and it was too severe. I hadn't slept since the ache began, and I started skipping meals because chewing was unthinkable. That's when Robin told the bishop.

He called me to his office on a bright afternoon. He looked at me calmly from across his desk and said, 'What are we going to do about your tooth?' I tried to relax my face.

'You can't go through the school year like this,' he said. 'But there's an easy solution. Very easy, in fact. How much does your father make?'

'Not much,' I said. 'He's been in debt since the boys wrecked all the equipment last year.'

'Excellent,' he said. 'I have the paperwork here for a grant. I'm sure you're eligible, and the best part is, you won't have to pay it back.'

I'd heard about Government grants. Dad said that to accept one was to indebt yourself to the Illuminati. 'That's how they get you,' he'd said. 'They give you free money, then the next thing you know, they *own* you.'

These words echoed in my head. I'd heard other students talk about their grants, and I'd recoiled from them. I would leave school before I would allow myself to be purchased.

'I don't believe in Government grants,' I said.
'Why not?'

I told him what my father said. He sighed and looked heavenward. 'How much will it cost to fix the tooth?'

'Fourteen hundred,' I said. 'I'll find the money.'

'The church will pay,' he said quietly. 'I have a discretionary fund.'

'That money is sacred.'

The bishop threw his hands in the air. We sat in silence, then he opened his desk drawer and withdrew a checkbook. I looked at the heading. It was for his personal account. He filled out a check, to me, for fifteen hundred dollars.

'I will *not* allow you to leave school over this,' he said.

The check was in my hand. I was so tempted, the pain in my jaw so savage, that I must have held it for ten seconds before passing it back.

★ ★ ★

I had a job at the campus creamery, flipping burgers and scooping ice cream. I got by between paydays by neglecting overdue bills and borrowing money from Robin, so twice a month, when a few hundred dollars went into my account, it was gone within hours. I was broke when I turned nineteen at the end of September. I had given up on fixing the tooth; I knew I would never have fourteen hundred dollars. Besides, the pain had lessened: either the nerve had died or my brain had adjusted to its shocks.

Still, I had other bills, so I decided to sell the only thing I had of any value — my horse, Bud. I called Shawn and asked how much I could get. Shawn said a mixed breed wasn't worth much, but that I could send him to auction like Grandpa's dog-food horses. I imagined Bud in a meat grinder, then said, 'Try to find a buyer first.' A few weeks later Shawn sent me a check for a few hundred dollars. When I called Shawn and asked who he'd sold Bud to, he mumbled something vague about a guy passing through from Tooele.

I was an incurious student that semester. Curiosity is a luxury reserved for the financially secure: my mind was absorbed with more immediate concerns, such as the exact balance of my bank account, who I owed how much, and whether there was anything in my room I could sell for ten or twenty dollars. I submitted my homework and studied for my exams, but I did so out of a terror — of losing my scholarship should my GPA fall a single decimal — not from real interest in my classes.

In December, after my last paycheck of the month, I had sixty dollars in my account. Rent was $110, due January 7. I needed quick cash. I'd heard there was a clinic near the mall that paid people for plasma. A clinic sounded like a part of the Medical Establishment, but I reasoned that as long as they were taking things out, not putting anything in, I'd be okay. The nurse stabbed at my veins for twenty minutes, then said they were too small.

I bought a tank of gas with my last thirty dollars and drove home for Christmas. On Christmas morning, Dad gave me a rifle — I didn't take it out of the box, so I have no idea what kind. I asked Shawn if he wanted to buy it off me, but Dad gathered it up and said he'd keep it safe.

That was it, then. There was nothing left to sell, no more childhood friends or Christmas presents. It was time to quit school and get a job.

I accepted that. My brother Tony was living in Las Vegas, working as a long-haul trucker, so on Christmas Day I called him. He said I could live with him for a few months and work at the In-N-Out Burger across the street.

I hung up and was walking down the hall, wishing I'd asked Tony if he could lend me the money to get to Vegas, when a gruff voice called to me. 'Hey, Siddle Lister. Come here a minute.'

Shawn's bedroom was filthy. Dirty clothes littered the floor, and I could see the butt of a handgun poking out from under a pile of stained T-shirts. The bookshelves strained under boxes of ammo and stacks of Louis L'Amour paperbacks. Shawn was sitting on the bed, his shoulders hunched, his legs bowed outward. He looked as if he'd been holding that posture for some time, contemplating the squalor. He let out a sigh, then stood and walked toward me, lifting his right arm. I took an involuntary step back, but he had only reached into his pocket. He pulled out his wallet, opened it and extracted a crisp hundred-dollar bill.

'Merry Christmas,' he said. 'You won't waste this like I will.'

★　★　★

I believed that hundred dollars was a sign from God. I was supposed to stay in school. I drove back to BYU and paid my rent. Then, because I knew I wouldn't be able to pay it in February, I took a second job as a domestic cleaner, driving twenty minutes north three days a week to scrub

288

expensive homes in Draper.

The bishop and I were still meeting every Sunday. Robin had told him that I hadn't bought my textbooks for the semester. 'This is ridiculous,' he said. 'Apply for the grant! You're poor! That's why these grants exist!'

My opposition was beyond rational, it was visceral.

'I make a lot of money,' the bishop said. 'I pay a lot of taxes. Just think of it as my money.' He had printed out the application forms, which he gave to me. 'Think about it. You need to learn to accept help, even from the Government.'

I took the forms. Robin filled them out. I refused to send them.

'Just get the paperwork together,' she said. 'See how it feels.'

I needed my parents' tax returns. I wasn't even sure my parents filed taxes, but if they did, I knew Dad wouldn't give them to me if he knew why I wanted them. I thought up a dozen fake reasons for why I might need them, but none were believable. I pictured the returns sitting in the large gray filing cabinet in the kitchen. Then I decided to steal them.

I left for Idaho just before midnight, hoping I would arrive at around three in the morning and the house would be quiet. When I reached the peak, I crept up the driveway, wincing each time a bit of gravel snapped beneath my tires. I eased the car door open noiselessly, then padded across the grass and slipped through the back door, moving silently through the house, reaching my hand out to feel my way to the filing cabinet.

I had only made it a few steps when I heard a familiar *clink*.

'Don't shoot!' I shouted. 'It's me!'

'Who?'

I flipped the light switch and saw Shawn sitting across the room, pointing a pistol at me. He lowered it. 'I thought you were . . . someone else.'

'Obviously,' I said.

We stood awkwardly for a moment, then I went to bed.

The next morning, after Dad left for the junkyard, I told Mother one of my fake stories about BYU needing her tax returns. She knew I was lying — I could tell because when Dad came in unexpectedly and asked why she was copying the returns, she said the duplicates were for her records.

I took the copies and returned to BYU. Shawn and I exchanged no words before I left. He never asked why I'd been sneaking into my own house at three in the morning, and I never asked who he'd been waiting for, sitting up in the middle of the night, with a loaded pistol.

★ ★ ★

The forms sat on my desk for a week before Robin walked with me to the post office and watched me hand them to the postal worker. It didn't take long, a week, maybe two. I was cleaning houses in Draper when the mail came, so Robin left the letter on my bed with a note that I was a Commie now.

290

I tore open the envelope and a check fell onto my bed. For four thousand dollars. I felt greedy, then afraid of my greed. There was a contact number. I dialed it.

'There's a problem,' I told the woman who answered. 'The check is for four thousand dollars, but I only need fourteen hundred.'

The line was silent.

'Hello? Hello?'

'Let me get this straight,' the woman said. 'You're saying the check is for too *much* money? What do you want me to do?'

'If I send it back, could you send me another one? I only need fourteen hundred. For a root canal.'

'Look, honey,' she said. 'You get that much because that's how much you get. Cash it or don't, it's up to you.'

I had the root canal. I bought my textbooks, paid rent, and had money left over. The bishop said I should treat myself to something, but I said I couldn't, I had to save the money. He told me I could afford to spend some. 'Remember,' he said, 'you can apply for the same amount next year.' I bought a new Sunday dress.

I'd believed the money would be used to control me, but what it did was enable me to keep my word to myself: for the first time, when I said I would never again work for my father, I believed it.

I wonder now if the day I set out to steal that tax return wasn't the first time I left *home* to go to Buck's Peak. That night I had entered my father's house as an intruder. It was a shift in mental language, a surrendering of where I was from.

My own words confirmed it. When other students asked where I was from, I said, 'I'm from Idaho,' a phrase that, as many times as I've had to repeat it over the years, has never felt comfortable in my mouth. When you are part of a place, growing that moment in its soil, there's never a need to say you're from there. I never uttered the words 'I'm from Idaho' until I'd left it.

24

A Knight, Errant

I had a thousand dollars in my bank account. It felt strange just to think that, let alone say it. A thousand dollars. Extra. That I did not immediately need. It took weeks for me to come to terms with this fact, but as I did, I began to experience the most powerful advantage of money: the ability to think of things besides money.

My professors came into focus, suddenly and sharply; it was as if before the grant I'd been looking at them through a blurred lens. My textbooks began to make sense, and I found myself doing more than the required reading.

It was in this state that I first heard the term bipolar disorder. I was sitting in Psychology 101 when the professor read the symptoms aloud from the overhead screen: depression, mania, paranoia, euphoria, delusions of grandeur and persecution. I listened with a desperate interest.

This is my father, I wrote in my notes. *He's describing Dad.*

A few minutes before the bell rang, a student asked what role mental disorders might have played in separatist movements. 'I'm thinking of famous conflicts like Waco, Texas, or Ruby Ridge, Idaho,' he said.

Idaho isn't famous for many things, so I figured I'd have heard of whatever 'Ruby Ridge' was. He'd said it was a conflict. I searched my memory, trying to recall if I'd ever heard the words. There was something familiar in them. Then images appeared in my mind, weak and distorted, as if the transmission were being disrupted at the source. I closed my eyes and the scene became vivid. I was in our house, crouching behind the birch wood cabinets. Mother was kneeling next to me, her breath slow and tired. She licked her lips and said she was thirsty, then before I could stop her she stood and reached for the tap. I felt the tremor of gunfire and heard myself shout. There was a thud as something heavy fell to the floor. I moved her arm aside and gathered up the baby.

The bell rang. The auditorium emptied. I went to the computer lab. I hesitated for a moment over the keyboard — struck by a premonition that this was information I might regret knowing — then typed 'Ruby Ridge' into the browser. According to Wikipedia, Ruby Ridge was the site of a deadly standoff between Randy Weaver and a number of Federal agencies, including the U.S. Marshals Service and the FBI.

The name Randy Weaver was familiar, and even as I read it I heard it falling from my father's lips. Then the story as it had lived in my imagination for thirteen years began replaying in my mind: the shooting of a boy, then of his father, then of his mother. The Government had murdered the entire family, parents and children, to cover up what they had done.

I scrolled past the backstory to the first shooting. Federal agents had surrounded the

Weaver cabin. The mission was surveillance only, and the Weavers were unaware of the agents until a dog began to bark. Believing the dog had sensed a wild animal, Randy's fourteen-year-old son, Sammy, charged into the woods. The agents shot the dog, and Sammy, who was carrying a gun, opened fire. The resulting conflict left two dead: a federal agent and Sammy, who was retreating, running up the hill toward the cabin, when he was shot in the back.

I read on. The next day, Randy Weaver was shot, also in the back, while trying to visit his son's body. The corpse was in the shed, and Randy was lifting the latch on the door, when a sniper took aim at his spine and missed. His wife, Vicki, moved toward the door to help her husband and again the sniper opened fire. The bullet struck her in the head, killing her instantly as she held their ten-month-old daughter. For nine days the family huddled in the cabin with their mother's body, until finally negotiators ended the standoff and Randy Weaver was arrested.

I read this last line several times before I understood it. Randy Weaver was alive? Did Dad know?

I kept reading. The nation had been outraged. Articles had appeared in nearly every major newspaper blasting the government's callous disregard for life. The Department of Justice had opened an investigation, and the Senate had held hearings. Both had recommended reforms to the rules of engagement, particularly concerning the use of deadly force.

The Weavers had filed a wrongful death suit for $200 million but settled out of court when the government offered Vicki's three daughters $1 million each. Randy Weaver was awarded $100,000 and all charges, except two related to court appearances, were dropped. Randy Weaver had been interviewed by major news organizations and had even co-written a book with his daughter. He now made his living speaking at gun shows.

If it was a cover-up, it was a very bad one. There had been media coverage, official inquiries, oversight. Wasn't that the measure of a democracy?

There was one thing I still didn't understand: Why had federal agents surrounded Randy Weaver's cabin in the first place? Why had Randy been targeted? I remembered Dad saying it could just as easy be us. Dad was always saying that one day the Government would come after folks who resisted its brainwashing, who didn't put their kids in school. For thirteen years, I'd assumed that this was why the Government had come for Randy: to force his children into school.

I returned to the top of the page and read the whole entry again, but this time I didn't skip the backstory. According to all the sources, including Randy Weaver himself, the conflict had begun when Randy sold two sawed-off shotguns to an undercover agent he'd met at an Aryan Nations gathering. I read this sentence more than once, many times in fact. Then I understood: white supremacy was at the heart of this story, not homeschool. The government, it seemed, had never been in the habit of murdering people for not submitting their children to a public education. This seemed so obvious to me now, it was difficult to understand why I had ever believed anything else.

For one bitter moment, I thought Dad had lied. Then I remembered the fear on his face, the heavy rattling of his breath, and I felt certain that he'd really believed we were in danger. I reached for some explanation and strange words came to mind, words I'd learned only minutes before: *paranoia, mania, delusions of grandeur and persecution*. And finally the story made sense — the one on the page, and the one that had lived in me through childhood. Dad must have read about Ruby Ridge or seen it on the news, and somehow as it passed through his feverish brain, it had ceased to be a story about someone else and had become a story about *him*. If the Government was after Randy Weaver, surely it must also be after Gene Westover, who'd been holding the front line in the war with the Illuminati for years. No longer content to read about the brave deeds of others, he had forged himself a helmet and mounted a nag.

★　★　★

I became obsessed with bipolar disorder. We were required to write a research paper for Psychology and I chose it as my subject, then used the paper as an excuse to interrogate every neuroscientist and cognitive specialist at the university. I described Dad's symptoms, attributing them not to my father but to a fictive uncle. Some of the symptoms fit perfectly; others did not. The professors told me that every case is different.

'What you're describing sounds more like schizophrenia,' one said. 'Did your uncle ever get treatment?'

'No,' I said. 'He thinks doctors are part of a Government conspiracy.'

'That does complicate things,' he said.

With all the subtlety of a bulldozer I wrote my paper on the effect bipolar parents have on their children. It was accusative, brutal. I wrote that children of bipolar parents are hit with double risk factors: first, because they are genetically predisposed to mood disorders and second, because of the *stressful environment and poor parenting of parents with such disorders*.

In class I had been taught about neurotransmitters and their effect on brain chemistry; I understood that disease is not a choice. This knowledge might have made me sympathetic to my father, but it didn't. I felt only anger. We were the ones who'd paid for it, I thought. Mother. Luke. Shawn. We had been bruised and gashed and concussed, had our legs set on fire and our heads cut open. We had lived in a state of alert, a kind of constant terror, our brains flooding with cortisol because we knew that any of those things might happen at any moment. Because Dad always put faith before safety. Because he believed himself right, and he kept on believing himself right — after the first car crash, after the second, after the bin, the fire, the pallet. And it was us who paid.

I visited Buck's Peak the weekend after I submitted my paper. I had been home for less than an hour when Dad and I got into an argument. He said I owed him for the car. He really only mentioned it but I became crazed, hysterical. For the first time in my life I shouted at my father — not about the car, but about the Weavers. I was so suffocated by rage, my words didn't come out as words but as choking, sputtering sobs. Why are you like this? Why did you terrify us like that? Why did you fight so hard against made-up monsters, but do nothing about the monsters in your own house?

Dad gaped at me, astonished. His mouth sagged and his hands hung limply at his sides, twitching, as if he wanted to raise them, to do something. I hadn't seen him look so helpless since he'd crouched next to our wrecked station wagon, watching Mother's face bulge and distend, unable even to touch her because electrified cables were sending a deadly pulse through the metal.

Out of shame or anger, I fled. I drove without stopping back to BYU. My father called a few hours later. I didn't answer. Screaming at him hadn't helped; maybe ignoring him would.

When the semester ended, I stayed in Utah. It was the first summer that I didn't return to Buck's Peak. I did not speak to my father, not even on the phone. This estrangement was not formalized: I just didn't feel like seeing him, or hearing his voice, so I didn't.

★ ★ ★

I decided to experiment with normality. For nineteen years I'd lived the way my father wanted. Now I would try something else.

I moved to a new apartment on the other side of town where no one knew me. I wanted a new start. At church my first week, my new bishop greeted me with a warm handshake, then moved on to the next newcomer. I reveled in his disinterest. If I could just pretend to be normal for a little while, maybe it would feel like the truth.

It was at church that I met Nick. Nick had square glasses and dark hair, which he gelled and teased into neat spikes. Dad would have scoffed at a man wearing hair gel, which is perhaps why I loved it. I also loved that Nick wouldn't have known an alternator from a crankshaft. What he *did* know were books and video games and clothing brands. And words. He had an astonishing vocabulary.

Nick and I were a couple from the beginning. He grabbed my hand the second time we met. When his skin touched mine, I prepared to fight that primal need to push him away, but it never came. It was strange and exciting, and no part of me wanted it to end. I wished I were still in my old congregation, so I could rush to my old bishop and tell him I wasn't broken anymore.

I overestimated my progress. I was so focused on what *was* working, I didn't notice what wasn't. We'd been together a few months, and I'd spent many evenings with his family, before I ever said a word about mine. I did it without thinking, casually mentioned one of Mother's oils when Nick said he had an ache in his shoulder. He was intrigued — he'd been waiting for me to bring them up — but I was angry at myself for the slip, and didn't let it happen again.

★ ★ ★

I began to feel poorly toward the end of May. A week passed in which I could hardly drag myself to my job, an internship at a law firm. I slept from early evening until late morning, then yawned through the day. My throat began to ache and my voice dropped, roughening into a deep crackle, as if my vocal cords had turned to sandpaper.

At first Nick was amused that I wouldn't see a doctor, but as the illness progressed his amusement turned to worry, then confusion. I blew him off. 'It's not that serious,' I said. 'I'd go if it were serious.'

Another week passed. I quit my internship and began sleeping through the days as well as the nights. One morning, Nick showed up unexpectedly.

'We're going to the doctor,' he said.

I started to say I wouldn't go, but then I saw his face. He looked as though he had a question but knew there was no point in asking it. The tense line of his mouth, the narrowing of his eyes. *This is what distrust looks like*, I thought.

Given the choice between seeing an evil socialist doctor, and admitting to my boyfriend that I believed doctors were evil socialists, I chose to see the doctor.

'I'll go today,' I said. 'I promise. But I'd rather go alone.'

'Fine,' he said.

He left, but now I had another problem. I didn't know *how* to go to a doctor. I called a friend from class and asked if she'd drive me. She picked me up an hour later and I watched, perplexed, as she drove right past the hospital a few blocks from my apartment. She took me to a small building north of campus, which she called a 'clinic.' I tried to feign nonchalance, act as though I'd done this before, but as we crossed the parking lot I felt as though Mother were watching me.

I didn't know what to say to the receptionist. My friend attributed my silence to my throat and explained my symptoms. We were told to wait. Eventually a nurse led me to a small white room where she weighed me, took my blood pressure, and swabbed my tongue. Sore throats this severe were usually caused by strep bacteria or the mono virus, she said. They would know in a few days.

When the results came back, I drove to the clinic alone. A balding middle-aged doctor gave me the results. 'Congratulations,' he said. 'You're positive for strep *and* mono. Only person I've seen in a month to get both.'

'Both?' I whispered. 'How can I have both?'

'Very, very bad luck,' he said. 'I can give you penicillin for the strep, but there's not much I can do for the mono. You'll have to wait it out. Still, once we've cleared out the strep, you should feel better.'

302

The doctor asked a nurse to bring some penicillin. 'We should start you on the antibiotics right away,' he said. I held the pills in my palm and was reminded of that afternoon when Charles had given me ibuprofen. I thought of Mother, and of the many times she'd told me that antibiotics poison the body, that they cause infertility and birth defects. That the spirit of the Lord cannot dwell in an unclean vessel, and that no vessel is clean when it forsakes God and relies on man. Or maybe Dad had said that last part.

I swallowed the pills. Perhaps it was desperation because I felt so poorly, but I think the reason was more mundane: curiosity. There I was, in the heart of the Medical Establishment, and I wanted to see, at long last, what it was I had always been afraid of. Would my eyes bleed? My tongue fall out? Surely something awful would happen. I needed to know what.

I returned to my apartment and called Mother. I thought confessing would alleviate my guilt. I told her I'd seen a doctor, and that I had strep and mono. 'I'm taking penicillin,' I said. 'I just wanted you to know.'

She began talking rapidly but I didn't hear much of it, I was so tired. When she seemed to be winding down, I said 'I love you' and hung up.

Two days later a package arrived, express from Idaho. Inside were six bottles of tincture, two vials of essential oil, and a bag of white clay. I recognized the formulas — the oils and tinctures were to fortify the liver and kidneys, and the clay was a foot soak to draw toxins. There was a note from Mother: *These herbs will flush the antibiotics from your system. Please use them for as long as you insist on taking the drugs. Love you.*

I leaned back into my pillow and fell asleep almost instantly, but before I did I laughed out loud. She hadn't sent any remedies for the strep or the mono. Only for the penicillin.

★ ★ ★

I awoke the next morning to my phone ringing. It was Audrey.

'There's been an accident,' she said.

Her words transported me to another moment, to the last time I'd answered a phone and heard those words instead of a greeting. I thought of that day, and of what Mother had said next. I hoped Audrey was reading from a different script.

'It's Dad,' she said. 'If you hurry — leave right now — you can say goodbye.'

25

The Work of Sulphur

There's a story I was told when I was young, told so many times and from such an early age, I can't remember who told it to me first. It was about Grandpa-down-the-hill and how he got the dent above his right temple.

When Grandpa was a younger man, he had spent a hot summer on the mountain, riding the white mare he used for cowboy work. She was a tall horse, calmed with age. To hear Mother tell it that mare was steady as a rock, and Grandpa didn't pay much attention when he rode her. He'd drop the knotted reins if he felt like it, maybe to pick a burr out of his boot or sweep off his red cap and wipe his face with his shirtsleeve. The mare stood still. But tranquil as she was, she was terrified of snakes.

'She must have glimpsed something slithering in the weeds,' Mother would say when she told the story, 'because she chucked Grandpa clean off.' There was an old set of harrows behind him. Grandpa flew into them and a disc caved in his forehead.

What exactly it was that shattered Grandpa's skull changed every time I heard the story. In some tellings it was harrows, but in others it was a rock. I suspect nobody knows for sure. There weren't any witnesses. The blow rendered Grandpa unconscious, and he doesn't remember much until Grandma found him on the porch, soaked to his boots in blood.

Nobody knows how he came to be on that porch.

From the upper pasture to the house is a distance of a mile — rocky terrain with steep, unforgiving hills, which Grandpa could not have managed in his condition. But there he was. Grandma heard a faint scratching at the door, and when she opened it there was Grandpa, lying in a heap, his brains dripping out of his head. She rushed him to town and they fitted him with a metal plate.

After Grandpa was home and recovering, Grandma went looking for the white mare. She walked all over the mountain but found her tied to the fence behind the corral, tethered with an intricate knot that nobody used except her father, Lott.

Sometimes, when I was at Grandma's eating the forbidden cornflakes and milk, I'd ask Grandpa to tell me how he got off the mountain. He always said he didn't know. Then he'd take a deep breath — long and slow, like he was settling into a mood rather than a story — and he'd tell the whole tale from start to finish. Grandpa was a quiet man, near silent. You could pass a whole afternoon clearing fields with him and never hear ten words strung together. Just 'Yep' and 'Not that one' and 'I reckon so.'

But ask how he got down the mountain that day and he'd talk for ten minutes, even though all he remembered was lying in the field, unable to open his eyes, while the hot sun dried the blood on his face.

'But I tell you this,' Grandpa would say, taking off his hat and running his fingers over the dent in his skull. 'I heard things while I was lyin' in them weeds. Voices, and they was talking. I recognized one, because it was Grandpa Lott. He was a tellin' somebody that Albert's son was in trouble. It was Lott sayin' that, I know it sure as I know I'm standing here.' Grandpa's eyes would shine a bit, then he'd say, 'Only thing is, Lott had been dead near ten years.'

This part of the story called for reverence. Mother and Grandma both loved to tell it but I liked Mother's telling best. Her voice hushed in the right places. It was angels, she would say, a small tear falling to the corner of her smile. Your great-grandpa Lott sent them, and they carried Grandpa down the mountain.

The dent was unsightly, a two-inch crater in his forehead. As a child, when I looked at it, sometimes I imagined a tall doctor in a white coat banging on a sheet of metal with a hammer. In my imagination the doctor used the same corrugated sheets of tin that Dad used to roof hay sheds.

But that was only sometimes. Usually I saw something else. Proof that my ancestors walked that peak, watching and waiting, angels at their command.

* * *

I don't know why Dad was alone on the mountain that day.

The car crusher was coming. I suppose he

307

wanted to remove that last fuel tank, but I can't imagine what possessed him to light his torch without first draining the fuel. I don't know how far he got, how many of the iron belts he managed to sever, before a spark from the torch made it into the tank. But I know Dad was standing next to the car, his body pressed against the frame, when the tank exploded.

He was wearing a long-sleeved shirt, leather gloves and a welding shield. His face and fingers took the brunt of the blast. The heat from the explosion melted through the shield as if it were a plastic spoon. The lower half of his face liquefied: the fire consumed plastic, then skin, then muscle. The same process was repeated with his fingers — the leather gloves were no match for the inferno that passed over and through them — then tongues of flame licked across his shoulders and chest. When he crawled away from the flaming vehicle, I imagine he looked more like a corpse than a living man.

It is unfathomable to me that he was able to move, let alone drag himself a quarter mile through fields and over ditches. If ever a man needed angels, it was that man. But against all reason he did it, and — as his father had years before — huddled outside his wife's door, unable to knock.

My cousin Kylie was working for my mother that day, filling vials of essential oil. A few other women worked nearby, weighing dried leaves or straining tinctures. Kylie heard a soft tap on the back door, as if someone was bumping it with their elbow. She opened it but has no memory of what was on the other side. 'I've blocked it out,' she would later tell me. 'I can't remember what I saw. I only remember what I thought, which was, *He has no skin.*'

My father was carried to the couch. Rescue Remedy — the homeopathic for shock — was poured into the lipless cavity that had been his mouth. They gave him lobelia and skullcap for the pain, the same mixture Mother had given Luke years before. Dad choked on the medicine. He couldn't swallow. He'd inhaled the fiery blast, and his insides were charred.

Mother tried to take him to the hospital, but between rasping breaths he whispered that he'd rather die than see a doctor. The authority of the man was such that she gave way.

The dead skin was gently cut away and he was slathered in salve — the same salve Mother had used on Luke's leg years before — from his waist to the tip of his head, then bandaged. Mother gave him ice cubes to suck on, hoping to hydrate him, but the inside of his mouth and throat were so badly burned, they absorbed no liquid, and without lips or muscles he couldn't hold the ice in his mouth. It would slide down his throat and choke him.

They nearly lost him many times that first night. His breathing would slow, then stop, and my mother — and the heavenly host of women who worked for her — would fly about, adjusting chakras and tapping pressure points, anything to coax his brittle lungs to resume their rattle.

That morning was when Audrey called me.[6] His heart had stopped twice during the night, she told me. It would probably be his heart that killed him, assuming his lungs didn't give out first. Either way, Audrey was sure he'd be dead by midday.

I called Nick. I told him I had to go to Idaho for a few days, for a family thing, nothing serious. He knew I wasn't telling him something — I could hear the hurt in his voice that I wouldn't confide in him — but I put him out of my mind the moment I hung up the phone.

I stood, keys in hand, hand on the doorknob, and hesitated. The strep. What if I gave it to Dad? I had been taking the penicillin for nearly three days. The doctor had said that after twenty-four hours I would no longer be contagious, but then he was a doctor, and I didn't trust him.

I waited a day. I took several times the prescribed dose of penicillin, then called Mother and asked what I should do.

'You should come home,' she said, and her voice broke. 'I don't think the strep will matter tomorrow.'

I don't recall the scenery from the drive. My eyes barely registered the patchwork of corn and potato fields, or the dark hills covered in pine. Instead I saw my father, the way he'd looked the last time I'd seen him, that twisted expression. I remembered the searing pitch of my voice as I'd screamed at him.

Like Kylie, I don't remember what I saw when I first looked at my father. I know that when Mother had removed the gauze that morning, she'd found that his ears were so burned, the

310

skin so glutinous, they had fused to the syrupy tissue behind them. When I walked through the back door, the first thing I saw was Mother grasping a butter knife, which she was using to pry my father's ears from his skull. I can still picture her gripping the knife, her eyes fixed, focused, but where my father should be, there's an aperture in my memory.

The smell in the room was powerful — of charred flesh, and of comfrey, mullein and plantain. I watched Mother and Audrey change his remaining bandages. They began with his hands. His fingers were slimy, coated in a pale ooze that was either melted skin or pus. His arms were not burned and neither were his shoulders or back, but a thick swath of gauze ran over his stomach and chest. When they removed it, I was pleased to see large patches of raw, angry skin. There were a few craters from where the flames must have concentrated in jets. They gave off a pungent smell, like meat gone to rot, and were filled with white pools.

But it was his face that visited my dreams that night. He still had a forehead and nose. The skin around his eyes and partway down his cheeks was pink and healthy. But below his nose, nothing was where it should be. Red, mangled, sagging, it looked like a plastic drama mask that had been held too close to a candle.

Dad hadn't swallowed anything — no food, no water — for nearly three days. Mother called a hospital in Utah and begged them to give her an IV. 'I need to hydrate him,' she said. 'He'll die if he doesn't get water.'

The doctor said he would send a chopper that very minute but Mother said no. 'Then I can't help you,' the doctor said. 'You're going to kill him, and I want no part of it.'

Mother was beside herself. In a final, desperate act, she gave Dad an enema, pushing the tube in as far as she dared trying to flush enough liquid through his rectum to keep him alive. She had no idea if it would work — if there was even an organ in that part of the body to absorb the water — but it was the only orifice that hadn't been scorched.

I slept on the living room floor that night so I could be there, in the room, when we lost him. I awoke several times to gasps and flights of movements and murmurs that it had happened again, he'd stopped breathing.

Once, an hour before dawn, his breath left him and I was sure it was the end: he was dead and would not be raised. I rested my hand on a small patch of bandages while Audrey and Mother rushed around me, chanting and tapping. The room was not at peace, or maybe it's just that I wasn't. For years my father and I had been locked in conflict, an endless battle of wills. I thought I had accepted it, accepted our relationship for what it was. But in that moment, I realized how much I'd been counting on that conflict coming to an end, how deeply I believed in a future in which we would be a father and daughter at peace.

I watched his chest, prayed for him to breathe, but he didn't. Then too much time had passed. I was preparing to move away, to let my mother and sister say goodbye, when he coughed — a brittle, rasping hack that sounded like crepe paper being crinkled. Then, like Lazarus reanimated, his chest began to rise and fall.

I told Mother I was leaving. Dad might survive, I said. And if he does, strep can't be what kills him.

★ ★ ★

Mother's business came to a halt. The women who worked for her stopped concocting tinctures and bottling oils and instead made vats of salve — a new recipe, of comfrey, lobelia and plantain, that Mother had concocted specifically for my father. Mother smeared the salve over Dad's upper body twice a day. I don't remember what other treatments they used, and I don't know enough about the energy work to give an account. I know they went through seventeen gallons of salve in the first two weeks, and that Mother was ordering gauze in bulk.

Tyler flew in from Purdue. He took over for Mother, changing the bandages on Dad's fingers every morning, scraping away the layers of skin and muscle that had necrotized during the night. It didn't hurt. The nerves were dead. 'I scraped off so many layers,' Tyler told me, 'I was sure that one morning I'd hit bone.'

Dad's fingers began to bow, bending unnaturally backward at the joint. This was because the tendons had begun to shrivel and contract. Tyler tried to curl Dad's fingers, to elongate the tendons and prevent the deformity from

313

becoming permanent, but Dad couldn't bear the pain.

I came back to Buck's Peak when I was sure the strep was gone. I sat by Dad's bed, dripping teaspoons of water into his mouth with a medical dropper and feeding him pureed vegetables as if he were a toddler. He rarely spoke. The pain made it difficult for him to focus; he could hardly get through a sentence before his mind surrendered to it. Mother offered to buy him pharmaceuticals, the strongest analgesics she could get her hands on, but he declined them. This was the Lord's pain, he said, and he would feel every part of it.

While I was away, I had scoured every video store within a hundred miles until I'd found the complete box set of *The Honeymooners*. I held it up for Dad. He blinked to show me he'd seen it. I asked if he wanted to watch an episode. He blinked again. I pushed the first tape into the VCR and sat beside him, searching his warped face, listening to his soft whimpers, while on the screen Alice Kramden outfoxed her husband again and again.

26

Waiting for Moving Water

Dad didn't leave his bed for two months unless one of my brothers was carrying him. He peed in a bottle, and the enemas continued. Even after it became clear that he would live, we had no idea what kind of life it would be. All we could do was wait, and soon it felt as though everything we did was just another form of waiting — waiting to feed him, waiting to change his bandages. Waiting to see how much of our father would grow back.

It was difficult to imagine a man like Dad — proud, strong, physical — permanently impaired. I wondered how he would adjust if Mother were forever cutting his food for him; if he could live a happy life if he wasn't able to grasp a hammer. So much had been lost.

But mixed in with the sadness, I also felt hope. Dad had always been a hard man — a man who knew the truth on every subject and wasn't interested in what anybody else had to say. We listened to *him*, never the other way around: when he was not speaking, he required silence.

The explosion transformed him from lecturer to observer. Speaking was difficult for him, because of the constant pain but also because his throat was burned. So he watched, he listened. He lay, hour after hour, day after day, his eyes alert, his mouth shut.

Within a few weeks, my father — who years earlier had not been able to guess my age within half a decade — knew about my classes, my boyfriend, my summer job. I hadn't told him any of it, but he'd listened to the chatter between me and Audrey as we changed his bandages, and he'd remembered.

'I'd like to hear more about them classes,' he rasped one morning near the end of the summer. 'It sounds real interesting.'

It felt like a new beginning.

★   ★   ★

Dad was still bedridden when Shawn and Emily announced their engagement. It was suppertime, and the family was gathered around the kitchen table, when Shawn said he guessed he'd marry Emily after all. There was silence while forks scraped plates. Mother asked if he was serious. He said he wasn't, that he figured he'd find somebody better before he actually had to go through with it. Emily sat next to him, wearing a warped smile.

I didn't sleep that night. I kept checking the bolt on the door. The present seemed vulnerable to the past, as if it might be overwhelmed by it, as if I might blink, and when my eyes opened I would be fifteen.

The next morning Shawn said he and Emily were planning a twenty-mile horse ride to Bloomington Lake. I surprised both of us by saying I wanted to go. I felt anxious when I imagined all those hours in the wilderness with Shawn, but I pushed the anxiety aside. There was something I had to do.

Fifty miles feels like five hundred on a horse, particularly if your body is more accustomed to a chair than a saddle. When we arrived at the lake, Shawn and Emily slipped nimbly off their horses and began to make camp; it was all I could do to unhitch Apollo's saddle and ease myself onto a fallen tree. I watched Emily set up the tent we were to share. She was tall and unthinkably slight, with long, straight hair so blond it was nearly silver.

We built a fire and sang campfire songs. We played cards. Then we went to our tents. I lay awake in the dark next to Emily, listening to the crickets. I was trying to imagine how to begin the conversation — how to tell her she shouldn't marry my brother — when she spoke. 'I want to talk to you about Shawn,' she said. 'I know he's got some problems.'

'He does,' I said.

'He's a spiritual man,' Emily said. 'God has given him a special calling. To help people. He told me how he helped Sadie. And how he helped you.'

'He didn't help me.' I wanted to say more, to explain to Emily what the bishop had explained to me. But they were his words, not mine. I had no words. I had come fifty miles to speak, and was mute.

'The devil tempts him more than other men,' Emily said. 'Because of his gifts, because he's a threat to Satan. That's why he has problems.

317

Because of his righteousness.'

She sat up. I could see the outline of her long ponytail in the dark. 'He said he'll hurt me,' she said. 'I know it's because of Satan. But sometimes I'm scared of him, I'm scared of what he'll do.'

I told her she shouldn't marry someone who scares her, that no one should, but the words left my lips stillborn. I believed them, but I didn't understand them well enough to make them live.

I stared into the darkness, searching it for her face, trying to understand what power my brother had over her. He'd had that power over me, I knew. He had some of it still. I was neither under his spell, nor free of it.

'He's a spiritual man,' she said again. Then she slipped into her sleeping bag, and I knew the conversation was over.

★   ★   ★

I returned to BYU a few days before the fall semester. I drove directly to Nick's apartment. We'd hardly spoken. Whenever he called, I always seemed to be needed somewhere to change a bandage or make salve. Nick knew my father had been burned, but he didn't know the severity of it. I'd withheld more information than I'd given, never saying that there had been an explosion, or that when I 'visited' my father it wasn't in a hospital but in our living room. I hadn't told Nick about his heart stopping. I hadn't described the gnarled hands, or the enemas, or the pounds of liquefied tissue we'd scraped off his body.

I knocked and Nick opened the door. He seemed surprised to see me. 'How's your dad?' he asked after I'd joined him on the sofa.

In retrospect, this was probably the most important moment of our friendship, the moment I could have done one thing, the better thing, and I did something else. It was the first time I'd seen Nick since the explosion. I might have told him everything right then: that my family didn't believe in modern medicine; that we were treating the burn at home with salves and homeopathy; that it had been terrifying, worse than terrifying; that for as long as I lived I would never forget the smell of charred flesh. I could have told him all that, could have surrendered the weight, let the relationship carry it and grow stronger. Instead I kept the burden for myself, and my friendship with Nick, already anemic, underfed and underused, dwindled in obsolescence.

I believed I could repair the damage — that now I was back, *this* would be my life, and it wouldn't matter that Nick understood nothing of Buck's Peak. But the peak refused to give me up. It clung to me. The black craters in my father's chest often materialized on chalkboards, and I saw the sagging cavity of his mouth on the pages of my textbooks. This remembered world was somehow more vivid than the physical world I inhabited, and I phased between them. Nick would take my hand, and for a moment I would be there with him, feeling the surprise of his skin on mine. But when I looked at our joined fingers, something would shift so that the hand

319

was not Nick's. It was bloody and clawed, not a hand at all.

When I slept, I gave myself wholly to the peak. I dreamed of Luke, of his eyes rolling back in his head. I dreamed of Dad, of the slow rattle in his lungs. I dreamed of Shawn, of the moment my wrist had cracked in the parking lot. I dreamed of myself, limping beside him, laughing that high, horrible cackle. But in my dreams I had long, silvery hair.

★ ★ ★

The wedding was in September.

I arrived at the church full of anxious energy, as though I'd been sent through time from some disastrous future to this moment, when my actions still had weight and my thoughts, consequences. I didn't know what I'd been sent to do, so I wrung my hands and chewed my cheeks, waiting for the crucial moment. Five minutes before the ceremony, I vomited in the women's bathroom.

When Emily said 'I do,' the vitality left me. I again became a spirit, and drifted back to BYU. I stared at the Rockies from my bedroom window and was struck by how implausible they seemed. Like paintings.

A week after the wedding I broke up with Nick — callously, I'm ashamed to say. I never told him of my life before, never sketched for him the world that had invaded and obliterated the one he and I had shared. I could have explained. I could have said, 'That place has a hold on me, which I may never break.' That would have got to the heart of it. Instead I sank through time. It was too late to confide in Nick, to take him with me wherever I was going. So I said goodbye.

27

If I Were a Woman

I'd come to BYU to study music, so that one day I could direct a church choir. But that semester — the fall of my junior year — I didn't enroll in a single music course. I couldn't have explained why I dropped advanced music theory in favor of geography and comparative politics, or gave up sight-singing to take History of the Jews. But when I'd seen those courses in the catalog, and read their titles aloud, I had felt something infinite, and I wanted a taste of that infinity.

For four months I attended lectures on geography and history and politics. I learned about Margaret Thatcher and the Thirty-Eighth Parallel and the Cultural Revolution; I learned about parliamentary politics and electoral systems around the world. I learned about the Jewish diaspora and the strange history of *The Protocols of the Elders of Zion*. By the end of the semester the world felt big, and it was hard to imagine returning to the mountain, to a kitchen, or even to a piano in the room next to the kitchen.

This caused a kind of crisis in me. My love of music, and my desire to study it, had been compatible with my idea of what a woman is. My love of history and politics and world affairs was not. And yet they called to me.

A few days before finals, I sat for an hour with my friend Josh in an empty classroom. He was reviewing his applications for law school. I was choosing my courses for the next semester.

'If you were a woman,' I asked, 'would you still study law?'

Josh didn't look up. 'If I were a woman,' he said, 'I wouldn't *want* to study it.'

'But you've talked about nothing except law school for as long as I've known you,' I said. 'It's your dream, isn't it?'

'It is,' he admitted. 'But it wouldn't be if I were a woman. Women are made differently. They don't have this ambition. Their ambition is for children.' He smiled at me as if I knew what he was talking about. And I did. I smiled, and for a few seconds we were in agreement.

Then: 'But what if you were a woman, and somehow you felt exactly as you do now?'

Josh's eyes fixed on the wall for a moment. He was really thinking about it. Then he said, 'I'd know something was wrong with me.'

I'd been wondering whether something was wrong with me since the beginning of the semester, when I'd attended my first lecture on world affairs. I'd been wondering how I could be a woman and yet be drawn to unwomanly things.

I knew someone must have the answer so I decided to ask one of my professors. I chose the professor of my Jewish history class, because he was quiet and soft-spoken. Dr. Kerry was a short man with dark eyes and a serious expression. He lectured in a thick wool jacket even in hot weather. I knocked on his office door quietly, as if I hoped he wouldn't answer, and soon was sitting silently across from him. I didn't know what my question was, and Dr. Kerry didn't ask. Instead he posed general questions — about my grades, what courses I was taking. He asked why I'd chosen Jewish history, and without thinking I blurted that I'd learned of the Holocaust only a few semesters before and wanted to learn the rest of the story.

'You learned of the Holocaust when?' he said.

'At BYU.'

'They didn't teach about it in your school?'

'They probably did,' I said. 'Only I wasn't there.'

'Where were you?'

I explained as best I could, that my parents didn't believe in public education, that they'd kept us home. When I'd finished, he laced his fingers as if he were contemplating a difficult problem. 'I think you should stretch yourself. See what happens.'

'Stretch myself how?'

He leaned forward suddenly, as if he'd just had an idea. 'Have you heard of Cambridge?' I hadn't. 'It's a university in England,' he said. 'One of the best in the world. I organize a study abroad program there for students. It's highly competitive and extremely demanding. You might not be accepted, but if you are, it may give you some idea of your abilities.'

I walked to my apartment wondering what to make of the conversation. I'd wanted moral advice, someone to reconcile my calling as a wife and mother with the call I heard of something else. But he'd put that aside. He'd seemed to say, 'First find out what you are capable of, then decide who you are.'

I applied to the program.

★ ★ ★

Emily was pregnant. The pregnancy was not going well. She'd nearly miscarried in the first trimester, and now that she was approaching twenty weeks, she was beginning to have contractions. Mother, who was the midwife, had given her Saint-John's-wort and other remedies. The contractions lessened but continued.

When I arrived at Buck's Peak for Christmas, I expected to find Emily on bed rest. She wasn't. She was standing at the kitchen counter straining herbs, along with half a dozen other women. She rarely spoke and smiled even more rarely, just moved about the house carrying vats of cramp bark and motherwort. She was quiet to the point of invisibility, and after a few minutes, I forgot she was there.

It had been six months since the explosion, and while Dad was back on his feet, it was clear he would never be the man he was. He could scarcely walk across a room without gasping for air, so damaged were his lungs. The skin on his lower face had regrown, but it was thin and waxy, as if someone had taken sandpaper and rubbed it to the point of transparency. His ears were thick with scars. He had thin lips and his mouth drooped, giving him the haggard appearance of a much older man. But it was his right hand, more than his face, that drew stares: each finger was frozen in its own pose, some curled, some bowed, twisting together into a gnarled claw. He could hold a spoon by wedging it between his index finger, which bowed upward, and his ring finger, which curved downward, but he ate with difficulty. Still, I wondered whether skin grafts could have achieved what Mother had with her comfrey and lobelia salve. It was a miracle, everyone said, so that was the new name they gave Mother's recipe: after Dad's burn it was known as Miracle Salve.

At dinner my first night on the peak, Dad described the explosion as a tender mercy from the Lord. 'It was a blessing,' he said. 'A miracle. God spared my life and extended to me a great calling. To testify of His power. To show people there's another way besides the Medical Establishment.'

I watched as he tried and failed to wedge his knife tightly enough to cut his roast. 'I was never in any danger,' he said. 'I'll prove it to you. As soon as I can walk across the yard without near passing out, I'll get a torch and cut off another tank.'

The next morning when I came out for breakfast, there was a crowd of women gathered around my father. They listened with hushed voices and glistening eyes as Dad told of the heavenly visitations he'd received while hovering between life and death. He had been ministered to by angels, he said, like the prophets of old. There was something in the way the women looked at him. Something like adoration.

I watched the women throughout the morning

326

and became aware of the change my father's miracle had wrought in them. Before, the women who worked for my mother had always approached her casually, with matter-of-fact questions about their work. Now their speech was soft, admiring. Dramas broke out between them as they vied for my mother's esteem, and for my father's. The change could be summed up simply: before, they had been employees; now they were followers.

The story of Dad's burn had become something of a founding myth: it was told over and over, to newcomers but also to the old. In fact, it was rare to spend an afternoon in the house without hearing some kind of recitation of the miracle, and occasionally these recitations were less than accurate. I heard Mother tell a room of devoted faces that sixty-five percent of Dad's upper body had been burned to the third degree. That was not what I remembered. In my memory the bulk of the damage had been skin-deep — his arms, back and shoulders had hardly been burned at all. It was only his lower face and hands that had been third-degree. But I kept this to myself.

For the first time, my parents seemed to be of one mind. Mother no longer moderated Dad's statements after he left the room, no longer quietly gave her own opinion. She had been transformed by the miracle — transformed into him. I remembered her as a young midwife, so cautious, so meek about the lives over which she had such power. There was little of that meekness in her now. The Lord Himself guided her hands, and no misfortune would occur except by the will of God.

★ ★ ★

A few weeks after Christmas, the University of Cambridge wrote to Dr. Kerry, rejecting my application. 'The competition was very steep,' Dr. Kerry told me when I visited his office.

I thanked him and stood to go.

'One moment,' he said. 'Cambridge instructed me to write if I felt there were any gross injustices.'

I didn't understand, so he repeated himself. 'I could only help one student,' he said. 'They have offered you a place, if you want it.'

It seemed impossible that I would really be allowed to go. Then I realized that I would need a passport, and that without a real birth certificate, I was unlikely to get one. Someone like me did not belong at Cambridge. It was as if the universe understood this and was trying to prevent the blasphemy of my going.

I applied in person. The clerk laughed out loud at my Delayed Certificate of Birth. 'Nine years!' she said. 'Nine years is *not* a delay. Do you have any other documentation?'

'Yes,' I said. 'But they have different birth dates. Also, one has a different name.'

She was still smiling. 'Different date and different name? No, that's not gonna work. There's no way you're gonna get a passport.'

I visited the clerk several more times, becoming more and more desperate, until, finally, a solution was found. My aunt Debbie visited the courthouse and swore an affidavit that I was who I said I was. I was issued a passport.

★ ★ ★

In February, Emily gave birth. The baby weighed one pound, four ounces.

When Emily had started having contractions at Christmas, Mother had said the pregnancy would unfold according to God's will. His will, it turned out, was that Emily give birth at home at twenty-six weeks' gestation.

There was a blizzard that night, one of those mighty mountain storms that clears the roads and closes the towns. Emily was in the advanced stages of labor when Mother realized she needed a hospital. The baby, which they named Peter, appeared a few minutes later, slipping from Emily so easily that Mother said she 'caught' him more than delivered him. He was still, and the color of ash. Shawn thought he was dead. Then Mother felt a tiny heartbeat — actually she *saw* his heart beating through a thin film of skin. My father rushed to the van and began scraping at the snow and ice. Shawn carried Emily and laid her on the back seat, then Mother placed the baby against Emily's chest and covered him, creating a makeshift incubator. Kangaroo care, she called it later.

My father drove; the storm raged. In Idaho we call it a whiteout: when the wind whips the snowfall so violently it bleaches the road, covers it as if with a veil, and you can't see the asphalt, or the fields or rivers; you can't see anything except billows of white. Somehow, skidding through snow and sleet, they made it to town but the hospital there was rural, unequipped to care for such a faint whimper of life. The doctors said they had to get him to McKay-Dee in Ogden as soon as possible, there was no time. He could not go by chopper because of the blizzard, so the doctors sent him in an ambulance. In fact they sent *two* ambulances, a second in case the first succumbed to the storm.

Many months would pass, and countless surgeries would be performed, before Shawn and Emily would bring home the little twig of flesh that I was told was my nephew. By then he was out of danger, but the doctors said his lungs might never develop fully. He might always be frail.

Dad said God had orchestrated the birth just as He had orchestrated the explosion. Mother echoed him, adding that God had placed a veil over her eyes so she wouldn't stop the contractions. 'Peter was supposed to come into the world this way,' she said. 'He is a gift from God, and God gives His gifts in whatever way He chooses.'

28

Pygmalion

The first time I saw King's College, Cambridge, I didn't think I was dreaming, but only because my imagination had never produced anything so grand. My eyes settled on a clock tower with stone carvings. I was led to the tower, then we passed through it and into the college. There was a lake of perfectly clipped grass and, across the lake, an ivory-tinted building I vaguely recognized as Greco-Roman. But it was the Gothic chapel, three hundred feet long and a hundred feet high, a stone mountain, that dominated the scene.

I was taken past the chapel and into another courtyard, then up a spiral staircase. A door was opened, and I was told that this was my room. I was left to make myself comfortable. The kindly man who'd given me this instruction did not realize how impossible it was.

Breakfast the next morning was served in a great hall. It was like eating in a church, the ceiling was cavernous, and I felt under scrutiny, as if the hall knew I was there and I shouldn't be. I'd chosen a long table full of other students from BYU. The women were talking about the clothes they had brought. Marianne had gone shopping when she learned she'd been accepted to the program. 'You need different *pieces* for Europe,' she said.

Heather agreed. Her grandmother had paid for her plane ticket, so she'd spent that money updating her wardrobe. 'The way people dress here,' she said, 'it's more refined. You can't get away with jeans.'

I thought about rushing to my room to change out of the sweatshirt and Keds I was wearing, but I had nothing to change into. I didn't own anything like what Marianne and Heather wore — bright cardigans accented with delicate scarves. I hadn't bought new clothes for Cambridge, because I'd had to take out a student loan just to pay the fees. Besides, I understood that even if I had Marianne's and Heather's clothes, I wouldn't know how to wear them.

Dr. Kerry appeared and announced that we'd been invited to take a tour of the chapel. We would even be allowed on the roof. There was a general scramble as we returned our trays and followed Dr. Kerry from the hall. I stayed near the back of the group as we made our way across the courtyard.

When I stepped inside the chapel, my breath caught in my chest. The room — if such a space can be called a room — was voluminous, as if it could hold the whole of the ocean. We were led through a small wooden door, then up a narrow spiraling staircase whose stone steps seemed numberless. Finally the staircase opened onto the roof, which was heavily slanted, an inverted V enclosed by stone parapets. The wind was gusting, rolling clouds across the sky; the view was spectacular, the city miniaturized, utterly dwarfed by the chapel. I forgot myself and climbed the slope, then walked along the ridge, letting the wind take me as I stared out at the expanse of crooked streets and stone courtyards.

'You're not afraid of falling,' a voice said. I turned. It was Dr. Kerry. He had followed me, but he seemed unsteady on his feet, nearly pitching with every rush of wind.

'We can go down,' I said. I ran down the ridge to the flat walkway near the buttress. Again Dr. Kerry followed but his steps were strange. Rather than walk facing forward, he rotated his body and moved sideways, like a crab. The wind continued its attack. I offered him an arm for the last few steps, so unsteady did he seem, and he took it.

'I meant it as an observation,' he said when we'd made it down. 'Here you stand, upright, hands in your pockets.' He gestured toward the other students. 'See how they hunch? How they cling to the wall?' He was right. A few were venturing onto the ridge but they did so cautiously, taking the same ungainly side steps Dr. Kerry had, tipping and swaying in the wind; everyone else was holding tightly to the stone parapet, knees bent, backs arched, as if unsure whether to walk or crawl.

I raised my hand and gripped the wall.

'You don't need to do that,' he said. 'It's not a criticism.'

He paused, as if unsure he should say more. 'Everyone has undergone a change,' he said. 'The other students were relaxed until we came to this height. Now they are uncomfortable, on edge. You seem to have made the opposite journey. This is the first time I've seen you at home in yourself. It's in the way you move: it's as if you've been on this roof all your life.'

A gust of wind swept over the parapet and Dr. Kerry teetered, clutching the wall. I stepped up onto the ridge so he could flatten himself against the buttress. He stared at me, waiting for an explanation.

'I've roofed my share of hay sheds,' I said finally.

'So your legs are stronger? Is that why you can stand in this wind?'

I had to think before I could answer. 'I can stand in this wind, because I'm not trying to stand in it,' I said. 'The wind is just wind. You could withstand these gusts on the ground, so you can withstand them in the air. There is no difference. Except the difference you make in your head.'

He stared at me blankly. He hadn't understood.

'I'm just standing,' I said. 'You are all trying to compensate, to get your bodies lower because the height scares you. But the crouching and the sidestepping are not natural. You've made yourselves vulnerable. If you could just control your panic, this wind would be nothing.'

'The way it is nothing to you,' he said.

★　★　★

I wanted the mind of a scholar, but it seemed that Dr. Kerry saw in me the mind of a roofer. The other students belonged in a library; I belonged in a crane.

The first week passed in a blur of lectures. In the second week, every student was assigned a supervisor to guide their research. My supervisor, I learned, was the eminent Professor Jonathan Steinberg, a former vice-master of a Cambridge college, who was much celebrated for his writings on the Holocaust.

My first meeting with Professor Steinberg took place a few days later. I waited at the porter's lodge until a thin man appeared and, producing a set of heavy keys, unlocked a wooden door set into the stone. I followed him up a spiral staircase and into the clock tower itself, where there was a well-lit room with simple furnishings: two chairs and a wooden table.

I could hear the blood pounding behind my ears as I sat down. Professor Steinberg was in his seventies but I would not have described him as an old man. He was lithe, and his eyes moved about the room with probing energy. His speech was measured and fluid.

'I am Professor Steinberg,' he said. 'What would you like to read?'

I mumbled something about historiography. I had decided to study not history, but historians. I suppose my interest came from the sense of groundlessness I'd felt since learning about the Holocaust and the civil rights movement — since realizing that what a person knows about the past is limited, and will always be limited, to what they are told by others. I knew what it was to have a misconception corrected — a misconception of such magnitude that shifting it shifted the world. Now I needed to understand how the great gatekeepers of history had come to terms with their own ignorance and partiality. I thought if I could accept that what they had written was not absolute but was the result of a biased process of conversation and revision, maybe I could reconcile myself with the fact that the history most people agreed upon was not the history I had been taught. Dad could be wrong, and the great historians Carlyle and Macaulay and Trevelyan could be wrong, but from the ashes of their dispute I could construct a world to live in. In knowing the ground was not ground at all, I hoped I could stand on it.

I doubt I managed to communicate any of this. When I finished talking, Professor Steinberg eyed me for a moment, then said, 'Tell me about your education. Where did you attend school?'

The air was immediately sucked from the room.

'I grew up in Idaho,' I said.

'And you attended school there?'

It occurs to me in retrospect that someone might have told Professor Steinberg about me, perhaps Dr. Kerry. Or perhaps he perceived that I was avoiding his question, and that made him curious. Whatever the reason, he wasn't satisfied until I had admitted that I'd never been to school.

'How marvelous,' he said, smiling. 'It's as if I've stepped into Shaw's Pygmalion.'

★ ★ ★

For two months I had weekly meetings with Professor Steinberg. I was never assigned readings. We read only what I asked to read, whether it was a book or a page.

None of my professors at BYU had examined my writing the way Professor Steinberg did. No comma, no period, no adjective or adverb was beneath his interest. He made no distinction between grammar and content, between form and substance. A poorly written sentence was a poorly conceived idea, and in his view the grammatical logic was as much in need of correction. 'Tell me,' he would say, 'why have you placed this comma here? What relationship between these phrases are you hoping to establish?' When I gave my explanation sometimes he would say, 'Quite right,' and other times he would correct me with lengthy explanations of syntax.

After I'd been meeting with Professor Steinberg for a month, I wrote an essay comparing Edmund Burke with Publius, the persona under which James Madison, Alexander Hamilton and John Jay had written *The Federalist Papers*. I barely slept for two weeks: every moment my eyes were open, I was either reading or thinking about those texts.

From my father I had learned that books were to be either adored or exiled. Books that were of God — books written by the Mormon prophets or the Founding Fathers — were not to be studied so much as cherished, like a thing perfect in itself. I had been taught to read the words of men like Madison as a cast into which I ought to pour the plaster of my own mind, to be reshaped according to the contours of their faultless model. I read them to learn what to think, not how to think for myself. Books that were not of God were banished; they were a danger, powerful and irresistible in their cunning.

To write my essay I had to read books differently, without giving myself over to either fear or adoration. Because Burke had defended the British monarchy, Dad would have said he was an agent of tyranny. He wouldn't have wanted the book in the house. There was a thrill in trusting myself to read the words. I felt a similar thrill in reading Madison, Hamilton and Jay, especially on those occasions when I discarded their conclusions in favor of Burke's, or when it seemed to me that their ideas were not really different in substance, only in form. There were wonderful suppositions embedded in this method of reading: that books are not tricks, and that I was not feeble.

I finished the essay and sent it to Professor Steinberg. Two days later, when I arrived for our next meeting, he was subdued. He peered at me from across the table. I waited for him to say the essay was a disaster, the product of an ignorant mind, that it had overreached, drawn too many conclusions from too little material.

'I have been teaching in Cambridge for thirty years,' he said. 'And this is one of the best essays I've read.'

I was prepared for insults but not for this.

Professor Steinberg must have said more about the essay but I heard nothing. My mind was consumed with a wrenching need to get out of that room. In that moment I was no longer in a clock tower in Cambridge. I was seventeen, in a red jeep, and a boy I loved had just touched my hand. I bolted.

I could tolerate any form of cruelty better than kindness. Praise was a poison to me; I choked on it. I wanted the professor to shout at me, wanted it so deeply I felt dizzy from the deprivation. The ugliness of me had to be given expression. If it was not expressed in his voice, I would need to express it in mine.

I don't remember leaving the clock tower, or how I passed the afternoon. That evening there was a black-tie dinner. The hall was lit by candlelight, which was beautiful, but it cheered me for another reason: I wasn't wearing formal clothing, just a black shirt and black pants, and I thought people might not notice in the dim lighting. My friend Laura arrived late. She explained that her parents had visited and taken her to France. She had only just returned. She was wearing a dress of rich purple with crisp pleats in the skirt. The hemline bounced several inches above her knee, and for a moment I thought the dress was whorish, until she said her father had bought it for her in Paris. A gift from one's father could not be whorish. A gift from one's father seemed to me the definitive signal that a woman was not a whore. I struggled with this dissonance — a whorish dress, gifted to a loved daughter — until the meal had been finished and the plates cleared away.

At my next supervision, Professor Steinberg

said that when I applied for graduate school, he would make sure I was accepted to whatever institution I chose. 'Have you visited Harvard?' he said. 'Or perhaps you prefer Cambridge?'

I imagined myself in Cambridge, a graduate student wearing a long black robe that swished as I strode through ancient corridors. Then I was hunching in a bathroom, my arm behind my back, my head in the toilet. I tried to focus on the student but I couldn't. I couldn't picture the girl in the whirling black gown without seeing that *other* girl. Scholar or whore, both couldn't be true. One was a lie.

'I can't go,' I said. 'I can't pay the fees.'

'Let me worry about the fees,' Professor Steinberg said.

★ ★ ★

In late August, on our last night in Cambridge, there was a final dinner in the great hall. The tables were set with more knives, forks and goblets than I'd ever seen; the paintings on the wall seemed ghostly in the candlelight. I felt exposed by the elegance and yet somehow made invisible by it. I stared at the other students as they passed, taking in every silk dress, every heavily lined eye. I obsessed over the beauty of them.

At dinner I listened to the cheerful chatter of my friends while longing for the isolation of my room. Professor Steinberg was seated at the high table. Each time I glanced at him, I felt that old instinct at work in me, tensing my muscles,

340

preparing me to take flight.

I left the hall the moment dessert was served. It was a relief to escape all that refinement and beauty — to be allowed to be unlovely and not a point of contrast. Dr. Kerry saw me leave and followed.

It was dark. The lawn was black, the sky blacker. Pillars of chalky light reached up from the ground and illuminated the chapel, which glowed, moonlike, against the night sky.

'You've made an impression on Professor Steinberg,' Dr. Kerry said, falling into step beside me. 'I only hope he has made some impression on you.'

I didn't understand.

'Come this way,' he said, turning toward the chapel. 'I have something to say to you.'

I walked behind him, noticing the silence of my own footfalls, aware that my Keds didn't click elegantly on stone the way the heels worn by other girls did.

Dr. Kerry said he'd been watching me. 'You act like someone who is impersonating someone else. And it's as if you think your life depends on it.'

I didn't know what to say, so I said nothing.

'It has never occurred to you,' he said, 'that you might have as much right to be here as anyone.' He waited for an explanation.

'I would enjoy serving the dinner,' I said, 'more than eating it.'

Dr. Kerry smiled. 'You should trust Professor Steinberg. If he says you're a scholar — 'pure gold,' I heard him say — then you are.'

'This is a magical place,' I said. 'Everything shines here.'

'You must stop yourself from thinking like that,' Dr. Kerry said, his voice raised. 'You are not fool's gold, shining only under a particular light. Whomever you become, whatever you make yourself into, that is who you always were. It was always in you. Not in Cambridge. In *you*. You are gold. And returning to BYU, or even to that mountain you came from, will not change who you are. It may change how others see you, it may even change how you see yourself — even gold appears dull in some lighting — but *that* is the illusion. And it always was.'

I wanted to believe him, to take his words and remake myself, but I'd never had that kind of faith. No matter how deeply I interred the memories, how tightly I shut my eyes against them, when I thought of my *self*, the images that came to mind were of *that* girl, in the bathroom, in the parking lot.

I couldn't tell Dr. Kerry about that girl. I couldn't tell him that the reason I couldn't return to Cambridge was that being here threw into great relief every violent and degrading moment of my life. At BYU I could almost forget, allow what had been to blend into what was. But the contrast here was too great, the world before my eyes too fantastical. The memories were more real — more believable — than the stone spires.

To myself I pretended there were other reasons I couldn't belong at Cambridge, reasons having to do with class and status: that it was because I was poor, had grown up poor. Because I could stand in the wind on the chapel roof and not tilt. *That* was the person who didn't belong in Cambridge: the roofer, not the whore. *I can go to school*, I had written in my journal that very afternoon. *And I can buy new clothes. But I am still Tara Westover. I have done jobs no Cambridge student would do. Dress us any way you like, we are not the same.* Clothes could not fix what was wrong with me. Something had rotted on the inside, and the stench was too powerful, the core too rancid, to be covered up by mere dressings.

Whether Dr. Kerry suspected any part of this, I'm not sure. But he understood that I had fixated on clothes as the symbol of why I didn't, and couldn't, belong. It was the last thing he said to me before he walked away, leaving me rooted, astonished, beside that grand chapel.

'The most powerful determinant of who you are is inside you,' he said. 'Professor Steinberg says this is Pygmalion. Think of the story, Tara.' He paused, his eyes fierce, his voice piercing. 'She was just a cockney in a nice dress. Until she believed in herself. Then it didn't matter what dress she wore.'

29

Graduation

The program ended and I returned to BYU. Campus looked the way it always had, and it would have been easy to forget Cambridge and settle back into the life I'd had there. But Professor Steinberg was determined that I not forget. He sent me an application for something called the Gates Cambridge Scholarship, which, he explained, was a little like the Rhodes Scholarship, but for Cambridge instead of Oxford. It would provide full funding for me to study at Cambridge, including tuition, room and board. As far as I was concerned it was comically out of reach for someone like me, but he insisted that it was not, so I applied.

Not long after, I noticed another difference, another small shift. I was spending an evening with my friend Mark, who studied ancient languages. Like me, and almost everyone at BYU, Mark was Mormon.

'Do you think people should study church history?' he asked.

'I do,' I said.

'What if it makes them unhappy?'

I thought I knew what he meant, but I waited for him to explain.

'Many women struggle with their faith after they learn about polygamy,' he said. 'My mother

344

did. I don't think she's ever understood it.'

'I've never understood it, either,' I said.

There was a tense silence. He was waiting for me to say my line: that I was praying for faith. And I *had* prayed for it, many, many times.

Perhaps both of us were thinking of our history, or perhaps only I was. I thought of Joseph Smith, who'd had as many as forty wives. Brigham Young had had fifty-five wives and fifty-six children. The church had ended the *temporal* practice of polygamy in 1890, but it had never recanted the doctrine. As a child I'd been taught — by my father but also in Sunday school — that in the fullness of time God would restore polygamy, and in the afterlife, I would be a plural wife. The number of my sister wives would depend on my husband's righteousness: the more nobly he lived, the more wives he would be given.

I had never made my peace with it. As a girl I had often imagined myself in heaven, dressed in a white gown, standing in a pearly mist across from my husband. But when the camera zoomed out there were ten women standing behind us, wearing the same white dress. In my fantasy I was the first wife but I knew there was no guarantee of that; I might be hidden anywhere in the long chain of wives. For as long as I could remember, this image had been at the core of my idea of paradise: my husband, and his wives. There was a sting in this arithmetic: in knowing that in the divine calculus of heaven, one man could balance the equation for countless women.

I remembered my great-great-grandmother. I

345

had first heard her name when I was twelve, which is the year that, in Mormonism, you cease to be a child and become a woman. Twelve was the age when lessons in Sunday school began to include words like *purity* and *chastity*. It was also the age that I was asked, as part of a church assignment, to learn about one of my ancestors. I asked Mother which ancestor I should choose, and without thinking she said, 'Anna Mathea.' I said the name aloud. It floated off my tongue like the beginning of a fairy tale. Mother said I should honor Anna Mathea because she had given me a gift: her voice.

'It was her voice that brought our family to the church,' Mother said. 'She heard Mormon missionaries preaching in the streets of Norway. She prayed, and God blessed her with faith, with the knowledge that Joseph Smith was His prophet. She told her father, but he'd heard stories about the Mormons and wouldn't allow her to be baptized. So she sang for him. She sang him a Mormon hymn called 'O My Father.' When she finished singing, her father had tears in his eyes. He said that any religion with music so beautiful must be the work of God. They were baptized together.'

After Anna Mathea converted her parents, the family felt called by God to come to America and meet the prophet Joseph. They saved for the journey, but after two years they could bring only half the family. Anna Mathea was left behind.

The journey was long and harsh, and by the time they made it to Idaho, to a Mormon settlement called Worm Creek, Anna's mother was sick, dying. It was her last wish to see her daughter again, so her father wrote to Anna, begging her to take what money she had and come to America. Anna had fallen in love and was to be married, but she left her fiancé in Norway and crossed the ocean. Her mother died before she reached the American shore.

The family was now destitute; there was no money to send Anna to her fiancé, to the marriage she had given up. Anna was a financial burden on her father, so a bishop persuaded her to marry a rich farmer as his second wife. His first wife was barren, and she flew into a jealous rage when Anna became pregnant. Anna worried the first wife might hurt her baby, so she returned to her father, where she gave birth to twins, though only one would survive the harsh winter on the frontier.

Mark was still waiting. Then he gave up and mumbled the words I was supposed to say, that he didn't understand fully, but that he knew polygamy was a principle from God.

I agreed. I said the words, then braced myself for a wave of humiliation — for that image to invade my thoughts, of me, one of many wives standing behind a solitary, faceless man — but it didn't come. I searched my mind and discovered a new conviction there: I would never be a plural wife. A voice declared this with unyielding finality; the declaration made me tremble. What if God commanded it? I asked. *You wouldn't do it*, the voice answered. And I knew it was true.

I thought again of Anna Mathea, wondering

what kind of world it was in which she, following a prophet, could leave her lover, cross an ocean, enter a loveless marriage as a second mistress, then bury her first child, only to have her granddaughter, in two generations, cross the same ocean an unbeliever. I was Anna Mathea's heir: she had given me her voice. Had she not given me her faith, also?

★ ★ ★

I was put on a short list for the Gates scholarship. There would be an interview in February in Annapolis. I had no idea how to prepare. Robin drove me to Park City, where there was an Ann Taylor discount outlet, and helped me buy a navy pantsuit and matching loafers. I didn't own a handbag so Robin lent me hers.

Two weeks before the interview my parents came to BYU. They had never visited me before, but they were passing through on their way to Arizona and stopped for dinner. I took them to the Indian restaurant across the street from my apartment.

The waitress stared a moment too long at my father's face, then her eyes bulged when they dropped to his hands. Dad ordered half the menu. I told him three mains would be enough, but he winked and said money was not a problem. It seemed the news of my father's miraculous healing was spreading, earning them more and more customers. Mother's products were being sold by nearly every midwife and natural healer in the Mountain West.

We waited for the food, and Dad asked about my classes. I said I was studying French. 'That's a socialist language,' he said, then he lectured for twenty minutes on twentieth-century history. He said Jewish bankers in Europe had signed secret agreements to start World War II, and that they had colluded with Jews in America to pay for it. They had engineered the Holocaust, he said, because they would benefit financially from worldwide disorder. They had sent their own people to the gas chambers for money.

These ideas were familiar to me, but it took me a moment to remember where I'd heard them: in a lecture Dr. Kerry had given on *The Protocols of the Elders of Zion*. The *Protocols*, published in 1903, purported to be a record of a secret meeting of powerful Jews planning world domination. The document was discredited as a fabrication but still it spread, fueling anti-Semitism in the decades before World War II. Adolf Hitler had written about the *Protocols* in *Mein Kampf*, claiming they were authentic, that they revealed the true nature of the Jewish people.

Dad was talking loudly, at a volume that would have suited a mountainside but was thunderous in the small restaurant. People at nearby tables had halted their own conversations and were sitting in silence, listening to ours. I regretted having chosen a restaurant so near my apartment.

Dad moved on from World War II to the United Nations, the European Union, and the imminent destruction of the world. He spoke as if the three were synonyms. The curry arrived and I focused my attention on it. Mother had grown tired of the lecture, and asked Dad to talk about something else.

'But the world is about to end!' he said. He was shouting now.

'Of course it is,' Mother said. 'But let's not discuss it over dinner.'

I put down my fork and stared at them. Of all the strange statements from the past half hour, for some reason this was the one that shocked me. The mere fact of them had never shocked me before. Everything they did had always made sense to me, adhering to a logic I understood. Perhaps it was the backdrop: Buck's Peak was theirs and it camouflaged them, so that when I saw them there, surrounded by the loud, sharp relics of my childhood, the setting seemed to absorb them. At least it absorbed the noise. But here, so near the university, they seemed so unreal as to be almost mythic.

Dad looked at me, waiting for me to give an opinion, but I felt alienated from myself. I didn't know who to be. On the mountain I slipped thoughtlessly into the voice of their daughter and acolyte. But here, I couldn't seem to find the voice that, in the shadow of Buck's Peak, came easily.

We walked to my apartment and I showed them my room. Mother shut the door, revealing a poster of Martin Luther King Jr. that I'd put up four years before, when I'd learned of the civil rights movement.

'Is that Martin Luther King?' Dad said. 'Don't you know he had ties to communism?' He chewed the waxy tissue where his lips had been.

They departed soon after to drive through the night. I watched them go, then took out my journal. *It's astonishing that I used to believe all this without the slightest suspicion*, I wrote. *The whole world was wrong; only Dad was right.*

I thought of something Tyler's wife, Stefanie, had told me over the phone a few days before. She said it had taken her years to convince Tyler to let her immunize their children, because some part of him still believed vaccines are a conspiracy by the Medical Establishment. Remembering that now, with Dad's voice still ringing in my ears, I sneered at my brother. *He's a scientist!* I wrote. *How can he not see beyond their paranoia!* I reread what I had written, and as I did so my scorn gave way to a sense of irony. *Then again*, I wrote. *Perhaps I could mock Tyler with more credibility if I had not remembered, as I did just now, that to this day I have never been immunized.*

★ ★ ★

My interview for the Gates scholarship took place at St. John's College in Annapolis. The campus was intimidating, with its immaculate lawns and crisp colonial architecture. I sat nervously in the corridor, waiting to be called in for my interview; I felt stiff in the pantsuit and clung awkwardly to Robin's handbag. But in the end, Professor Steinberg had written such a powerful letter of recommendation that there was little left for me to do.

I received confirmation the next day: I'd won the scholarship.

The phone calls began — from BYU's student paper and the local news. I did half a dozen interviews. I was on TV. I awoke one morning to find my picture plastered on BYU's homepage. I was the third BYU student ever to win a Gates scholarship, and the university was taking full advantage of the press. I was asked about my high school experience, and which of my grade school teachers had prepared me for my success. I dodged, I parried, I lied when I had to. I didn't tell a single reporter that I'd never gone to school.

I didn't know why I couldn't tell them. I just couldn't stand the thought of people patting me on the back, telling me how impressive I was. I didn't want to be Horatio Alger in someone's tear-filled homage to the American dream. I wanted my life to make sense, and nothing in that narrative made sense to me.

★ ★ ★

A month before my graduation, I visited Buck's Peak. Dad had read the articles about my scholarship, and what he said was, 'You didn't mention home school. I'd think you'd be more grateful that your mother and I took you out of them schools, seeing how it's worked out. You should be telling people that's what done it: home school.'

I said nothing. Dad took it as an apology.

He disapproved of my going to Cambridge. 'Our ancestors risked their lives to cross the ocean, to escape those socialist countries. And what do you do? You turn around and go back?'

Again, I said nothing.

'I'm looking forward to your graduation,' he said. 'The Lord has a few choice rebukes for me to give them professors.'

'You will not,' I said quietly.

'If the Lord moves me, I will stand and speak.'

'You will not,' I repeated.

'I won't go anywhere that the Lord's spirit isn't welcome.'

That was the conversation. I hoped it would blow over, but Dad was so hurt that I hadn't mentioned homeschooling in my interviews that this new wound festered.

There was a dinner the night before my graduation where I was to receive the 'most outstanding undergraduate' award from the history department. I waited for my parents at the entrance, but they never appeared. I called Mother, thinking they were running late. She said they weren't coming. I went to the dinner and was presented with a plaque. My table had the only empty seats in the hall. The next day there was a luncheon for honors graduates, and I was seated with the college dean and the director of the honors program. Again, there were two empty seats. I said my parents had had car trouble.

I phoned my mother after the luncheon.

'Your father won't come unless you apologize,'

she said. 'And I won't, either.'

I apologized. 'He can say whatever he wants. But please come.'

They missed most of the ceremony; I don't know if they saw me accept my diploma. What I remember is waiting with my friends before the music began, watching their fathers snap pictures and their mothers fix their hair. I remember that my friends were wearing colorful leis and recently gifted jewelry.

After the ceremony I stood alone on the lawn, watching the other students with their families. Eventually I saw my parents. Mother hugged me. My friend Laura snapped two photos. One is of me and Mother, smiling our forced smiles; the other is of me wedged between my parents, looking squeezed, under pressure.

I was leaving the Mountain West that night. I had packed before graduation. My apartment was empty, my bags by the door. Laura had volunteered to drive me to the airport, but my parents asked if they could take me.

I expected them to drop me at the curb, but Dad insisted that they walk with me through the airport. They waited while I checked my bags, then followed me to the security gate. It was as if Dad wanted to give me until the last second to change my mind. We walked in silence. When we arrived at security I hugged them both and said goodbye. I removed my shoes, laptop, camera, then I passed through the checkpoint, reassembled my pack, and headed for the terminal.

It was only then that I glanced back and saw Dad, still standing at the checkpoint, watching me walk away, his hands in his pockets, his shoulders slumping, his mouth slackened. I waved and he stepped forward, as if to follow, and I was reminded of the moment, years before, when power lines had covered the station wagon, with Mother inside it, and Dad had stood next to her, exposed.

He was still holding that posture when I turned the corner. That image of my father will always stay with me: that look on his face, of love and fear and loss. I knew why he was afraid. He'd let it slip my last night on Buck's Peak, the same night he'd said he wouldn't come to see me graduate.

'If you're in America,' he'd whispered, 'we can come for you. Wherever you are. I've got a thousand gallons of fuel buried in the field. I can fetch you when The End comes, bring you home, make you safe. But if you cross the ocean . . .'

PART THREE

PART THREE

30

Hand of the Almighty

A stone gate barred the entrance to Trinity College. Cut into the gate was a small wooden door. I stepped through it. A porter in a black overcoat and bowler hat showed me around the college, leading me through Great Court, the largest of the courtyards. We walked through a stone passageway and into a covered corridor whose stone was the color of ripe wheat.

'This is the north cloister,' the porter said. 'It is here that Newton stomped his foot to measure the echo, calculating the speed of sound for the first time.'

We returned to the Great Gate. My room was directly opposite it, up three flights of stairs. After the porter left I stood, bookended by my suitcases, and stared out my little window at the mythic stone gate and its otherworldly battlements. Cambridge was just as I remembered: ancient, beautiful. I was different. I was not a visitor, not a guest. I was a member of the university. My name was painted on the door. According to the paperwork, I belonged here.

I dressed in dark colors for my first lecture, hoping I wouldn't stand out, but even so I didn't think I looked like the other students. I certainly didn't *sound* like them, and not just because they were British. Their speech had a lilting cadence that made me think of singing more than speaking. To my ears they sounded refined, educated; I had a tendency to mumble, and when nervous, to stutter.

I chose a seat around the large square table and listened as the two students nearest me discussed the lecture topic, which was Isaiah Berlin's two concepts of liberty. The student next to me said he'd studied Isaiah Berlin at Oxford; the other said he'd already heard this lecturer's remarks on Berlin when he was an undergraduate at Cambridge. I had never heard of Isaiah Berlin.

The lecturer began his presentation. He spoke calmly but moved through the material quickly, as if he assumed we were already familiar with it. This was confirmed by the other students, most of whom were not taking notes. I scribbled down every word.

'So what are Isaiah Berlin's two concepts?' the lecturer asked. Nearly everyone raised a hand. The lecturer called on the student who had studied at Oxford. 'Negative liberty,' he said, 'is the freedom from external obstacles or constraints. An individual is free in this sense if they are not physically prevented from taking action.' I was reminded for a moment of Richard, who had always seemed able to recite with exactness anything he'd ever read.

'Very good,' the lecturer said. 'And the second?'

'Positive liberty,' another student said, 'is freedom from internal constraints.'

I wrote this definition in my notes, but I didn't understand it.

The lecturer tried to clarify. He said positive

liberty is self-mastery — the rule of the self, by the self. To have positive liberty, he explained, is to take control of one's own mind; to be liberated from irrational fears and beliefs, from addictions, superstitions and all other forms of self-coercion.

I had no idea what it meant to self-coerce. I looked around the room. No one else seemed confused. I was one of the few students taking notes. I wanted to ask for further explanation, but something stopped me — the certainty that to do so would be to shout to the room that I didn't belong there.

After the lecture, I returned to my room, where I stared out my window at the stone gate with its medieval battlements. I thought of positive liberty, and of what it might mean to self-coerce, until my head thrummed with a dull ache.

I called home. Mother answered. Her voice rose with excitement when she recognized my weepy 'Hello, Mom.' I told her I shouldn't have come to Cambridge, that I didn't understand anything. She said she'd been muscle-testing and had discovered that one of my chakras was out of balance. She could adjust it, she said. I reminded her that I was five thousand miles away.

'That doesn't matter,' she said. 'I'll adjust the chakra on Audrey and wing it to you.'

'You'll what it to me?'

'*Wing* it,' she said. 'Distance is nothing to living energy. I can send the corrected energy to you from here.'

'How fast does energy travel?' I asked. 'At the

speed of sound, or is it more like a jetliner? Does it fly direct, or will it have to lay over in Minneapolis?'

Mother laughed and hung up.

* * *

I studied most mornings in the college library, near a small window. I was there on a particular morning when Drew, a friend from BYU, sent me a song via email. He said it was a classic but I had never heard of it, nor of the singer. I played the song through my headphones. It gripped me immediately. I listened to it over and over while staring out at the north cloister.

> Emancipate yourselves from mental slavery
> None but ourselves can free our mind

I scratched those lines into notebooks, into the margins of the essays I was writing. I wondered about them when I should have been reading. From the Internet I learned about the cancer that had been discovered on Bob Marley's foot. I also learned that Marley had been a Rastafarian, and that Rastafari believe in a 'whole body,' which is why he had refused surgery to amputate the toe. Four years later, at age thirty-six, he died.

Emancipate yourselves from mental slavery. Marley had written that line a year before his death, while an operable melanoma was, at that moment, metastasizing to his lungs, liver, stomach and brain. I imagined a greedy surgeon

362

with sharp teeth and long, skeletal fingers urging Marley to have the amputation. I shrank from this frightening image of the doctor and his corrupt medicine, and only then did I understand, as I had not before, that although I had renounced my father's world, I had never quite found the courage to live in this one.

I flipped through my notebook to the lecture on negative and positive liberty. In a blank corner I scratched the line, *None but ourselves can free our mind*. Then I picked up my phone and dialed.

'I need to get my vaccinations,' I told the nurse.

★ ★ ★

I attended a seminar on Wednesday afternoons, where I noticed two women, Katrina and Sophie, who nearly always sat together. I never spoke to them until one afternoon a few weeks before Christmas, when they asked if I'd like to get a coffee. I'd never 'gotten a coffee' before — I'd never even tasted coffee, because it is forbidden by the church — but I followed them across the street and into a café. The cashier was impatient so I chose at random. She passed me a doll-sized cup with a tablespoon of mud-colored liquid in it, and I looked longingly at the foamy mugs Katrina and Sophie carried to our table. They debated concepts from the lecture; I debated whether to drink my coffee.

They used complex phrases with ease. Some of them, like 'the second wave,' I'd heard before even if I didn't know what they meant; others, like 'the hegemonic masculinity,' I couldn't get my tongue around let alone my mind. I'd taken several sips of the grainy, acrid fluid before I understood that they were talking about feminism. I stared at them as if they were behind glass. I'd never heard anyone use the word 'feminism' as anything but a reprimand. At BYU, 'You sound like a feminist' signaled the end of the argument. It also signaled that I had lost.

I left the café and went to the library. After five minutes online and a few trips to the stacks, I was sitting in my usual place with a large pile of books written by what I now understood to be second-wave writers — Betty Friedan, Germaine Greer, Simone de Beauvoir. I read only a few pages of each book before slamming it shut. I'd never seen the word 'vagina' printed out, never said it aloud.

I returned to the Internet and then to the shelves, where I exchanged the books of the second wave for those that preceded the first — Mary Wollstonecraft and John Stuart Mill. I read through the afternoon and into the evening, developing for the first time a vocabulary for the uneasiness I'd felt since childhood.

From the moment I had first understood that my brother Richard was a boy and I was a girl, I had wanted to exchange his future for mine. My future was motherhood; his, fatherhood. They sounded similar but they were not. To be one was to be a decider. To preside. To call the family to order. To be the other was to be among those called.

I knew my yearning was unnatural. This knowledge, like so much of my self-knowledge, had come to me in the voice of people I knew, people I loved. All through the years that voice had been with me, whispering, wondering, worrying. That I was *not right*. That my dreams were perversions. That voice had many timbres, many tones. Sometimes it was my father's voice; more often it was my own.

I carried the books to my room and read through the night. I loved the fiery pages of Mary Wollstonecraft, but there was a single line written by John Stuart Mill that, when I read it, moved the world: 'It is a subject on which nothing final can be known.' The subject Mill had in mind was the nature of women. Mill claimed that women have been coaxed, cajoled, shoved and squashed into a series of feminine contortions for so many centuries, that it is now quite impossible to define their natural abilities or aspirations.

Blood rushed to my brain; I felt an animating surge of adrenaline, of possibility, of a frontier being pushed outward. *Of the nature of women, nothing final can be known.* Never had I found such comfort in a void, in the black absence of knowledge. It seemed to say: whatever you are, you are woman.

★ ★ ★

In December, after I had submitted my last essay, I took a train to London and boarded a plane. Mother, Audrey and Emily picked me up at the airport in Salt Lake City, and together we skidded onto the interstate. It was nearly midnight when the mountain came into view. I could only just make out her grand form against the inky sky.

When I entered the kitchen I noticed a gaping hole in the wall, which led to a new extension Dad was building. Mother walked with me through the hole and switched on the light.

'Amazing, isn't it?' she said. 'Amazing' was the word.

It was a single massive room the size of the chapel at church, with a vaulted ceiling that rose some sixteen feet into the air. The size of the room was so ridiculous, it took me a moment to notice the decor. The walls were exposed Sheet-rock, which contrasted spectacularly with the wood paneling on the vaulted ceiling. Crimson suede sofas sat cordially next to the stained upholstery love seat my father had dragged in from the dump many years before. Thick rugs with intricate patterns covered half the floor, while the other half was raw cement. There were several pianos, only one of which looked playable, and a television the size of a dining table. The room suited my father perfectly: it was larger than life and wonderfully incongruous.

Dad had always said he wanted to build a room the size of a cruise ship but I'd never thought he'd have the money. I looked to Mother for an explanation but it was Dad who answered. The business was a roaring success, he explained. Essential oils were popular, and

Mother had the best on the market. 'Our oils are so good,' he said, 'we've started eating into the profits of the large corporate producers. They know all about them Westovers in Idaho.' Dad told me that one company had been so alarmed by the success of Mother's oils, they had offered to buy her out for an astonishing three million dollars. My parents hadn't even considered it. Healing was their calling. No amount of money could tempt them. Dad explained that they were taking the bulk of their profits and reconsecrating them to God in the form of supplies — food, fuel, may be even a real bomb shelter. I suppressed a grin. From what I could tell, Dad was on track to become the best-funded lunatic in the Mountain West.

Richard appeared on the stairwell. He was finishing his undergraduate degree in chemistry at Idaho State. He'd come home for Christmas, and he'd brought his wife, Kami, and their one-month-old son, Donavan. When I'd met Kami a year before, just before the wedding, I'd been struck by how *normal* she was. Like Tyler's wife, Stefanie, Kami was an outsider: she was a Mormon, but she was what Dad would have called 'mainstream.' She thanked Mother for her herbal advice but seemed oblivious to the expectation that she renounce doctors. Donavan had been born in a hospital.

I wondered how Richard was navigating the turbulent waters between his normal wife and his abnormal parents. I watched him closely that night, and to me it seemed he was trying to live in both worlds, to be a loyal adherent to all creeds. When my father condemned doctors as minions of Satan, Richard turned to Kami and gave a small laugh, as if Dad were joking. But when my father's eyebrows rose, Richard's expression changed to one of serious contemplation and accord. He seemed in a state of constant transition, phasing in and out of dimensions, unsure whether to be my father's son or his wife's husband.

★ ★ ★

Mother was overwhelmed with holiday orders, so I passed my days on Buck's Peak just as I had as a child: in the kitchen, making homeopathics. I poured the distilled water and added the drops from the base formula, then passed the tiny glass bottle through the ring made by my thumb and index fingers, counting to fifty or a hundred, then moving on to the next. Dad came in for a drink of water. He smiled when he saw me.

'Who knew we'd have to send you to Cambridge to get you in the kitchen where you belong?' he said.

In the afternoons, Shawn and I saddled the horses and fought our way up the mountain, the horses half-jumping to clamber through snowdrifts that reached their bellies. The mountain was beautiful and crisp; the air smelled of leather and pine. Shawn talked about the horses, about their training, and about the colts he expected in the spring, and I remembered that he was always at his best when he was with his horses.

I had been home about a week when the

mountain was gripped by an intense cold spell. The temperature plunged, dropping to zero, then dropping further still. We put the horses away, knowing that if they worked up a sweat, it would turn to ice on their backs. The trough froze solid. We broke the ice but it refroze quickly, so we carried buckets of water to each horse.

That night everyone stayed indoors. Mother was blending oils in the kitchen. Dad was in the extension, which I had begun to jokingly call the Chapel. He was lying on the crimson sofa, a Bible resting on his stomach, while Kami and Richard, played hymns on the piano. I sat with my laptop on the love seat, near Dad, and listened to the music. I had just begun a message to Drew when something struck the back door. The door burst open, and Emily flew into the room.

Her thin arms were wrapped around her body and she was shaking, gasping for breath. She wore no coat, no shoes, nothing but jeans, an old pair I'd left behind, and one of my worn T-shirts. Mother helped her to the sofa, wrapping her in the nearest blanket. Emily bawled, and for several minutes not even Mother could get her to say what had happened. Was everyone all right? Where was Peter? He was fragile, half the size he should have been, and he wore oxygen tubes because his lungs had never fully developed. Had his tiny lungs collapsed, his breathing stopped?

The story came out haltingly, between erratic sobs and the clattering of teeth. From what I could tell, when Emily had gone to Stokes that afternoon to buy groceries, she had returned home with the wrong crackers for Peter. Shawn had exploded. 'How can he grow if you can't buy the right food!' he had screamed, then he'd gathered her up and flung her from their trailer, into a snowbank. She'd pounded on the door, begging to be let in, then she'd run up the hillside to the house. I stared at her bare feet as she said this. They were so red, they looked as if they'd been burned.

My parents sat with Emily on the sofa, one on each side of her, patting her shoulders and squeezing her hands. Richard paced a few feet behind them. He seemed frustrated, anxious, as if he wanted to explode into action and was only just being held in check.

Kami was still seated at the piano. She was staring at the group huddled on the couch, confused. She had not understood Emily. She did not understand why Richard was pacing, or why he paused every few seconds to glance at Dad, waiting for a word or gesture — any signal of what should be done.

I looked at Kami and felt a tightening in my chest. I resented her for witnessing this. I imagined myself in Emily's place, which was easy to do — I couldn't stop myself from doing it — and in a moment I was in a parking lot, laughing my high-pitched cackle, trying to convince the world that my wrist wasn't breaking. Before I knew what I was doing I had crossed the room. I grasped my brother's arm and pulled him with me to the piano. Emily was still sobbing, and I used her sobs to muffle my whispers. I told Kami that what we were witnessing was private, and that Emily would be embarrassed by it tomorrow. For Emily's sake, I said, we should all go to our rooms and leave it in Dad's hands.

Kami stood. She had decided to trust me. Richard hesitated, giving Dad a long look, then he followed her from the room.

I walked with them down the hallway then I doubled back. I sat at the kitchen table and watched the clock. Five minutes passed, then ten. *Come on, Shawn,* I chanted under my breath. *Come now.*

I'd convinced myself that if Shawn appeared in the next few minutes, it would be to make sure Emily had made it to the house — that she hadn't slipped on the ice and broken a leg, wasn't freezing to death in a field. But he didn't come.

Twenty minutes later, when Emily finally stopped shaking, Dad picked up the phone. 'Come get your wife!' he shouted into it. Mother was cradling Emily's head against her shoulder. Dad returned to the sofa and patted Emily's arm. As I stared at the three of them huddling together, I had the impression that all of this had happened before, and that everyone's part was well rehearsed. Even mine.

It would be many years before I would understand what had happened that night, and what my role in it had been. How I had opened my mouth when I should have stayed silent, and shut it when I should have spoken out. What was needed was a revolution, a reversal of the ancient, brittle roles we'd been playing out since my childhood. What was needed — what Emily needed — was a woman emancipated from pretense, a woman who could show herself to be a man. Voice an opinion. Take action in scorn of deference. A father.

The French doors my father had installed squawked as they opened. Shawn shuffled in wearing heavy boots and a thick winter coat. Peter emerged from the folds of thick wool, where Shawn had been shielding him from the cold, and reached out for Emily. She clung to him. Dad stood. He motioned for Shawn to take the seat next to Emily. I stood and went to my room, pausing to take a last look at my father, who was inhaling deeply, readying himself to deliver a lengthy lecture.

'It was very stern,' Mother assured me twenty minutes later, when she appeared at my door asking if I could lend Emily a pair of shoes and a coat. I fetched them and watched from the kitchen as she disappeared, tucked under my brother's arm.

31

Tragedy Then Farce

The day before I returned to England, I drove seven miles along the mountain range, then turned onto a narrow dirt road and stopped in front of a powder-blue house. I parked behind an RV that was nearly as large as the house itself. I knocked; my sister answered.

She stood in the doorway in flannel pajamas, a toddler on her hip and two small girls clinging to her leg. Her son, about six, stood behind her. Audrey stepped aside to let me pass, but her movements were stiff, and she avoided looking directly at me. We'd spent little time together since she'd married.

I moved into the house, stopping abruptly in the entryway when I saw a three-foot hole in the linoleum that plunged to the basement. I walked past the hole and into the kitchen, which was filled with the scent of our mother's oils — birch, eucalyptus, ravensara.

The conversation was slow, halting. Audrey asked me no questions about England or Cambridge. She had no frame of reference for my life, so we talked about hers — how the public school system was corrupt so she was teaching her children herself, at home. Like me, Audrey had never attended a public school. When she was seventeen, she had made a fleeting effort to get her GED. She had even enlisted the help of our cousin Missy, who had come up from Salt Lake City to tutor her. Missy had worked with Audrey for an entire summer, at the end of which she'd declared that Audrey's education hovered somewhere between the fourth- and fifth-grade levels, and that a GED was out of the question. I chewed my lip and stared at her daughter, who had brought me a drawing, wondering what education she could hope to receive from a mother who had none herself.

We made breakfast for the children, then played with them in the snow. We baked, we watched crime dramas and designed beaded bracelets. It was as if I had stepped through a mirror and was living a day in the life I might have had, if I'd stayed on the mountain. But I hadn't stayed. My life had diverged from my sister's, and it felt as though there was no common ground between us. The hours passed; it was late afternoon; and still she felt distant from me, still she refused to meet my gaze.

I had brought a small porcelain tea set for her children, and when they began to quarrel over the teapot, I gathered up the pieces. The oldest girl reminded me that she was five now, which she said was too old to have a toy taken away. 'If you act like a child,' I said, 'I'll treat you like one.'

I don't know why I said it; I suppose Shawn was on my mind. I regretted the words even as they left my lips, hated myself for saying them. I turned to pass the tea set to my sister, so she could administer justice however she saw fit, but when I saw her expression I nearly dropped it. Her mouth hung open in a perfect circle.

'Shawn used to say that,' she said, fixing her eyes on mine.

That moment would stay with me. I would remember it the next day, when I boarded a plane in Salt Lake City, and it would still be on my mind when I landed in London. It was the shock of it that I couldn't shake. Somehow, it had never occurred to me that my sister might have lived my life before I did.

★ ★ ★

That term, I presented myself to the university like resin to a sculptor. I believed I could be remade, my mind recast. I forced myself to befriend other students, clumsily introducing myself again and again until I had a small circle of friends. Then I set out to obliterate the barriers that separated me from them. I tasted red wine for the first time, and my new friends laughed at my pinched face. I discarded my high-necked blouses and began to wear more fashionable cuts — fitted, often sleeveless, with less restrictive necklines. In photos from this period I'm struck by the symmetry: I look like everyone else.

In April I began to do well. I wrote an essay on John Stuart Mill's concept of self-sovereignty, and my supervisor, Dr. David Runciman, said that if my dissertation was of the same quality, I might be accepted to Cambridge for a PhD. I was stunned: I, who had sneaked into this grand place as an impostor, might now enter through the front door. I set to work on my dissertation, again choosing Mill as the topic.

One afternoon near the end of term, when I was eating lunch in the library cafeteria, I recognized a group of students from my program. They were seated together at a small table. I asked if I could join them, and a tall Italian named Nic nodded. From the conversation I gathered that Nic had invited the others to visit him in Rome during the spring holiday. 'You can come, too,' he said.

We handed in our final essays for the term, then boarded a plane. On our first evening in Rome, we climbed one of the seven hills and looked out over the metropolis. Byzantine domes hovered over the city like rising balloons. It was nearly dusk; the streets were bathed in amber. It wasn't the color of a modern city, of steel, glass and concrete. It was the color of sunset. It didn't look real. Nic asked me what I thought of his home, and that was all I could say: it didn't look real.

At breakfast the next morning, the others talked about their families. Someone's father was a diplomat; another's was an Oxford don. I was asked about my parents. I said my father owned a junkyard.

Nic took us to the conservatory where he'd studied violin. It was in the heart of Rome and was richly furnished, with a grand staircase and resonant halls. I tried to imagine what it would have been like to study in such a place, to walk across marble floors each morning and, day after day, come to associate learning with beauty. But my imagination failed me. I could only imagine the school as I was experiencing it now, as a kind of museum, a relic from someone else's life.

For two days we explored Rome, a city that is both a living organism and a fossil. Bleached structures from antiquity lay like dried bones, embedded in pulsating cables and thrumming traffic, the arteries of modern life. We visited the Pantheon, the Roman Forum, the Sistine Chapel. My instinct was to worship, to venerate. That was how I felt toward the whole city: that it should be behind glass, adored from a distance, never touched, never altered. My companions moved through the city differently, aware of its significance but not subdued by it. They were not hushed by the Trevi Fountain; they were not silenced by the Colosseum. Instead, as we moved from one relic to the next, they debated philosophy — Hobbes and Descartes, Aquinas and Machiavelli. There was a kind of symbiosis in their relationship to these grand places: they gave life to the ancient architecture by making it the backdrop of their discourse, by refusing to worship at its altar as if it were a dead thing.

On the third night there was a rainstorm. I stood on Nic's balcony and watched streaks of lightning race across the sky, claps of thunder chasing them. It was like being on Buck's Peak, to feel such power in the earth and sky.

The next morning was cloudless. We took a picnic of wine and pastries to the grounds of the Villa Borghese. The sun was hot, the pastries ambrosial. I could not remember ever feeling more present. Someone said something about Hobbes, and without thinking I recited a line from Mill. It seemed the natural thing, to bring this voice from the past into a moment so saturated with the past already, even if the voice was mixed with my own. There was a pause while everyone checked to see who had spoken, then someone asked which text the line was from, and the conversation moved forward.

For the rest of the week, I experienced Rome as they did: as a place of history, but also as a place of life, of food and traffic and conflict and thunder. The city was no longer a museum; it was as vivid to me as Buck's Peak. The Piazza del Popolo. The Baths of Caracalla. Castel Sant'Angelo. These became as real to my mind as the Princess, the red railway car, the Shear. The world they represented, of philosophy, science, literature — an entire civilization — took on a life that was distinct from the life I had known. At the Galleria Nazionale d'Arte Antica, I stood before Caravaggio's *Judith Beheading Holofernes* and did not once think about chickens.

I don't know what caused the transformation, why suddenly I could engage with the great thinkers of the past, rather than revere them to the point of muteness. But there was something about that city, with its white marble and black asphalt, crusted with history, ablaze in traffic lights, that showed me I could admire the past without being silenced by it.

I was still breathing in the fustiness of ancient stone when I arrived in Cambridge. I rushed up

378

the staircase, anxious to check my email, knowing there would be a message from Drew. When I opened my laptop, I saw that Drew had written, but so had someone else: my sister.

★   ★   ★

I opened Audrey's message. It was written in one long paragraph, with little punctuation and many spelling errors, and at first I fixated on these grammatical irregularities as a way to mute the text. But the words would not be hushed; they shouted at me from the screen.

Audrey said she should have stopped Shawn many years ago, before he could do to me what he'd done to her. She said that when she was young, she'd wanted to tell Mother, to ask for help, but she'd thought Mother wouldn't believe her. She'd been right. Before her wedding, she'd experienced nightmares and flashbacks, and she'd told Mother about them. Mother had said the memories were false, impossible. *I should have helped you*, Audrey wrote. *But when my own mother didn't believe me, I stopped believing myself.*[1]

It was a mistake she was going to correct. *I believe God will hold me accountable if I don't stop Shawn from hurting anyone else*, she wrote. She was going to confront him, and our parents, and she was asking me to stand with her. *I am*

---

[1] The italics used on this page indicate that the language from the referenced email is paraphrased, not directly quoted.

doing this with or without you. But without you, I will probably lose.

I sat in the dark for a long time. I resented her for writing me. I felt she had torn me from one world, one life, where I was happy, and dragged me back into another.

I typed a response. I told her she was right, that of course we should stop Shawn, but I asked her to do nothing until I could return to Idaho. I don't know why I asked her to wait, what benefit I thought time would yield. I don't know what I thought would happen when we talked to our parents, but I understood instinctively what was at stake. As long as we had never asked, it was possible to believe that they would help. To tell them was to risk the unthinkable: it was to risk learning that they already knew.

Audrey did not wait, not even a day. The next morning she showed my email to Mother. I cannot imagine the details of that conversation, but I know that for Audrey it must have been a tremendous relief, laying my words before our mother, finally able to say, I'm not crazy. It happened to Tara, too.

For all of that day, Mother pondered it. Then she decided she had to hear the words from me. It was late afternoon in Idaho, nearly midnight in England, when my mother, unsure how to place an international call, found me online. The words on the screen were small, confined to a tiny text box in the corner of the browser, but somehow they seemed to swallow the room. She told me she had read my letter. I braced myself for her rage.

It is painful to face reality, she wrote. *To realize there was something ugly, and I refused to see it.*[1]

I had to read those lines a number of times before I understood them. Before I realized that she was not angry, not blaming me, or trying to convince me I had only imagined. She believed me.

Don't blame yourself, I told her. Your mind was never the same after the accident.

Maybe, she said. *But sometimes I think we choose our illnesses, because they benefit us in some way.*

I asked Mother why she'd never stopped Shawn from hurting me.

Shawn always said you picked the fights, and I guess I wanted to believe that, because it was easier. Because you were strong and rational, and anyone could see that Shawn was not.

That didn't make sense. If I had seemed rational, why had Mother believed Shawn when he'd told her I was picking fights? That I needed to be subdued, disciplined.

I'm a mother, she said. *Mothers protect. And Shawn was so damaged.*

I wanted to say that she was also *my* mother but I didn't. I don't think Dad will believe any of this, I typed.

He will, she wrote. *But it's hard for him. It reminds him of the damage his bipolar has*

---

[1] The italicized language in the description of the referenced text exchange is paraphrased, not directly quoted.

caused to our family.

I had never heard Mother admit that Dad might be mentally ill. Years before, I had told her what I'd learned in my psychology class about bipolar disorder and schizophrenia, but she had shrugged it off. Hearing her say it now felt liberating. The illness gave me something to attack besides my father, so when Mother asked why I hadn't come to her sooner, why I hadn't asked for help, I answered honestly.

Because you were so bullied by Dad, I said. You were not powerful in the house. Dad ran things, and he was not going to help us.

I am stronger now, she said. *I no longer run scared.*

When I read this, I imagined my mother as a young woman, brilliant and energetic, but also anxious and complying. Then the image changed, her body thinning, elongating, her hair flowing, long and silver.

Emily is being bullied, I wrote.

She is, Mother said. *Like I was.*

She is you, I said.

She is me. But we know better now. We can rewrite the story.

I asked about a memory. It was from the weeks before I'd left for BYU, after Shawn had had a particularly bad night. He'd brought Mother to tears, then plopped onto the sofa and turned on the TV. I'd found her sobbing at the kitchen table, and she'd asked me not to go to BYU. 'You're the only one strong enough to handle him,' she'd said. 'I can't, and your father can't. It has to be you.'

I typed slowly, reluctantly: Do you remember telling me not to go to school, that I was the only one who could handle Shawn?

Yes, I remember that.

There was a pause, then more words appeared — words I hadn't known I needed to hear, but once I saw them, I realized I'd been searching my whole life for them.

You were my child. I should have protected you.

I lived a lifetime in the moment I read those lines, a life that was not the one I had actually lived. I became a different person, who remembered a different childhood. I didn't understand the magic of those words then, and I don't understand it now. I know only this: that when my mother told me she had not been the mother to me that she wished she'd been, she became that mother for the first time.

I love you, I wrote, and closed my laptop.

★ ★ ★

Mother and I spoke only once about that conversation, on the phone, a week later. 'It's being dealt with,' she said. 'I told your father what you and your sister said. Shawn will get help.'

I put the issue from my mind. My mother had taken up the cause. She was strong. She had built that business, with all those people working for her, and it dwarfed my father's business, and all the other businesses in the whole town; she, that docile woman, had a power in her the rest of us couldn't contemplate. And Dad. He had changed. He was softer, more prone to laugh. The future could be different from the past. Even the past could be different from the past, because my memories could change: I no longer remembered Mother listening in the kitchen while Shawn pinned me to the floor, pressing my windpipe. I no longer remembered her looking away.

My life in Cambridge was transformed — or rather, I was transformed into someone who believed she belonged in Cambridge. The shame I'd long felt about my family leaked out of me almost overnight. For the first time in my life I talked openly about where I'd come from. I admitted to my friends that I'd never been to school. I described Buck's Peak, with its many junkyards, barns, corrals. I even told them about the root cellar full of supplies in the wheat field, and the gasoline buried near the old barn.

I told them I'd been poor, I told them I'd been ignorant, and in telling them this I felt not the slightest prick of shame. Only then did I understand where the shame had come from: it wasn't that I hadn't studied in a marble conservatory, or that my father wasn't a diplomat. It wasn't that Dad was half out of his mind, or that Mother followed him. It had come from having a father who shoved me toward the chomping blades of the shear, instead of pulling me away from them. It had come from those moments on the floor, from knowing that Mother was in the next room, closing her eyes and ears to me, and choosing, for that moment, not to be my mother at all.

I fashioned a new history for myself. I became a popular dinner guest, with my stories of hunting and horses, of scrapping and fighting mountain fires. Of my brilliant mother, midwife and entrepreneur; of my eccentric father, junkman and zealot. I thought I was finally being honest about the life I'd had before. It wasn't the truth exactly, but it was true in a larger sense: true to what *would* be, in the future, now that everything had changed for the better. Now that Mother had found her strength.

The past was a ghost, insubstantial, unaffecting. Only the future had weight.

32

A Brawling Woman in a Wide House

When I next returned to Buck's Peak, it was autumn and Grandma-down-the-hill was dying. For nine years she had battled the cancer in her bone marrow; now the contest was ending. I had just learned that I'd won a place at Cambridge to study for a PhD when Mother wrote to me. 'Grandma is in the hospital again,' she said. 'Come quick. I think this will be the last time.'

When I landed in Salt Lake, Grandma was drifting in and out of consciousness. Drew met me at the airport. We were more than friends by then, and Drew said he would drive me to Idaho, to the hospital in town.

I hadn't been back there since I'd taken Shawn years before, and as I walked down its white, antiseptic hallway, it was difficult not to think of him. We found Grandma's room. Grandpa was seated at her bedside, holding her speckled hand. Her eyes were open and she looked at me. 'It's my little Tara, come all the way from England,' she said, then her eyes closed. Grandpa squeezed her hand but she was asleep. A nurse told us she would likely sleep for hours.

Drew said he would drive me to Buck's Peak. I agreed, and it wasn't until the mountain came into view that I wondered whether I'd made a mistake. Drew had heard my stories, but still there was a risk in bringing him here: this was not a story, and I doubted whether anyone would play the part I had written for them.

The house was in chaos. There were women everywhere, some taking orders over the phone, others mixing oils or straining tinctures. There was a new annex on the south side of the house, where younger women were filling bottles and packaging orders for shipment. I left Drew in the living room and went to the bathroom, which was the only room in the house that still looked the way I remembered it. When I came out I walked straight into a thin old woman with wiry hair and large, square glasses.

'This bathroom is for senior management only,' she said. 'Bottle fillers must use the bathroom in the annex.'

'I don't work here,' I said.

She stared at me. Of course I worked here. Everyone worked here.

'This bathroom is for senior management,' she repeated, straightening to her full height. '*You* are not allowed to leave the annex.'

She walked away before I could reply.

I still hadn't seen either of my parents. I weaved my way back through the house and found Drew on the sofa, listening to a woman explain that aspirin can cause infertility. I grasped his hand and pulled him behind me, cutting a path through the strangers.

'Is this place for real?' he said.

I found Mother in a windowless room in the basement. I had the impression that she was hiding there. I introduced her to Drew and she smiled warmly. 'Where's Dad?' I said. I suspected that he was sick in bed, as he had been prone to pulmonary illnesses since the explosion had charred his lungs.

'I'm sure he's in the fray,' she said, rolling her eyes at the ceiling, which thrummed with the thudding of feet.

Mother came with us upstairs. The moment she appeared on the landing, she was hailed by several of her employees with questions from clients. Everyone seemed to want her opinion — about their burns, their heart tremors, their underweight infants. She waved them off and pressed forward. The impression she gave as she moved through her own house was of a celebrity in a crowded restaurant, trying not to be recognized.

My father's desk was the size of a car. It was parked in the center of the chaos. He was on the phone, which he'd wedged between his cheek and shoulder so it wouldn't slip through his waxy hands. 'Doctors can't help with them diabetes,' he said, much too loudly. 'But the Lord can!'

I looked sideways at Drew, who was smiling. Dad hung up and turned toward us. He greeted Drew with a large grin. He radiated energy, feeding off the general bedlam of the house. Drew said he was impressed with the business, and Dad seemed to grow six inches. 'We've been blessed for doing the Lord's work,' he said.

The phone rang again. There were at least three employees tasked with answering it, but Dad leapt for the receiver as if he'd been waiting for an important call. I'd never seen him so full of life.

'The power of God on earth,' he shouted into the mouthpiece. 'That's what these oils are: God's pharmacy!'

The noise in the house was disorienting, so I took Drew up the mountain. We strolled through fields of wild wheat and from there into the skirt of pines at the mountain base. The fall colors were soothing and we stayed for hours, gazing down at the quiet valley. It was late afternoon when we finally made our way back to the house and Drew left for Salt Lake City.

I entered the Chapel through the French doors and was surprised by the silence. The house was empty, every phone disconnected, every workstation abandoned. Mother sat alone in the center of the room.

'The hospital called,' she said. 'Grandma's gone.'

★ ★ ★

My father lost his appetite for the business. He started getting out of bed later and later, and when he did, it seemed it was only to insult or accuse. He shouted at Shawn about the junkyard and lectured Mother about her management of the employees. He snapped at Audrey when she tried to make him lunch, and barked at me for typing too loudly. It was as if he wanted to fight, to punish himself for the old woman's death. Or maybe the punishment was for her life, for the conflict that had been between them, which had only ended now she was dead.

The house slowly filled again. The phones were reconnected, and women materialized to answer them. Dad's desk remained empty. He spent his days in bed, gazing up at the stucco ceiling. I brought him supper, as I had as a child, and wondered now, as I'd wondered then, whether he knew I was there.

Mother moved about the house with the vitality of ten people, mixing tinctures and essential oils, directing her employees between making funeral arrangements and cooking for every cousin and aunt who dropped in unannounced to reminisce about Grandma. As often as not I'd find her in an apron, hovering over a roast with a phone in each hand, one a client, the other an uncle or friend calling to offer condolences. Through all this my father remained in bed.

Dad spoke at the funeral. His speech was a twenty-minute sermon on God's promises to Abraham. He mentioned my grandmother twice. To strangers it must have seemed he was hardly affected by the loss of his mother, but we knew better, we who could see the devastation.

When we arrived home from the service, Dad was incensed that lunch wasn't ready. Mother scrambled to serve the stew she'd left to slow-cook, but after the meal Dad seemed equally frustrated by the dishes, which Mother hurriedly cleaned, and then by his grandchildren, who played noisily while Mother dashed about trying to hush them.

That evening, when the house was empty and

quiet, I listened from the living room as my parents argued in the kitchen.

'The least you could do,' Mother said, 'is fill out these thank-you cards. It was *your* mother, after all.'

'That's wifely work,' Dad said. 'I've never heard of a man writing cards.'

He had said the exact wrong thing. For ten years, Mother had been the primary breadwinner, while continuing to cook meals, clean the house, do the laundry, and I had never once heard her express anything like resentment. Until now.

'Then you should do the *husband's work*,' she said, her voice raised.

Soon they were both shouting. Dad tried to corral her, to subdue her with a show of anger, the way he always had, but this only made her more stubborn. Eventually she tossed the cards on the table and said, 'Fill them out or don't. But if you don't, no one will.' Then she marched downstairs. Dad followed, and for an hour their shouts rose up through the floor. I'd never heard my parents shout like that — at least, not my mother. I'd never seen her refuse to give way.

The next morning I found Dad in the kitchen, dumping flour into a glue-like substance I assumed was supposed to be pancake batter. When he saw me, he dropped the flour and sat at the table. 'You're a woman, ain'tcha?' he said. 'Well, this here's a kitchen.' We stared at each other and I contemplated the distance that had sprung up between us — how natural those words sounded to his ears, how grating to mine.

It wasn't like Mother to leave Dad to make his own breakfast. I thought she might be ill and went downstairs to check on her. I'd barely made it to the landing when I heard it: deep sobs coming from the bathroom, muffled by the steady drone of a blow-dryer. I stood outside the door and listened for more than a minute, paralyzed. Would she want me to leave, to pretend I hadn't heard? I waited for her to catch her breath, but her sobs only grew more desperate.

I knocked. 'It's me,' I said.

The door opened, a sliver at first, then wider, and there was my mother, her skin glistening from the shower, wrapped in a towel that was too small to cover her. I had never seen my mother so exposed, and instinctively I closed my eyes. The world went black. I heard a thud, the cracking of plastic, and opened my eyes. Mother had dropped the blow-dryer and it had struck the floor, its roar now doubled as it rebounded off the exposed concrete. I looked at her, and as I did she pulled me to her and held me. The wet from her body seeped into my clothes, and I felt droplets slide from her hair and onto my shoulder.

33

Sorcery of Physics

I didn't stay long on Buck's Peak, maybe a week. On the day I left the mountain, Audrey asked me not to go. I have no memory of the conversation, but I remember writing the journal entry about it. I wrote it my first night back in Cambridge, while sitting on a stone bridge and staring up at King's College Chapel. I remember the river, which was calm; I remember the slow drift of autumn leaves resting on the glassy surface. I remember the scratch of my pen moving across the page, recounting in detail, for a full eight pages, precisely what my sister had said. But the memory of her saying it is gone: it is as if I wrote in order to forget.

Audrey asked me to stay. Shawn was too strong, she said, too persuasive, for her to confront him alone. I told her she wasn't alone, she had Mother. Audrey said I didn't understand. No one had believed us after all. If we asked Dad for help, she was sure he'd call us both liars. I told her our parents had changed and we should trust them. Then I boarded a plane and took myself five thousand miles away.

If I felt guilty to be documenting my sister's fears from such a safe distance, surrounded by grand libraries and ancient chapels, I gave only one indication of it, in the last line of the entry: *Cambridge is less beautiful tonight.*

★　★　★

Drew had come with me to Cambridge, having been admitted to a master's program in Middle Eastern studies. I told him about my conversation with Audrey. He was the first boyfriend in whom I confided about my family — really confided, the truth and not just amusing anecdotes. Of course all that is in the past, I said. My family is different now. But you should know. So you can watch me. In case I do something crazy.

The first term passed in a flurry of dinners and late-night parties, punctuated by even later nights in the library. To qualify for a PhD, I had to produce a piece of original academic research. In other words, having spent five years reading history, I was now being asked to write it.

But to write what? While reading for my master's thesis, I'd been surprised to discover echoes of Mormon theology in the great philosophers of the nineteenth century. I mentioned this to David Runciman, my supervisor. '*That's* your project,' he said. 'You can do something no one has done: you can examine Mormonism not just as a religious movement, but as an intellectual one.'

I began to reread the letters of Joseph Smith and Brigham Young. As a child I'd read those letters as an act of worship; now I read them with different eyes, not the eyes of a critic, but also not the eyes of a disciple. I examined polygamy, not as a doctrine but as a social policy. I measured it against its own aims, as well as against other movements and theories from the same period. It felt like a radical act.

My friends in Cambridge had become a kind of family, and I felt a sense of belonging with them that, for many years, had been absent on Buck's Peak. Sometimes I felt damned for those feelings. No natural sister should love a stranger more than a brother, I thought, and what sort of daughter prefers a teacher to her own father?

But although I wished it were otherwise, I did not want to go home. I preferred the family I had chosen to the one I had been given, so the happier I became in Cambridge, the more my happiness was made fetid by my feeling that I had betrayed Buck's Peak. That feeling became a physical part of me, something I could taste on my tongue or smell on my own breath.

I bought a ticket to Idaho for Christmas. The night before my flight, there was a feast in my college. One of my friends had formed a chamber choir that was to sing carols during dinner. The choir had been rehearsing for weeks, but on the day of the feast the soprano fell ill with bronchitis. My phone rang late that afternoon. It was my friend. 'Please tell me you know someone who can sing,' he said.

I had not sung for years, and never without my father to hear me, but a few hours later I joined the chamber choir on a platform near the rafters, above the massive Christmas tree that dominated the hall. I treasured the moment, taking pleasure in the lightness I felt to have music once again floating up from my chest, and wondering whether Dad, if he were here, would have braved the university and all its socialism to hear me sing. I believed he would.

★ ★ ★

Buck's Peak was unchanged. The Princess was buried in snow but I could see the deep contours of her legs. Mother was in the kitchen when I arrived, stirring a stew with one hand and with the other holding the phone and explaining the properties of motherwort. Dad's desk was still empty. He was in the basement, Mother said, in bed. Something had hold of his lungs.

A burly stranger shuffled through the back door. Several seconds passed before I recognized my brother. Luke's beard was so thick, he looked like one of his goats. His left eye was white and dead: he'd been shot in the face with a paintball gun a few months before. He crossed the room and clapped me on the back, and I stared into his remaining eye, looking for something familiar. But it wasn't until I saw the raised scar on his forearm, a curved check mark two inches wide from where the Shear had bitten his flesh, that I was sure this man was my brother.[7] He told me he was living with his wife and a pack of kids in a mobile home behind the barn, making his money working oil rigs in North Dakota.

Two days passed. Dad came upstairs every evening and settled himself into a sofa in the Chapel, where he would cough and watch TV or read the Old Testament. I spent my days studying or helping Mother.

On the third evening I was at the kitchen table, reading, when Shawn and Benjamin shuffled through the back door. Benjamin was telling Shawn about a punch he'd thrown after a fender bender in town. He said that before climbing out of his truck to confront the other driver, he'd slipped his handgun into the waistband of his jeans. 'The guy didn't know what he was getting into,' Benjamin said, grinning.

'Only an idiot brings a gun into a mess like that,' Shawn said.

'I wasn't gonna use it,' Benjamin muttered.

'Then don't bring it,' Shawn said. 'Then you *know* you won't use it. If you bring it you *might* use it, that's how things are. A fistfight can turn into a gunfight real quick.'

Shawn spoke calmly, thoughtfully. His blond hair was filthy and uncut, growing wild, and his face was covered in stubble the color of shale. His eyes shone from under the oil and dirt, blazes of blue in clouds of ash. His expression, as well as his words, seemed to belong to a much older man, a man whose hot blood had cooled, who was at peace.

Shawn turned to me. I had been avoiding him, but suddenly that seemed unfair. He had changed; it was cruel to pretend he hadn't. He asked if I'd like to go for a drive, and I said I would. Shawn wanted ice cream so we got milkshakes. The conversation was calm, comfortable, like it had been years before on those dusky evenings in the corral. He told me about running the crew without Dad, about Peter's frail lungs — about the surgeries and the oxygen tubes he still wore at night.

We were nearly home, only a mile from Buck's Peak, when Shawn cranked the wheel and the car skidded on the ice. He accelerated through the spin, the tires caught, and the car leapt onto a side road.

'Where we going?' I asked, but the road only went one place.

The church was dark, the parking lot deserted.

Shawn circled the lot, then parked near the main entrance. He switched off the ignition and the headlights faded. I could barely make out the curve of his face in the dark.

'You talk much to Audrey?' he said.

'Not really,' I said.

He seemed to relax, then he said, 'Audrey is a lying piece of shit.'

I looked away, fixing my eyes on the church spire, visible against the light from the stars.

'I'd put a bullet in her head,' Shawn said, and I felt his body shift toward me. 'But I don't want to waste a good bullet on a worthless bitch.'

It was crucial that I not look at him. As long as I kept my eyes on the spire, I almost believed he couldn't touch me. Almost. Because even while I clung to this belief, I waited to feel his hands on my neck. I knew I would feel them, and soon, but I didn't dare do anything that might break the spell of waiting. In that moment part of me believed, as I had always believed, that it would be me who broke the spell, who caused it to break. When the stillness shattered and his fury rushed at me, I would know that something I had done was the catalyst, the cause. There is hope in such a superstition; there is the illusion of control.

I stayed still, without thought or motion.

The ignition clicked, the engine growled to life. Warm air flooded through the vents.

'You feel like a movie?' Shawn said. His voice was casual. I watched the world revolve as the car spun around and lurched back to the highway. 'A movie sounds just right,' he said.

I said nothing, unwilling to move or speak lest I offend the strange sorcery of physics that I still believed had saved me. Shawn seemed unaware of my silence. He drove the last mile to Buck's Peak chatting cheerfully, almost playfully, about whether to watch *The Man Who Knew Too Little*, or not.

34

The Substance of Things

I didn't feel particularly brave as I approached my father in the Chapel that night. I saw my role as reconnaissance: I was there to relay information, to tell Dad that Shawn had threatened Audrey, because Dad would know what to do.

Or perhaps I was calm because I was not there, not really. Maybe I was across an ocean, on another continent, reading Hume under a stone archway. Maybe I was racing through King's College, the *Discourse on Inequality* tucked under my arm.

'Dad, I need to tell you something.'

I said that Shawn had made a joke about shooting Audrey, and that I thought it was because Audrey had confronted him about his behavior. Dad stared at me, and the skin where his lips had been tightened. He shouted for Mother and she appeared. Her mood was somber; I couldn't understand why she wouldn't look me in the eye.

'What exactly are you saying?' Dad said.

From that moment it was an interrogation. Every time I suggested that Shawn was violent or manipulative in any way, Dad shouted at me: 'Where's your proof? Do you have proof?'

'I have journals,' I said.

'Get them, I'm going to read them.'

'I don't have them with me.' This was a lie;

400

they were under my bed.

'What the hell am I supposed to think if you ain't got proof?' Dad was still shouting. Mother sat on the sofa's edge, her mouth open in a slant. She looked in agony.

'You don't need proof,' I said quietly. 'You've seen it. You've both seen it.'

Dad said I wouldn't be happy until Shawn was rotting in prison, that I'd come back from Cambridge just to raise hell. I said I didn't want Shawn in prison but that some type of intervention was needed. I turned to Mother, waiting for her to add her voice to mine, but she was silent. Her eyes were fixed on the floor as if Dad and I were not there.

There was a moment when I realized she would not speak, that she would sit there and say nothing, that I was alone. I tried to calm Dad but my voice trembled, cracked. Then I was wailing — sobs erupted from somewhere, some part of me I had not felt in years, that I had forgotten existed. I thought I might vomit.

I ran to the bathroom. I was shaking from my feet to my fingers.

I had to strangle the sobs quickly — Dad would never take me seriously if I couldn't — so I stopped the bawling using the old methods: staring my face down in the mirror and scolding it for every tear. It was such a familiar process, that in doing it I shattered the illusion I'd been building so carefully for the past year. The fake past, the fake future, both gone.

I stared at the reflection. The mirror was mesmeric, with its triple panels trimmed with false oak. It was the same mirror I'd gazed into as a child, then as a girl, then as a youth, half woman, half girl. Behind me was the same toilet Shawn had put my head in, holding me there until I confessed I was a whore.

I had often locked myself in this bathroom after Shawn let me go. I would move the panels until they showed my face three times, then I would glare at each one, contemplating what Shawn had said and what he had made me say, until it all began to feel true instead of just something I had said to make the pain stop. And here I was still, and here was the mirror. The same face, repeated in the same three panels.

Except it wasn't. This face was older, and floating above a soft cashmere sweater. But Dr. Kerry was right: it wasn't the clothes that made this face, this woman, different. It was something behind her eyes, something in the set of her jaw — a hope or belief or conviction — that a life is not a thing unalterable. I don't have a word for what it was I saw, but I suppose it was something like *faith*.

I had regained a fragile sense of calm, and I left the bathroom carrying that calmness delicately, as if it were a china plate balancing on my head. I walked slowly down the hall, taking small, even steps.

'I'm going to bed,' I said when I'd made it to the Chapel. 'We'll talk about this tomorrow.'

Dad was at his desk, holding a phone in his left hand. 'We'll talk about it now,' he said. 'I told Shawn what you said. He is coming.'

*   *   *

I considered making a run for it. Could I get to my car before Shawn made it to the house? Where were the keys? I need my laptop, I thought, with my research. *Leave it*, the girl from the mirror said.

Dad told me to sit and I did. I don't know how long I waited, paralyzed with indecision, but I was still wondering if there was time to escape when the French doors opened and Shawn walked in. Suddenly the vast room felt tiny. I looked at my hands. I couldn't raise my eyes.

I heard footsteps. Shawn had crossed the room and was now sitting next to me on the sofa. He waited for me to look at him, and when I didn't he reached out and took my hand. Gently, as if he were unfolding the petals of a rose, he peeled open my fingers and dropped something into them. I felt the cold of the blade before I saw it, and sensed the blood even before I glimpsed the red streak staining my palm.

The knife was small, only five or six inches long and very thin. The blade glowed crimson. I rubbed my thumb and index finger together, then brought them to my nose and inhaled. Metallic. It was definitely blood. Not mine — he'd merely handed me the knife — but whose?

'If you're smart, Siddle Lister,' Shawn said, 'you'll use this on yourself. Because it will be better than what I'll do to you if you don't.'

'That's uncalled for,' Mother said.

I gaped at Mother, then at Shawn. I must have

seemed like an idiot to them, but I couldn't grasp what was happening well enough to respond to it. I half-wondered if I should return to the bathroom and climb through the mirror, then send out the other girl, the one who was sixteen. *She* could handle this, I thought. She would not be afraid, like I was. She would not be hurt, like I was. She was a thing of stone, with no fleshy tenderness. I did not yet understand that it was this fact of being tender — of having lived some years of a life that allowed tenderness — that would, finally, save me.

I stared at the blade. Dad began a lecture, pausing often so Mother could ratify his remarks. I heard voices, among them my own, chanting harmonies in an ancient hall. I heard laughter, the slosh of wine being poured from a bottle, the tinkle of butter knives tapping porcelain. I heard little of my father's speech, but I remember exactly, as if it were happening now, being transported over an ocean and back through three sunsets, to the night I had sung with my friends in the chamber choir. *I must have fallen asleep*, I thought. *Too much wine. Too much Christmas turkey.*

Having decided I was dreaming, I did what one does in dreams: I tried to understand and use the rules of this queer reality. I reasoned with the strange shadows impersonating my family, and when reasoning failed, I lied. The impostors had bent reality. Now it was my turn. I told Shawn I hadn't said anything to Dad. I said things like 'I don't know how Dad got that idea' and 'Dad must have misheard me,' hoping that if

I rejected their percipience, they would simply dissipate. An hour later, when the four of us were still seated on the sofas, I finally came to terms with their physical persistence. They were here, and so was I.

The blood on my hands had dried. The knife lay on the carpet, forgotten by everyone except me. I tried not to stare at it. Whose was the blood? I studied my brother. He had not cut himself.

Dad had begun a new lecture, and this time I was present enough to hear it. He explained that little girls need to be instructed in how to behave appropriately around men, so as not to be too inviting. He'd noticed indecent habits in my sister's daughters, the oldest of whom was six. Shawn was calm. He had been worn down by the sheer duration of Dad's droning. More than that, he felt protected, justified, so that when the lecture finally ended he said to me, 'I don't know what you said to Dad tonight, but I can tell just by looking at you that I've hurt you. And I'm sorry.'

We hugged. We laughed like we always did after a fight. I smiled at him like I'd always done, like *she* would have. But *she* wasn't there, and the smile was a fake.

★ ★ ★

I went to my room and shut the door, quietly sliding the bolt, and called Drew. I was nearly incoherent with panic but eventually he understood. He said I should leave, right now, and he'd meet me halfway. I can't, I said. At this moment things are calm. If I try to run off in the middle of the night, I don't know what will happen.

I went to bed but not to sleep. I waited until six in the morning, then I found Mother in the kitchen. I'd borrowed the car I was driving from Drew, so I told Mother something had come up unexpectedly, that Drew needed his car in Salt Lake. I said I'd be back in a day or two.

A few minutes later I was driving down the hill. The highway was in sight when I saw something and stopped. It was the trailer where Shawn lived with Emily and Peter. A few feet from the trailer, near the door, the snow was stained with blood. Something had died there.

From Mother I would later learn it was Diego, a German shepherd Shawn had purchased a few years before. The dog had been a pet, much beloved by Peter. After Dad had called, Shawn had stepped outside and slashed the dog to death, while his young son, only feet away, listened to the dog scream. Mother said the execution had nothing to do with me, that it had to be done because Diego was killing Luke's chickens. It was a coincidence, she said.

I wanted to believe her but didn't. Diego had been killing Luke's chickens for more than a year. Besides, Diego was a purebred. Shawn had paid five hundred dollars for him. He could have been sold.

But the real reason I didn't believe her was the knife. I'd seen my father and brothers put down dozens of dogs over the years — strays mostly,

406

that wouldn't stay out of the chicken coop. I'd never seen anyone use a knife on a dog. We shot them, in the head or the heart, so it was quick. But Shawn chose a knife, and a knife whose blade was barely bigger than his thumb. It was the knife you'd choose to experience a slaughter, to feel the blood running down your hand the moment the heart stopped beating. It wasn't the knife of a farmer, or even of a butcher. It was a knife of rage.

I don't know what happened in the days that followed. Even now, as I scrutinize the components of the confrontation — the threat, the denial, the lecture, the apology — it is difficult to relate them. When I considered it weeks later, it seemed I had made a thousand mistakes, driven a thousand knives into the heart of my own family. Only later did it occur to me that whatever damage was done that night might not have been done solely by me. And it was more than a year before I understood what should have been immediately apparent: that my mother had not confronted my father and my father had not confronted Shawn. Dad had never promised to help me and Audrey. Mother had lied.

Now, when I reflect on my mother's words, remembering the way they appeared as if by magic on the screen, one detail stands above the rest: that Mother described my father as bipolar. It was the exact disorder that I myself suspected. It was *my* word, not hers. Then I wonder if perhaps my mother, who had always reflected so perfectly the will of my father, had that night merely been reflecting mine.

No, I tell myself. They were her words. But hers or not, those words, which had so comforted and healed me, were hollow. I don't believe they were faithless, but sincerity failed to give them substance, and they were swept away by other, stronger currents.

35

West of the Sun

I fled the mountain with my bags half packed and did not retrieve anything that was left behind. I went to Salt Lake and spent the rest of the holidays with Drew.

I tried to forget that night. For the first time in fifteen years, I closed my journal and put it away. Journaling is contemplative, and I didn't want to contemplate anything.

After the New Year I returned to Cambridge, but I withdrew from my friends. I had seen the earth tremble, felt the preliminary shock; now I waited for the seismic event that would transform the landsape. I knew how it would begin. Shawn would think about what Dad had told him on the phone, and sooner or later he would realize that my denial — my claim that Dad had misunderstood me — was a lie. When he realized the truth, he would despise himself for perhaps an hour. Then he would transfer his loathing to me.

It was early March when it happened. Shawn sent me an email. It contained no greeting, no message whatsoever. Just a chapter from the Bible, from Matthew, with a single verse set apart in bold: *O generation of vipers, how can ye, being evil, speak good things?* It froze my blood.

Shawn called an hour later. His tone was casual, and we talked for twenty minutes about Peter, about how his lungs were developing. Then he said, 'I have a decision to make, and I'd like your advice.'

'Sure.'

'I can't decide,' he said. He paused, and I thought perhaps the connection had failed. 'Whether I should kill you myself, or hire an assassin.' There was a static-filled silence. 'It might be cheaper to hire someone, when you figure in the cost of the flight.'

I pretended I hadn't understood, but this only made him aggressive. Now he was hurling insults, snarling. I tried to calm him but it was pointless. We were seeing each other at long last. I hung up on him but he called again, and again and again, each time repeating the same lines, that I should watch my back, that his assassin was coming for me. I called my parents.

'He didn't mean it,' Mother said. 'Anyway, he doesn't have that kind of money.'

'Not the point,' I said.

Dad wanted evidence. 'You didn't record the call?' he said. 'How am I supposed to know if he was serious?'

'He sounded like he did when he threatened me with the bloody knife,' I said.

'Well, he wasn't serious about that.'

'Not the point,' I said again.

The phone calls stopped, eventually, but not because of anything my parents did. They stopped when Shawn cut me out of his life. He wrote, telling me to stay away from his wife and child, and to stay the hell away from him. The email was long, a thousand words of accusation and bile, but by the end his tone was mournful. He said he loved his brothers, that they were the best men he knew. *I loved you the best of all of them,* he wrote, *but you had a knife in my back the whole time.*

It had been years since I'd had a relationship with my brother, but the loss of it, even with months of foreknowledge, stunned me.

My parents said he was justified in cutting me off. Dad said I was hysterical, that I'd thrown thoughtless accusations when it was obvious my memory couldn't be trusted. Mother said my rage was a real threat and that Shawn had a right to protect his family. 'Your anger that night,' she told me on the phone, meaning the night Shawn had killed Diego, 'was twice as dangerous as Shawn has ever been.'

Reality became fluid. The ground gave way beneath my feet, dragging me downward, spinning fast, like sand rushing through a hole in the bottom of the universe. The next time we spoke, Mother told me that the knife had never been meant as a threat. 'Shawn was trying to make you more comfortable,' she said. 'He knew you'd be scared if *he* were holding a knife, so he gave it to you.' A week later she said there had never been any knife at all.

'Talking to you,' she said, 'your reality is so *warped*. It's like talking to someone who wasn't even there.'

I agreed. It was exactly like that.

I had a grant to study that summer in Paris. Drew came with me. Our flat was in the sixth arrondissement, near the Luxembourg Gardens. My life there was entirely new, and as near to a cliché as I could make it. I was drawn to those parts of the city where one could find the most tourists so I could throw myself into their center. It was a hectic form of forgetting, and I spent the summer in pursuit of it: of losing myself in swarms of travelers, allowing myself to be wiped clean of all personality and character, of all history. The more crass the attraction, the more I was drawn to it.

I had been in Paris for several weeks when, one afternoon, returning from a French lesson, I stopped at a café to check my email. There was a message from my sister.

My father had visited her — this I understood immediately — but I had to read the message several times before I understood what exactly had taken place. Our father had testified to her that Shawn had been cleansed by the Atonement of Christ, that he was a new man. Dad had warned Audrey that if she ever again brought up the past, it would destroy our entire family. It was God's will that Audrey and I forgive Shawn, Dad said. If we did not, ours would be the greater sin.

I could easily imagine this meeting, the gravity of my father as he sat across from my sister, the reverence and power in his words.

Audrey told Dad that she had accepted the

power of the Atonement long ago, and had forgiven her brother. She said that I had provoked her, had stirred up anger in her. That I had betrayed her because I'd given myself over to fear, the realm of Satan, rather than walking in faith with God. I was dangerous, she said, because I was controlled by that fear, and by the Father of Fear, Lucifer.

That is how my sister ended her letter, by telling me I was not welcome in her home, or even to call her unless someone else was on the line to supervise, to keep her from succumbing to my influence. When I read this, I laughed out loud. The situation was perverse but not without irony: a few months before, Audrey had said that Shawn should be supervised around children. Now, after our efforts, the one who would be supervised was me.

★ ★ ★

When I lost my sister, I lost my family.

I knew my father would pay my brothers the same visit he'd paid her. Would they believe him? I thought they would. After all, Audrey would confirm it. My denials would be meaningless, the rantings of a stranger. I'd wandered too far, changed too much, bore too little resemblance to the scabby-kneed girl they remembered as their sister.

There was little hope of overpowering the history my father and sister were creating for me. Their account would claim my brothers first, then it would spread to my aunts, uncles,

413

cousins, the whole valley. I had lost an entire kinship, and for what?

It was in this state of mind that I received another letter: I had won a visiting fellowship to Harvard. I don't think I have ever received a piece of news with more indifference. I knew I should be drunk with gratitude that I, an ignorant girl who'd crawled out of a scrap heap, should be allowed to study there, but I couldn't summon the fervor. I had begun to conceive of what my education might cost me, and I had begun to resent it.

★ ★ ★

After I read Audrey's letter, the past shifted. It started with my memories of her. They transformed. When I recalled any part of our childhood together, moments of tenderness or humor, of the little girl who had been me with the little girl who had been her, the memory was immediately changed, blemished, turned to rot. The past became as ghastly as the present.

The change was repeated with every member of my family. My memories of them became ominous, indicting. The female child in them, who had been me, stopped being a child and became something else, something threatening and ruthless, something that would consume them.

This monster child stalked me for a month before I found a logic to banish her: that I was likely insane. If I was insane, everything could be made to make sense. If I was sane, nothing could. This logic seemed damning. It was also a

414

relief. I was not evil; I was clinical.

I began to defer, always, to the judgment of others. If Drew remembered something differently than I did, I would immediately concede the point. I began to rely on Drew to tell me the facts of our lives. I took pleasure in doubting myself about whether we'd seen a particular friend last week or the week before, or whether our favorite *crêperie* was next to the library or the museum. Questioning these trivial facts, and my ability to grasp them, allowed me to doubt whether anything I remembered had happened at all.

My journals were a problem. I knew that my memories were not memories only, that I had recorded them, that they existed in black and white. This meant that more than my memory was in error. The delusion was deeper, in the core of my mind, which invented in the very moment of occurrence, then recorded the fiction.

In the month that followed, I lived the life of a lunatic. Seeing sunshine, I suspected rain. I felt a relentless desire to ask people to verify whether they were seeing what I was seeing. Is this book blue? I wanted to ask. Is that man tall?

Sometimes this skepticism took the form of uncompromising certainty: there were days when the more I doubted my own sanity, the more violently I defended my own memories, my own 'truth,' as the only truth possible. Shawn was violent, dangerous, and my father was his protector. I couldn't bear to hear any other opinion on the subject.

In those moments I searched feverishly for a reason to think myself sane. Evidence. I craved it like air. I wrote to Erin — the woman Shawn had dated before and after Sadie, who I hadn't seen since I was sixteen. I told her what I remembered and asked her, bluntly, if I was deranged. She replied immediately that I was not. To help me trust myself, she shared her memories — of Shawn screaming at her that she was a whore. My mind snagged on that word. I had not told her that that was *my* word.

Erin told me another story. Once, when she had talked back to Shawn — just a little, she said, as if her manners were on trial — he'd ripped her from her house and slammed her head against a brick wall so hard she'd thought he was going to kill her. His hands locked around her throat. *I was lucky*, she wrote. *I had screamed before he began choking me, and my grandpa heard it and stopped him in time. But I know what I saw in his eyes.*

Her letter was like a handrail fixed to reality, one I could reach out and grasp when my mind began to spin. That is, until it occurred to me that she might be as crazy as I was. She was damaged, obviously, I told myself. How could I trust her account after what she'd been through? I could not give this woman credence because I, of all people, knew how crippling her psychological injuries were. So I continued searching for testimony from some other source.

Four years later, by pure chance, I would get it.

While traveling in Utah for research, I would meet a young man who would bristle at my last name.

'Westover,' he would say, his face darkening. 'Any relation to Shawn?'

'My brother.'

'Well, the last time I saw your *brother*,' he would say, emphasizing this last word as if he were spitting on it, 'he had both hands wrapped around my cousin's neck, and he was smashing her head into a brick wall. He would have killed her, if it weren't for my grandfather.'

And there it was. A witness. An impartial account. But by the time I heard it, I no longer needed to hear it. The fever of self-doubt had broken long ago. That's not to say I trusted my memory absolutely, but I trusted it as much as I trusted anybody else's, and more than some people's.

But that was years away.

36

Four Long Arms, Whirling

It was a sunny September afternoon when I heaved my suitcase through Harvard Yard. The colonial architecture felt foreign but also crisp and unimposing compared to the Gothic pinnacles of Cambridge. The central library, called the Widener, was the largest I had ever seen, and for a few minutes I forgot the past year and stared up at it, wonderstruck.

My room was in the graduate dorms near the law school. It was small and cavelike — dark, moist, frigid, with ashen walls and cold tiles the color of lead. I spent as little time in it as possible. The university seemed to offer a new beginning, and I intended to take it. I enrolled in every course I could squeeze into my schedule, from German idealism to the history of secularism to ethics and law. I joined a weekly study group to practice French, and another to learn knitting. The graduate school offered a free course on charcoal sketching. I had never drawn in my life but I signed up for that, too.

I began to read — Hume, Rousseau, Smith, Godwin, Wollstonecraft and Mill. I lost myself in the world they had lived in, the problems they had tried to solve. I became obsessed with their ideas about the family — with how a person ought to weigh their special obligations to kin

418

against their obligations to society as a whole. Then I began to write, weaving the strands I'd found in Hume's *Principles of Morals* with filaments from Mill's *The Subjection of Women*. It was good work, I knew it even as I wrote it, and when I'd finished I set it aside. It was the first chapter of my PhD.

I returned from my sketching class one Saturday morning to find an email from my mother. We're coming to Harvard, she said. I read that line at least three times, certain she was joking. My father did not travel — I'd never known him to go anywhere except Arizona to visit his mother — so the idea that he would fly across the country to see a daughter he believed taken by the devil seemed ludicrous. Then I understood: he was coming to save me. Mother said they had already booked their flights and would be staying in my dorm room.

'Do you want a hotel?' I asked. They didn't.

★   ★   ★

A few days later, I signed in to an old chat program I hadn't used in years. There was a cheerful jingle and a name turned from gray to green. *Charles is online*, it said. I'm not sure who started the chat, or who suggested moving the conversation to the phone. We talked for an hour, and it was as if no time had passed.

He asked where I was studying; when I answered, he said, 'Harvard! Holy hell!'

'Who woulda thought?' I said.

'I did,' he said, and it was true. He had always

419

seen me like that, long before there was any reason to.

I asked what he'd done after graduating from college and there was a strained silence. 'Things didn't go the way I planned,' he said. He'd never graduated. He'd dropped out his sophomore year after his son was born, because his wife was sick and there was a mound of medical bills. He'd signed on to work the oil rigs in Wyoming. 'It was only supposed to be for a few months,' he said. 'That was a year ago.'

I told him about Shawn, how I'd lost him, how I was losing the rest of my family. He listened quietly, then let out a long sigh and said, 'Have you ever thought maybe you should just let them go?'

I hadn't, not once. 'It's not permanent,' I said. 'I can fix it.'

'Funny how you can change so much,' Charles said, 'but still sound the same as when we were seventeen.'

★　★　★

My parents arrived as the leaves began to turn, when campus was at its most beautiful, the reds and yellows of autumn mingling with the burgundy of colonial brick. With his hay-seed grammar, denim shirt and lifetime-member NRA cap, Dad would have always been out of place at Harvard, but his scarring intensified the effect. I had seen him many times in the years since the explosion, but it wasn't until he came to Harvard, and I saw him set against my life

420

there, that I realized how severely he'd disfigured himself. That awareness reached me through the eyes of others — strangers whose faces changed when he passed them in the street, who turned to get a second look. Then I would look at him, too, and notice how the skin on his chin was taut and plastic; how his lips lacked natural roundness; how his cheeks sucked inward at an angle that was almost skeletal. His right hand, which he often raised to point at some feature or other, was knotted and twisted, and when I gazed at it, set against Harvard's antediluvian steeples and columns, it seemed to me the claw of some mythical creature.

Dad had little interest in the university, so I took him into the city. I taught him how to take the T — how to feed his card through the slot and push through the rotating gate. He laughed out loud, as if it were a fabulous technology. A homeless man passed through our subway car and asked for a dollar. Dad gave him a crisp fifty.

'You keep that up in Boston, you won't have any money left,' I said.

'Doubt it,' Dad said with a wink. 'The business is rolling. We got more than we can spend!'

Because his health was fragile, my father took the bed. I had purchased an air mattress, which I gave to Mother. I slept on the tile floor. Both my parents snored loudly, and I lay awake all night. When the sun finally rose I stayed on the floor, eyes closed, breathing slow, deep breaths, while my parents ransacked my mini fridge and discussed me in hushed tones.

'The Lord has commanded me to testify,' Dad said. 'She may yet be brought to the Lord.'

While they plotted how to reconvert me, I plotted how to let them. I was ready to yield, even if it meant an exorcism. A miracle would be useful: if I could stage a convincing rebirth, I could dissociate from everything I'd said and done in the last year. I could take it all back — blame Lucifer and be given a clean slate. I imagined how esteemed I would be, as a newly cleansed vessel. How loved. All I had to do was swap my memories for theirs, and I could have my family.

My father wanted to visit the Sacred Grove in Palmyra, New York — the forest where, according to Joseph Smith, God had appeared and commanded him to found the true church. We rented a car and six hours later entered Palmyra. Near the grove, off the highway, there was a shimmering temple topped by a golden statue of the angel Moroni. Dad pulled over and asked me to cross the temple grounds. 'Touch the temple,' he said. 'Its power will cleanse you.'

I studied his face. His expression was stretched — earnest, desperate. With all that was in him, he was willing me to touch the temple and be saved.

My father and I looked at the temple. He saw God; I saw granite. We looked at each other. He saw a woman damned; I saw an unhinged old man, literally disfigured by his beliefs. And yet, triumphant. I remembered the words of Sancho Panza: *An adventuring knight is someone who's beaten and then finds himself emperor.*

When I reflect on that moment now, the image blurs, reconstituting itself into that of a zealous knight astride a steed, charging into an imaginary battle, striking at shadows, hacking into thin air. His jaw is set, his back straight. His eyes blaze with conviction, throwing sparks that burn where they lie. My mother gives me a pale, disbelieving look, but when he turns his gaze on her they become of one mind, then they are both tilting at windmills.

I crossed the grounds and held my palm to the temple stone. I closed my eyes and tried to believe that this simple act could bring the miracle my parents prayed for. That all I had to do was touch this relic and, by the power of the Almighty, all would be put right. But I felt nothing. Just cold rock.

I returned to the car. 'Let's go,' I said.

When life itself seems lunatic, who knows where madness lies?

In the days that followed, I wrote that passage everywhere — unconsciously, compulsively. I find it now in books I was reading, in my lecture notes, in the margins of my journal. Its recitation was a mantra. I willed myself to believe it — to believe there was no real difference between what I knew to be true and what I knew to be false. To convince myself that there was some dignity in what I planned to do, in surrendering my own perceptions of right and wrong, of reality, of sanity itself, to earn the love of my parents. For them I believed I could don armor and charge at giants, even if I saw only windmills.

We entered the Sacred Grove. I walked ahead

and found a bench beneath a canopy of trees. It was a lovely wood, heavy with history. It was the reason my ancestors had come to America. A twig snapped, my parents appeared. They sat, one on either side of me.

My father spoke for two hours. He testified that he had beheld angels and demons. He had seen physical manifestations of evil and had been visited by the Lord Jesus Christ, like the prophets of old, like Joseph Smith had been in this very grove. His faith was no longer a faith, he said, but a perfect knowledge.

'You have been taken by Lucifer,' he whispered, his hand on my shoulder. 'I could feel it the moment I entered your room.'

I thought of my dorm room — of the murky walls and frigid tiles, but also of the sunflowers Drew had sent, and of the textile wall hanging a friend from Zimbabwe had brought from his village.

Mother said nothing. She stared at the dirt, her eyes glossy, her lips pursed. Dad prodded me for a response. I searched myself, reaching deep, groping for the words he needed to hear. But they were not in me, not yet.

Before we returned to Harvard, I convinced my parents to take a detour to Niagara Falls. The mood in the car was heavy, and at first I regretted having suggested the diversion, but the moment Dad saw the falls he was transformed, elated. I had a camera. Dad had always hated cameras but when he saw mine his eyes shone with excitement. 'Tara! Tara!' he shouted, running ahead of me and Mother. 'Get yourself a picture of this angle. Ain't that pretty!' It was as if he realized we were making a memory, something beautiful we might need later. Or perhaps I'm projecting, because that was how I felt. *There are some photos from today that might help me forget the grove,* I wrote in my journal. *There's a picture of me and Dad happy, together. Proof that's possible.*

★   ★   ★

When we returned to Harvard, I offered to pay for a hotel. They refused to go. For a week we stumbled over one another in my dorm room. Every morning my father trudged up a flight of stairs to the communal shower in nothing but a small white towel. This would have humiliated me at BYU, but at Harvard I shrugged. I had transcended embarrassment. What did it matter who saw him, or what he said to them, or how shocked they were? It was *his* opinion I cared about; he was the one I was losing.

Then it was their last night, and still I had not been reborn.

Mother and I shuffled around the shared kitchen making a beef and potato casserole, which we brought into the room on trays. My father studied his plate quietly, as if he were alone. Mother made a few observations about the food, then she laughed nervously and was silent.

When we'd finished, Dad said he had a gift for me. 'It's why I came,' he said. 'To offer you a priesthood blessing.'

In Mormonism, the priesthood is God's power

425

to act on earth — to advise, to counsel, to heal the sick, and to cast out demons. It is given to men. This was the moment: if I accepted the blessing, he would cleanse me. He would lay his hands on my head and cast out the evil thing that had made me say what I had said, that had made me unwelcome in my own family. All I had to do was yield, and in five minutes it would be over.

I heard myself say no.

Dad gaped at me in disbelief, then he began to testify — not about God, but about Mother. The herbs, he said, were a divine calling from the Lord. Everything that happened to our family, every injury, every near death, was because we had been chosen, we were special. God had orchestrated all of it so we could denounce the Medical Establishment and testify of His power.

'Remember when Luke burned his leg?' Dad said, as if I could forget. 'That was the Lord's plan. It was a curriculum. For your mother. So she would be ready for what would happen to me.'

The explosion, the burn. It was the highest of spiritual honors, he said, to be made a living testament of God's power. Dad held my hands in his mangled fingers and told me that his disfiguration had been foreordained. That it was a tender mercy, that it had brought souls to God.

Mother added her testimony in low, reverent whispers. She said she could stop a stroke by adjusting a chakra; that she could halt heart attacks using only energy; that she could cure cancer if people had faith. She herself had had

426

breast cancer, she said, and she had cured it.

My head snapped up. 'You have cancer?' I said. 'You're sure? You had it tested?'

'I didn't need to have it tested,' she said. 'I muscle-tested it. It was cancer. I cured it.'

'We could have cured Grandma, too,' Dad said. 'But she turned away from Christ. She lacked faith and that's why she's dead. God won't heal the faithless.'

Mother nodded but never looked up.

'Grandma's sin was serious,' Dad said. 'But your sins are more serious still, because you were given the truth and have turned from it.'

The room was quiet except for the dull hum of traffic on Oxford Street.

Dad's eyes were fixed on me. It was the gaze of a seer, of a holy oracle whose power and authority were drawn from the very universe. I wanted to meet it head-on, to prove I could withstand its weight, but after a few seconds something in me buckled, some inner force gave way, and my eyes dropped to the floor.

'I am called of God to testify that disaster lies ahead of you,' Dad said. 'It is coming soon, very soon, and it will break you, break you utterly. It will knock you down into the depths of humility. And when you are there, when you are lying broken, you will call on the Divine Father for mercy.' Dad's voice, which had risen to fever pitch, now fell to a murmur. 'And He will not hear you.'

I met his gaze. He was burning with conviction; I could almost feel the heat rolling off him. He leaned forward so that his face was

427

nearly touching mine and said, 'But I will.'

The silence settled, undisturbed, oppressive.

'I will offer, one final time, to give you a blessing,' he said.

The blessing was a mercy. He was offering me the same terms of surrender he had offered my sister. I imagined what a relief it must have been for her, to realize she could trade her reality — the one she shared with me — for his. How grateful she must have felt to pay such a modest price. I could not judge her for her choice, but in that moment I knew I could not choose it for myself. Everything I had worked for, all my years of study, had been to purchase for myself this one privilege: to see and experience more truths than those given to me by my father, and to use those truths to construct my own mind. I had come to believe that the ability to evaluate many ideas, many histories, many points of view, was at the heart of what it means to self-create. If I yielded now, I would lose more than an argument. I would lose custody of my own mind. This was the price I was being asked to pay, I understood that now. What my father wanted to cast from me wasn't a demon: it was me.

Dad reached into his pocket and withdrew a vial of consecrated oil, which he placed in my palm. I studied it. This oil was the only thing needed to perform the ritual, that and the holy authority resting in my father's misshapen hands. I imagined my surrender, imagined closing my eyes and recanting my blasphemies. I imagined how I would describe my change, my divine transformation, what words of gratitude I would shout. The words were ready, fully formed and waiting to leave my lips.

But when my mouth opened they vanished.

'I love you,' I said. 'But I can't. I'm sorry, Dad.'

My father stood abruptly.

He said again there was an evil presence in my room, that he couldn't stay another night. Their flight was not until morning, but Dad said it was better to sleep on a bench than with the devil.

My mother bustled about the room, shoveling shirts and socks into their suitcase. Five minutes later, they were gone.

37

Gambling for Redemption

Someone was screaming, a long, steady holler, so loud it woke me up. It was dark. There were streetlights, pavement, the rumble of distant cars. I was standing in the middle of Oxford Street, half a block from my dorm room. My feet were bare, and I was wearing a tank top and flannel pajama bottoms. It felt like people were gawking at me, but it was two in the morning and the street was empty.

Somehow I got back into my building, then I sat on my bed and tried to reconstruct what had happened. I remembered going to sleep. I remembered the dream. What I did *not* remember was flying from my bed and sprinting down the hall and into the street, shouting, but that is what I had done.

The dream had been of home. Dad had built a maze on Buck's Peak and trapped me inside it. The walls were ten feet high and made of supplies from his root cellar — sacks of grain, cases of ammunition, drums of honey. I was searching for something, something precious I could never replace. I had to escape the maze to recover it, but I couldn't find the way out, and Dad was pursuing me, sealing the exits with sacks of grain stacked into barricades.

I stopped going to my French group, then to my sketching class. Instead of reading in the library or attending lectures, I watched TV in my room, working my way through every popular series from the past two decades. When one episode ended, I would begin the next without thinking, the way one breath follows another. I watched TV eighteen or twenty hours a day. When I slept I dreamed of home, and at least once a week I awoke standing in the street in the middle of the night, wondering if it was my own cry that I'd heard just before waking.

I did not study. I tried to read but the sentences meant nothing. I needed them to mean nothing. I couldn't bear to string sentences into strands of thought, or to weave those strands into ideas. Ideas were too similar to reflection, and my reflections were always of the expression on my father's stretched face the moment before he'd fled from me.

The thing about having a mental breakdown is that no matter how obvious it is that you're having one, it is somehow not obvious to you. *I'm fine*, you think. *So what if I watched TV for twenty-four straight hours yesterday. I'm not falling apart. I'm just lazy.* Why it's better to think yourself lazy than think yourself in distress, I'm not sure. But it *was* better. More than better: it was vital.

By December I was so far behind in my work that, pausing one night to begin a new episode of *Breaking Bad*, I realized that I might fail my

PhD. I laughed maniacally for ten minutes at this irony: that having sacrificed my family to my education, I might lose that, also.

After a few more weeks of this, I stumbled from my bed one night and decided that I'd made a mistake, that when my father had offered me the blessing, I should have accepted it. But it wasn't too late. I could repair the damage, put it right.

I purchased a ticket to Idaho for Christmas. Two days before the flight, I awoke in a cold sweat. I'd dreamed I was in a hospital, lying on crisp white sheets. Dad was at the foot of the gurney, telling a policeman I had stabbed myself. Mother echoed him, her eyes panicked. I was surprised to hear Drew's voice, shouting that I needed to be moved to another hospital. 'He'll find her here,' he kept saying.

I wrote to Drew, who was living in the Middle East. I told him I was going to Buck's Peak. When he replied his tone was urgent and sharp, as if he was trying to cut through whatever fog I was living in. *My dear Tara*, he wrote. *If Shawn stabs you, you won't be taken to a hospital. You'll be put in the basement and given some lavender for the wound.* He begged me not to go, saying a hundred things I already knew and didn't care about, and when that didn't work, he said: *You told me your story so I could stop you if you ever did something crazy. Well, Tara, this is it. This is crazy.*

I can still fix this, I chanted as the plane lifted off the tarmac.

* * *

It was a bright winter morning when I arrived on Buck's Peak. I remember the crisp smell of frozen earth as I approached the house and the feel of ice and gravel crunching beneath my boots. The sky was a shocking blue. I breathed in the welcome scent of pine.

My gaze dropped below the mountain and my breath caught. When Grandma had been alive, she had, by nagging, shouting and threats, kept my father's junkyard contained. Now refuse covered the farm and was creeping toward the mountain base. The rolling hills, once perfect lakes of snow, were dotted with mangled trucks and rusted septic tanks.

Mother was ecstatic when I stepped through the door. I hadn't told her I was coming, hoping that, if no one knew, I might avoid Shawn. She talked rapidly, nervously. 'I'm going to make you biscuits and gravy!' she said, then flew to the kitchen.

'I'll help in a minute,' I said. 'I just need to send an email.'

The family computer was in the old part of the house, what had been the front room before the renovation. I sat down to write Drew, because I'd promised, as a kind of compromise between us, that while on the mountain I would write to him every two hours. I nudged the mouse and the screen flickered on. The browser was already open; someone had forgotten to sign out. I moved to open a different browser but stopped when I saw my name. It was in the message that was open on the screen, which Mother had sent only moments before. To Shawn's ex-girlfriend Erin.

The premise of the message was that Shawn had been reborn, spiritually cleansed. That the Atonement had healed our family, and that all had been restored. All except me. *The spirit has whispered to me the truth about my daughter,* Mother wrote. *My poor child has given herself over to fear, and that fear has made her desperate to validate her misperceptions. I do not know if she is a danger to our family, but I have reasons to think she might be.*[1]

I had known, even before reading the message, that my mother shared my father's dark vision, that she believed the devil had a hold of me, that I was dangerous. But there was something in seeing the words on the page, in reading them and hearing *her* voice in them, the voice of my mother, that turned my body cold.

There was more to the email. In the final paragraph, Mother described the birth of Emily's second child, a daughter, who had been born a month before. Mother had midwifed the child. The birth had taken place at home and, according to Mother, Emily had nearly bled to death before they could get to a hospital. Mother finished the story by testifying: God had worked through her hands that night, she said. The birth was a testament of His power.

---

[1] The italicized language in the description of the referenced email exchange is paraphrased, not directly quoted.

I remembered the drama of Peter's birth: how he'd slipped out of Emily weighing little more than a pound; how he'd been such a shocking shade of gray, they'd thought he was dead; how they'd fought through a snowstorm to the hospital in town, only to be told it wasn't enough, and there were no choppers flying; how two ambulances had been dispatched to McKay-Dee in Ogden. That a woman with this medical history, a woman so obviously high-risk, should be advised to attempt a second birth at home seemed reckless to the point of delusion.

If the first fall was God's will, whose was the second?

I was still wondering at the birth of my niece when Erin's response appeared. *You are right about Tara*, she said. *She is lost without faith.* Erin told Mother that my doubting myself — my writing to her, Erin, to ask if I might be mistaken, if my memories might be false — was evidence that my soul was in jeopardy, that I couldn't be trusted: *She is building her life on fear. I will pray for her.* Erin ended the message by praising my mother's skill as a midwife. *You are a true hero*, she wrote.

I closed the browser and stared at the wallpaper behind the screen. It was the same floral print from my childhood. For how long had I been dreaming of seeing it? I had come to reclaim that life, to save it. But there was nothing here to save, nothing to grasp. There was only shifting sand, shifting loyalties, shifting histories.

I remembered the dream, the maze. I remembered the walls made of grain sacks and ammunition boxes, of my father's fears and paranoias, his scriptures and prophecies. I had wanted to escape the maze with its disorienting switchbacks, its ever-modulating pathways, to find the precious thing. But now I understood: the precious thing, that was the maze. That's all that was left of the life I'd had here: a puzzle whose rules I would never understand, because they were not rules at all but a kind of cage meant to enclose me. I could stay, and search for what had been home, or I could go, now, before the walls shifted and the way out was shut.

Mother was sliding biscuits into the oven when I entered the kitchen. I looked around, mentally searching the house. *What do I need from this place?* There was only one thing: my memories. I found them under my bed, in a box, where I had left them. I carried them to the car and put them in the backseat.

'I'm going for a drive,' I told Mother. I tried to keep my voice smooth. I hugged her, then took a long look at Buck's Peak, memorizing every line and shadow. Mother had seen me take my journals to the car. She must have known what that meant, must have sensed the farewell in it, because she fetched my father. He gave me a stiff hug and said, 'I love you, you know that?'

'I do,' I said. 'That has never been the issue.'

Those words are the last I said to my father.

★ ★ ★

I drove south; I didn't know where I was going. It was nearly Christmas. I had decided to go to

436

the airport and board the next flight to Boston when Tyler called.

I hadn't spoken to my brother in months — after what happened with Audrey, it had seemed pointless to confide in my siblings. I was sure Mother would have told every brother, cousin, aunt and uncle the story she had told Erin: that I was possessed, dangerous, taken by the devil. I wasn't wrong: Mother *had* warned them. But then she made a mistake.

After I left Buck's Peak, she panicked. She was afraid I might contact Tyler, and that if I did, he might sympathize with me. She decided to get to Tyler first, to deny anything I might tell him, but she miscalculated. She didn't stop to think how the denials would sound, coming from nowhere like that.

'Of course Shawn didn't stab Diego and threaten Tara with the knife,' Mother reassured Tyler, but to Tyler, who had never heard any part of this story, not from me or anyone else, this was somewhat less than reassuring. A moment after he said goodbye to Mother, Tyler called me, demanding to know what had happened and why I hadn't come to him.

I thought he'd say I was lying but he didn't. He accepted almost immediately the reality I'd spent a year denying. I didn't understand why he was trusting me, but then he told me his own stories and I remembered: Shawn had been *his* older brother, too.

In the weeks that followed, Tyler began to test my parents in the subtle, nonconfrontational way that was uniquely his. He suggested that perhaps

437

the situation had been mishandled, that perhaps I was not possessed. Perhaps I was not evil at all.

I might have taken comfort in Tyler's trying to help me, but the memory of my sister was too raw, and I didn't trust him. I knew that if Tyler confronted my parents — really confronted them — they would force him to choose between me and them, between me and the rest of the family. And from Audrey I had learned: he would not choose me.

*　*　*

My fellowship at Harvard finished in the spring. I flew to the Middle East, where Drew was completing a Fulbright. It took some effort, but I managed to hide from Drew how poorly I was doing, or at least I thought I did. I probably didn't. He was, after all, the one chasing me through his flat when I awoke in the middle of the night, screaming and sprinting, with no idea where I was but a desperate need to escape it.

We left Amman and drove south. We were in a Bedouin camp in the Jordanian desert on the day the navy SEALs killed bin Laden. Drew spoke Arabic, and when the news broke he spent hours in conversation with our guides. 'He's no Muslim,' they told Drew as we sat on cold sand watching the dying flames of a campfire. 'He does not understand Islam, or he would not do the terrible things he's done.'

I watched Drew talk with the Bedouins, heard the strange, smooth sounds falling from his lips, and was struck by the implausibility of my

438

presence there. When the twin towers had fallen ten years before, I had never heard of Islam. Now I was drinking sugary tea with Zalabia Bedouins and squatting on a sand drift in Wadi Rum, the Valley of the Moon, less than twenty miles from the Saudi Arabian border.

The distance — physical and mental — that had been traversed in the last decade nearly stopped my breath, and I wondered if perhaps I had changed *too* much. All my studying, reading, thinking, traveling, had it transformed me into someone who no longer belonged anywhere? I thought of the girl who, knowing nothing beyond her junkyard and her mountain, had stared at a screen, watching as two planes sailed into strange white pillars. Her classroom was a heap of junk. Her textbooks, slates of scrap. And yet she had something precious that I — despite all my opportunities, or maybe because of them — did not.

★ ★ ★

I returned to England, where I continued to unravel. My first week back in Cambridge, I awoke nearly every night in the street, having run there, shouting, asleep. I developed headaches that lasted for days. My dentist said I was grinding my teeth. My skin broke out so severely that twice perfect strangers stopped me in the street and asked if I was having an allergic reaction. No, I said. I always look like this.

One evening, I got into an argument with a friend about something trivial, and before I knew what was happening I had pressed myself into the wall and was hugging my knees to my chest, trying to keep my heart from leaping out of my body. My friend rushed toward me to help and I screamed. It was an hour before I could let her touch me, before I could will myself away from the wall. *So that's a panic attack*, I thought the next morning.

Soon after, I sent a letter to my father. I'm not proud of that letter. It's full of rage, a fractious child screaming, 'I hate you' at a parent. It's filled with words like 'thug' and 'tyrant,' and it goes on for pages, a torrent of frustration and abuse.

That is how I told my parents I was cutting off contact with them. Between insults and fits of temper, I said I needed a year to heal myself; then perhaps I could return to their mad world to try to make sense of it.

My mother begged me to find another way. My father said nothing.

38

Family

I was failing my PhD.

If I had explained to my supervisor, Dr. Runciman, why I was unable to work, he would have helped me, would have secured additional funding, petitioned the department for more time. But I didn't explain, I couldn't. He had no idea why it had been nearly a year since I'd sent him work, so when we met in his office one overcast July afternoon, he suggested that I quit.

'The PhD is exceptionally demanding,' he said. 'It's okay if you can't do it.'

I left his office full of fury at myself. I went to the library and gathered half a dozen books, which I lugged to my room and arranged on my desk. But my mind was made nauseous by rational thought, and by the next morning the books had moved to my bed, where they propped up my laptop while I worked steadily through *Buffy the Vampire Slayer*.

★ ★ ★

That autumn, Tyler confronted my father. He talked to Mother first, on the phone. He called me after and related their conversation. He said Mother was 'on our side,' that she thought the situation with Shawn was unacceptable and had convinced Dad to do something. 'Dad is taking care of it,' Tyler said. 'Everything is going to be fine. You can come home.'

My phone rang again two days later, and I paused *Buffy* to answer it. It was Tyler. The whole thing had exploded in his face. He had felt uneasy after his conversation with Mother, so he had called Dad to see exactly what was being done about Shawn. Dad had become angry, aggressive. He'd shouted at Tyler that if he brought this up again, he would be disowned, then he'd hung up the phone.

I dislike imagining this conversation. Tyler's stutter was always worse when he talked to our father. I picture my brother hunched over the receiver, trying to concentrate, to push out the words that have jammed in his throat, while his father hurls an arsenal of ugly words.

Tyler was still reeling from Dad's threat when his phone rang. He thought it was Dad calling to apologize, but it was Shawn. Dad had told him everything. 'I can have you out of this family in two minutes,' Shawn said. 'You know I can do it. Just ask Tara.'

I listened to Tyler relate this story while staring at the frozen image of Sarah Michelle Gellar. Tyler talked for a long time, moving through the events quickly but lingering in a wasteland of rationalization and self-recrimination. Dad must have misunderstood, Tyler said. There had been a mistake, a miscommunication. Maybe it was *his* fault, maybe he hadn't said the right thing in the right way. That was it. *He* had done this, and *he* could repair it.

442

As I listened, I felt a strange sensation of distance that bordered on disinterestedness, as if my future with Tyler, this brother I had known and loved all my life, was a film I had already seen and knew the ending of. I knew the shape of this drama because I had lived it already, with my sister. This was the moment I had lost Audrey: this was the moment the costs had become real, when the tax was levied, the rent due. This was the moment she had realized how much easier it was to walk away: what a poor trade it was to swap an entire family for a single sister.

So I knew even before it happened that Tyler would go the same way. I could hear his hand-wringing through the long echo of the telephone. He was deciding what to do, but I knew something he did not: that the decision had already been made, and what he was doing now was just the long work of justifying it.

It was October when I got the letter.

It came in the form of a PDF attached to an email from Tyler and Stefanie. The message explained that the letter had been drafted carefully, thoughtfully, and that a copy would be sent to my parents. When I saw that, I knew what it meant. It meant Tyler was ready to denounce me, to say my father's words, that I was possessed, dangerous. The letter was a kind of voucher, a pass that would admit him back into the family.

I couldn't get myself to open the attachment; some instinct had seized my fingers. I remembered Tyler as he'd been when I was young, the quiet older brother reading his books while I lay under his desk, staring at his socks and breathing in his music. I wasn't sure I could bear it, to hear *those* words in *his* voice.

I clicked the mouse, the attachment opened. I was so far removed from myself that I read the entire letter without understanding it: *Our parents are held down by chains of abuse, manipulation, and control . . . They see change as dangerous and will exile anyone who asks for it. This is a perverted idea of family loyalty . . . They claim faith, but this is not what the gospel teaches. Keep safe. We love you.*

From Tyler's wife, Stefanie, I would learn the story of this letter, how in the days after my father had threatened disownment, Tyler had gone to bed every night saying aloud to himself, over and over, 'What am I supposed to do? She's my sister.'

When I heard this story, I made the only good decision I had made for months: I enrolled in the university counseling service. I was assigned to a sprightly middle-aged woman with tight curls and sharp eyes, who rarely spoke in our sessions, preferring to let me talk it out, which I did, week after week, month after month. The counseling did nothing at first — I can't think of a single session I would describe as 'helpful' — but their collective power over time was undeniable. I didn't understand it then, and I don't understand it now, but there was something nourishing in setting aside that time each week, in the act of admitting that I needed something I could not provide for myself.

Tyler did send the letter to my parents, and

once committed he never wavered. That winter I spent many hours on the phone with him and Stefanie, who became a sister to me. They were available whenever I needed to talk, and back then I needed to talk quite a lot.

Tyler paid a price for that letter, though the price is hard to define. He was not disowned, or at least his disownment was not permanent. Eventually he worked out a truce with my father, but their relationship may never be the same.

I've apologized to Tyler more times than I can count for what I've cost him, but the words are awkwardly placed and I stumble over them. What is the proper arrangement of words? How do you craft an apology for weakening someone's ties to his father, to his family? Perhaps there aren't words for that. How do you thank a brother who refused to let you go, who seized your hand and wrenched you upward just as you had decided to stop kicking, and sink? There aren't words for that, either.

* * *

Winter was long that year, the dreariness punctuated only by my weekly counseling sessions and the odd sense of loss, almost bereavement, I felt whenever I finished one TV series and had to find another.

Then it was spring, then summer, and finally as summer turned to fall, I found I could read with focus. I could hold thoughts in my head besides anger and self-accusation. I returned to the chapter I had written nearly two years before

445

at Harvard. Again I read Hume, Rousseau, Smith, Godwin, Wollstonecraft and Mill. Again I thought about the family. There was a puzzle in it, something unresolved. What is a person to do, I asked, when their obligations to their family conflict with *other* obligations — to friends, to society, to themselves?

I began the research. I narrowed the question, made it academic, specific. In the end, I chose four intellectual movements from the nineteenth century and examined how they had struggled with the question of family obligation. One of the movements I chose was nineteenth-century Mormonism. I worked for a solid year, and at the end of it I had a draft of my thesis: 'The Family, Morality, and Social Science in Anglo-American Cooperative Thought, 1813–1890.'

The chapter on Mormonism was my favorite. As a child in Sunday school, I'd been taught that all history was a preparation for Mormonism: that every event since the death of Christ had been fashioned by God to make possible the moment when Joseph Smith would kneel in the Sacred Grove and God would restore the one true church. Wars, migrations, natural disasters — these were mere preludes to the Mormon story. On the other hand, secular histories tended to overlook spiritual movements like Mormonism altogether.

My dissertation gave a different shape to history, one that was neither Mormon nor anti-Mormon, neither spiritual nor profane. It didn't treat Mormonism as the objective of human history, but neither did it discount the contribution Mormonism had made in grappling with the questions of the age. Instead, it treated the Mormon ideology as a chapter in the larger human story. In my account, history did not set Mormons apart from the rest of the human family; it bound them to it.

I sent Dr. Runciman the draft, and a few days later we met in his office. He sat across from me and, with a look of astonishment, said it was good. 'Some parts of it are very good,' he said. He was smiling now. 'I'll be surprised if it doesn't earn a doctorate.'

As I walked home carrying the heavy manuscript, I remembered attending one of Dr. Kerry's lectures, which he had begun by writing, 'Who writes history?' on the blackboard. I remembered how strange the question had seemed to me then. My idea of a historian was not human; it was of someone like my father, more prophet than man, whose visions of the past, like those of the future, could not be questioned, or even augmented. Now, as I passed through King's College, in the shadow of the enormous chapel, my old diffidence seemed almost funny. *Who writes history?* I thought. *I do.*

★ ★ ★

On my twenty-seventh birthday, the birthday I had chosen, I submitted my PhD dissertation. The defense took place in December, in a small, simply furnished room. I passed and returned to London, where Drew had a job and we'd rented a flat. In January, nearly ten years to the day

447

since I'd set foot in my first classroom at BYU, I received confirmation from the University of Cambridge: I was Dr. Westover.

I had built a new life, and it was a happy one, but I felt a sense of loss that went beyond family. I had lost Buck's Peak, not by leaving but by leaving silently. I had retreated, fled across an ocean and allowed my father to tell my story for me, to define me to everyone I had ever known. I had conceded too much ground — not just the mountain, but the entire province of our shared history.

It was time to go home.

39

Watching the Buffalo

It was spring when I arrived in the valley. I drove along the highway to the edge of town, then pulled over at the drop-off overlooking the Bear River. From there I could look out over the basin, a patchwork of expectant fields stretching to Buck's Peak. The mountain was crisp with evergreens, which were luminous set against the browns and grays of shale and limestone. The Princess was as bright as I'd ever seen her. She stood facing me, the valley between us, radiating permanence.

The Princess had been haunting me. From across the ocean I'd heard her beckoning, as if I were a troublesome calf who'd wandered from her herd. Her voice had been gentle at first, coaxing, but when I didn't answer, when I stayed away, it had turned to fury. I had betrayed her. I imagined her face contorted with rage, her stance heavy and threatening. She had been living in my mind like this for years, a deity of contempt.

But seeing her now, standing watch over her fields and pastures, I realized that I had misunderstood her. She was not angry with me for leaving, because *leaving* was a part of her cycle. Her role was not to corral the buffalo, not to gather and confine them by force. It was to celebrate their return.

I backtracked a quarter mile into town and parked beside Grandma-over-in-town's white picket fence. In my mind it was still *her* fence, even though she didn't live here anymore: she had been moved to a hospice facility near Main Street.

I had not seen my grandparents in three years, not since my parents had begun telling the extended family that I was possessed. My grandparents loved their daughter. I was sure they had believed her account of me. So I had surrendered them. It was too late to reclaim Grandma — she was suffering from Alzheimer's and would not have known me — so I had come to see my grandfather, to find out whether there would be a place for me in his life.

We sat in the living room; the carpet was the same crisp white from my childhood. The visit was short and polite. He talked about Grandma, whom he had cared for long after she ceased to recognize him. I talked about England. Grandpa mentioned my mother, and when he spoke of her it was with the same look of awe that I had seen in the faces of her followers. I didn't blame him. From what I'd heard, my parents were powerful people in the valley. Mother was marketing her products as a spiritual alternative to Obamacare, and she was selling product as fast as she could make it, even with dozens of employees.

God had to be behind such a wondrous success, Grandpa said. My parents must have been called by the Lord to do what they have done, to be great healers, to bring souls to God. I smiled and stood to go. He was the same gentle old man I remembered, but I was overwhelmed by the distance between us. I hugged him at the door, and gave him a long look. He was eighty-seven. I doubted whether, in the years he had left, I would be able to prove to him that I was not what my father said I was, that I was not a wicked thing.

★ ★ ★

Tyler and Stefanie lived a hundred miles north of Buck's Peak, in Idaho Falls. It was there I planned to go next, but before leaving the valley, I wrote my mother. It was a short message. I said I was nearby and wanted her to meet me in town. I wasn't ready to see Dad, I said, but it had been years since I'd seen her face. Would she come?

I waited for her reply in the parking lot at Stokes. I didn't wait long.

It pains me that you think it is acceptable to ask this. A wife does not go where her husband is not welcome. I will not be party to such blatant disrespect.[1]

The message was long and reading it made me tired, as if I'd run a great distance. The bulk of it was a lecture on loyalty: that families forgive, and that if I could not forgive mine, I would regret it for the rest of my life. *The past*, she wrote,

---

[1] The italicized language in the description of the referenced exchange is paraphrased, not directly quoted.

whatever it was, ought to be shoveled fifty feet under and left to rot in the earth.

Mother said I was welcome to come to the house, that she prayed for the day when I would run through the back door, shouting, 'I'm home!'

I wanted to answer her prayer — I was barely more than ten miles from the mountain — but I knew what unspoken pact I would be making as I walked through that door. I could have my mother's love, but there were terms, the same terms they had offered me three years before: that I trade my reality for theirs, that I take my own understanding and bury it, leave it to rot in the earth.

Mother's message amounted to an ultimatum: I could see her *and* my father, or I would never see her again. She has never recanted.

★ ★ ★

The parking lot had filled while I was reading. I let her words settle, then started the engine and pulled onto Main Street. At the intersection I turned west, toward the mountain. Before I left the valley, I would set eyes on my home.

Over the years I'd heard many rumors about my parents: that they were millionaires, that they were building a fortress on the mountain, that they had hidden away enough food to last decades. The most interesting, by far, were the stories about Dad hiring and firing employees. The valley had never recovered from the recession; people needed work. My parents were one of the largest employers in the county, but

452

from what I could tell Dad's mental state made it difficult for him to maintain employees long-term: when he had a fit of paranoia, he tended to fire people with little cause. Months before, he had fired Diane Hardy, Rob's ex-wife, the same Rob who'd come to fetch us after the second accident. Diane and Rob had been friends with my parents for twenty years. Until Dad fired Diane.

It was perhaps in another such fit of paranoia that Dad fired my mother's sister Angie. Angie had spoken to Mother, believing her sister would never treat family that way. When I was a child it had been Mother's business; now it was hers and Dad's together. But at this test of whose it was really, my father won: Angie was dismissed.

It is difficult to piece together what happened next, but from what I later learned, Angie filed for unemployment benefits, and when the Department of Labor called my parents to confirm that she had been terminated, Dad lost what little reason remained to him. It was not the Department of Labor on the phone, he said, but the Department of Homeland Security, pretending to be the Department of Labor. Angie had put his name on the terrorist watch list, he said. The Government was after him now — after his money and his guns and his fuel. It was Ruby Ridge all over again.

I pulled off the highway and onto the gravel, then stepped out of the car and gazed up at Buck's Peak. It was clear immediately that at least some of the rumors were true — for one, that my parents were making huge sums of money. The house was massive. The home I'd grown up in had had five bedrooms; now it had been expanded in all directions and looked as though it had at least forty.

It would only be a matter of time, I thought, before Dad started using the money to prepare for the End of Days. I imagined the roof lined with solar panels, laid out like a deck of cards. 'We need to be self-sufficient,' I imagined Dad would say as he dragged the panels across his titanic house. In the coming year, Dad would spend hundreds of thousands of dollars buying equipment and scouring the mountain for water. He didn't want to be dependent on the Government, and he knew Buck's Peak must have water, if he could only find it. Gashes the size of football fields would appear at the mountain base, leaving a desolation of broken roots and upturned trees where once there had been a forest. He was probably chanting, 'Got to be self-reliant' the day he climbed into a crawler and tore into the fields of satin wheat.

★ ★ ★

Grandma-over-in-town died on Mother's Day.

I was doing research in Colorado when I heard the news. I left immediately for Idaho, but while traveling realized I had nowhere to stay. It was then that I remembered my aunt Angie, and that my father was telling anyone who would listen that she had put his name on a terrorist watch list. Mother had cast her aside; I hoped I could reclaim her.

454

Angie lived next door to my grandfather, so again I parked along the white picket fence. I knocked. Angie greeted me politely, the way Grandpa had done. It was clear that she had heard much about me from my mother and father in the past five years.

'I'll make you a deal,' I said. 'I'll forget everything my dad has said about you, if you'll forget everything he's said about me.' She laughed, closing her eyes and throwing back her head in a way that nearly broke my heart, she looked so much like my mother.

I stayed with Angie until the funeral.

In the days before the service, my mother's siblings began to gather at their childhood home. They were my aunts and uncles, but some of them I hadn't seen since I was a child. My uncle Daryl, who I barely knew, suggested that his brothers and sisters should spend an afternoon together at a favorite restaurant in Lava Hot Springs. My mother refused to come. She would not go without my father, and he would have nothing to do with Angie.

It was a bright May afternoon when we all piled into a large van and set off on the hour-long drive. I was uncomfortably aware that I had taken my mother's place, going with her siblings and her remaining parent on an outing to remember her mother, a grandmother I had not known well. I soon realized that my not knowing her was wonderful for her children, who were bursting with remembrances and loved answering questions about her. With every story my grandmother came into sharper focus, but the woman taking shape from their collective memories was nothing like the woman I remembered. It was then I realized how cruelly I had judged her, how my perception of her had been distorted, because I'd been looking at her through my father's harsh lens.

During the drive back, my aunt Debbie invited me to visit her in Utah. My uncle Daryl echoed her. 'We'd love to have you in Arizona,' he said. In the space of a day, I had reclaimed a family — not mine, hers.

The funeral was the next day. I stood in a corner and watched my siblings trickle in.

There were Tyler and Stefanie. They had decided to home school their seven children, and from what I'd seen, the children were being educated to a very high standard. Luke came in next, with a brood so numerous I lost count. He saw me and crossed the room, and we made small talk for several minutes, neither of us acknowledging that we hadn't seen each other in half a decade, neither of us alluding to why. *Do you believe what Dad says about me?* I wanted to ask. *Do you believe I'm dangerous?* But I didn't. Luke worked for my parents, and without an education, he needed that job to support his family. Forcing him to take a side would only end in heartache.

Richard, who was finishing a PhD in chemistry, had come down from Oregon with Kami and their children. He smiled at me from the back of the chapel. A few months before, Richard had written to me. He'd said he was sorry for believing Dad, that he wished he'd done more to help me when I needed it, and that from then on, I could count on his support. We were family, he said.

Audrey and Benjamin chose a bench near the back. Audrey had arrived early, when the chapel was empty. She had grabbed my arm and whispered that my refusing to see our father was a grave sin. 'He is a great man,' she said. 'For the rest of your life you will regret not humbling yourself and following his counsel.' These were the first words my sister had said to me in years, and I had no response to them.

Shawn arrived a few minutes before the service, with Emily and Peter and a little girl I had never met. It was the first time I had been in a room with him since the night he'd killed Diego. I was tense, but there was no need. He did not look at me once during the service.

My oldest brother, Tony, sat with my parents, his five children fanning out in the pew. Tony had a GED and had built a successful trucking company in Las Vegas, but it hadn't survived the recession. Now he worked for my parents, as did Shawn and Luke and their wives, as well as Audrey and her husband, Benjamin. Now I thought about it, I realized that all my siblings, except Richard and Tyler, were economically dependent on my parents. My family was splitting down the middle — the three who had left the mountain, and the four who had stayed. The three with doctorates, and the four without high school diplomas. A chasm had appeared, and was growing.

★ ★ ★

A year would pass before I would return to Idaho.

A few hours before my flight from London, I wrote to my mother — as I always did, as I always will do — to ask if she would see me. Again, her response was swift. She would not, she would never, unless I would see my father. To see me without him, she said, would be to disrespect her husband.

For a moment it seemed pointless, this annual pilgrimage to a home that continued to reject me, and I wondered if I should go. Then I received another message, this one from Aunt Angie. She said Grandpa had canceled his plans for the next day, and was refusing even to go to the temple, as he usually did on Wednesdays, because he wanted to be at home in case I came by. To this Angie added: *I get to see you in about twelve hours! But who's counting?*

40

Educated

When I was a child, I waited for my mind to grow, for my experiences to accumulate and my choices to solidify, taking shape into the likeness of a person. That person, or that likeness of one, had belonged. I was *of* that mountain, the mountain that had made me. It was only as I grew older that I wondered if how I had started is how I would end — if the first shape a person takes is their only true shape.

As I write the final words of this story, I've not seen my parents in years, since my grandmother's funeral. I'm close to Tyler, Richard and Tony, and from them, as well as from other family, I hear of the ongoing drama on the mountain — the injuries, violence and shifting loyalties. But it comes to me now as distant hearsay, which is a gift. I don't know if the separation is permanent, if one day I will find a way back, but it has brought me peace.

That peace did not come easily. I spent two years enumerating my father's flaws, constantly updating the tally, as if reciting every resentment, every real and imagined act of cruelty, of neglect, would justify my decision to cut him from my life. Once justified, I thought the strangling guilt would release me and I could catch my breath.

But vindication has no power over guilt. No

amount of anger or rage directed at others can subdue it, because guilt is never about *them*. Guilt is the fear of one's own wretchedness. It has nothing to do with other people.

I shed my guilt when I accepted my decision on its own terms, without endlessly prosecuting old grievances, without weighing his sins against mine. Without thinking of my father at all. I learned to accept my decision for my own sake, because of me, not because of him. Because I needed it, not because he deserved it.

It was the only way I could love him.

When my father was in my life, wrestling me for control of that life, I perceived him with the eyes of a soldier, through a fog of conflict. I could not make out his tender qualities. When he was before me, towering, indignant, I could not remember how, when I was young, his laugh used to shake his gut and make his glasses shine. In his stern presence, I could never recall the pleasant way his lips used to twitch, before they were burned away, when a memory tugged tears from his eyes. I can only remember those things now, with a span of miles and years between us.

But what has come between me and my father is more than time or distance. It is a change in the self. I am not the child my father raised, but he is the father who raised her.

If there was a single moment when the breach between us, which had been cracking and splintering for two decades, was at last too vast to be bridged, I believe it was that winter night, when I stared at my reflection in the bathroom mirror, while, without my knowing it, my father

460

grasped the phone in his knotted hands and dialed my brother. Diego, the knife. What followed was very dramatic. But the real drama had already played out in the bathroom.

It had played out when, for reasons I don't understand, I was unable to climb through the mirror and send out my sixteen-year-old self in my place.

Until that moment she had always been there. No matter how much I appeared to have changed — how illustrious my education, how altered my appearance — I was still *her*. At best I was two people, a fractured mind. *She* was inside, and emerged whenever I crossed the threshold of my father's house.

That night I called on her and she didn't answer. She left me. She stayed in the mirror. The decisions I made after that moment were not the ones she would have made. They were the choices of a changed person, a new self.

You could call this selfhood many things. Transformation. Metamorphosis. Falsity. Betrayal.

I call it an education.

Acknowledgements

To my brothers Tyler, Richard and Tony I owe the greatest debt for making this book possible, first in the living of it, then in the writing of it. From them and their wives, Stefanie, Kami and Michele, I learned much of what I know about family.

Tyler and Richard in particular were generous with their time and their memories, reading multiple drafts, adding their own details, and in general helping me make the book as accurate as possible. Though our perspectives may have differed in some particulars, their willingness to verify the facts of this story enabled me to write it.

Professor David Runciman encouraged me to write this memoir and was among the first to read the manuscript. Without his confidence in it, I might never have had confidence in it myself.

I am grateful to those who make books their life's work and who gave a portion of that life to this book: my agents, Anna Stein and Karolina Sutton; and my wonderful editors, Hilary Redmon and Andy Ward at Random House, and Jocasta Hamilton at Hutchinson; as well as the many other people who worked to edit, typeset and launch this story. Most notably, Boaty Boatright at ICM was a tireless champion. Special thanks are owed to Ben Phelan, who was given the difficult task of fact checking this book, and who did so rigorously but with great sensitivity and professionalism.

I am especially grateful to those who believed in this book before it was a book, when it was just a jumble of home-printed papers. Among those early readers are Dr. Marion Kant, Dr. Paul Kerry, Annie Wilding, Livia Gainham, Sonya Teich, Dunni Alao and Suraya Sidhi Singh.

My aunts Debbie and Angie came back into my life at a crucial moment, and their support means everything. For believing in me, always, thanks to Professor Jonathan Steinberg. For granting me haven, emotional as well as practical, in which to write this book, I am indebted to my dear friend, Drew Mecham.

Notes

1   p. 2 Except for my sister Audrey, who broke an arm and a leg when she was young. She was taken to get a cast.

2   p. 28 While everyone agrees that there were many years in which my parents did not have a phone, there is considerable disagreement in the family about which years they were. I've asked my brothers, aunts, uncles and cousins, but I have not been able to definitively establish a timeline, and have therefore relied on my own memories.

3   p. 110 Since the writing of this story, I have spoken to Luke about the incident. His account differs from both mine and Richard's. In Luke's memory, Dad took Luke to the house, administered a homeopathic for shock, then put him in a tub of cold water, where he left him to go fight the fire. This goes against my memory, and against Richard's. Still, perhaps our memories are in error. Perhaps I found Luke in a tub, alone, rather than on the grass. What everyone agrees upon, strangely, is that somehow Luke ended up on the front lawn, his leg in a garbage can.

4   p. 183 My account of Shawn's fall is based on the story as it was told to me at the time. Tyler was told the same story; in fact, many of the details in this account come from his memory. Asked fifteen years later, others

remember it differently. Mother says Shawn was not standing on a pallet, only on forklift tines. Luke remembers the pallet, but substitutes a metal drain, with the grating removed, in place of the rebar. He says the fall was twelve feet, and that Shawn began acting strangely as soon as he regained consciousness. Luke has no memory of who dialed 9-11, but says there were men working in a nearby mill, and he suspects that one of them called immediately after Shawn fell.

5   p. 208 Asked fifteen years later, Dwain did not recall being there. But he is there, vividly, in my memory.

6   p. 309 It is possible that my timeline is off here by one or two days. According to some who were there, although my father was horribly burned, he did not seem in any real danger until the third day, when the scabbing began, making it difficult to breathe. Dehydration compounded the situation. In this account, it was then that they feared for his life, and that is when my sister called me, only I misunderstood and assumed that the explosion had happened the day before.

7   p. 396 I remember this as the scar Luke got from working the Shear; however, it might have come from a roofing accident.

A Note on the Text

Certain footnotes have been included to give a voice to memories that differ from mine. The notes concerning two stories — Luke's burn and Shawn's fall from the pallet — are significant and require additional commentary.

In both events, the discrepancies between accounts are many and varied. Take Luke's burn. Everyone who was there that day either saw someone who wasn't there, or failed to see someone who was. Dad saw Luke, and Luke saw Dad. Luke saw me, but I did not see Dad and Dad did not see me. I saw Richard and Richard saw me, but Richard did not see Dad, and neither Dad nor Luke saw Richard. What is one to make of such a carousel of contradiction? After all the turning around and round, when the music finally stops, the only person everyone can agree was actually present that day, is Luke.

Shawn's fall from the pallet is even more bewildering. I was not there. I heard my account from others, but was confident it was true because I'd heard it told that way for years, by many people, and because Tyler had heard the same story. He remembered it the way I did, fifteen years later. So I put it in writing. Then this other story appeared. *There was no waiting*, it insists. *The chopper was called right away.*

I'd be lying if I said these details are unimportant; that the 'big picture' is the same no matter which version you believe. These details matter. Either my father sent Luke down the mountain alone, or he did not; either he left Shawn in the sun with a serious head injury, or he did not. A different father, a different man, is born from those details.

I don't know which account of Shawn's fall to believe. More remarkably, I don't know which account of Luke's burn to believe, and *I was there*. I can return to that moment. Luke is on the grass. I look around me. There is no one else, no shadow of my father, not even the idea of him pushing in on the periphery of my memory. He is not there. But in Luke's memory he *is* there, laying him gently in the bathtub, administering a homeopathic for shock.

What I take from this is a correction, not to my memory but to my understanding. We are all of us more complicated than the roles we are assigned in the stories other people tell. This is especially true in families. When one of my brothers first read my account of Shawn's fall, he wrote to me: 'I can't imagine Dad calling 9-11. Shawn would have died first.' But maybe not. Maybe, after hearing his son's skull crack, the desolate thud of bone and brain on concrete, our father was not the man we thought he would be, and assumed he had been for years after. I have always known that my father loves his children and powerfully; I have always believed that his hatred of doctors was more powerful. But maybe not. Maybe, in that moment, a moment of real crisis, his love subdued his fear and hatred both.

Maybe the real tragedy is that he could live in

our minds this way, in my brother's and mine, because his response in other moments — thousands of smaller dramas and lesser crises — had led us to see him in that role. To believe that should *we* fall, he would not intervene. We would die first.

We are all more complicated than the roles we are assigned in stories. Nothing has revealed that truth to me more than writing this memoir — trying to pin down the people I love on paper, to capture the whole meaning of them in a few words, which is of course impossible. This is the best I can do: to tell that *other* story next to the one I remember. Of a summer day, a fire, the smell of charred flesh, and a father helping his son down the mountain.

We do hope that you have enjoyed reading this large print book.

Did you know that all of our titles are available for purchase?

We publish a wide range of high quality large print books including:
Romances, Mysteries, Classics
General Fiction
Non Fiction and Westerns

Special interest titles available in large print are:
The Little Oxford Dictionary
Music Book
Song Book
Hymn Book
Service Book

Also available from us courtesy of Oxford University Press:
Young Readers' Dictionary
(large print edition)
Young Readers' Thesaurus
(large print edition)

For further information or a free brochure, please contact us at:
Ulverscroft Large Print Books Ltd.,
The Green, Bradgate Road, Anstey,
Leicester, LE7 7FU, England.
Tel: (00 44) **0116 236 4325**
Fax: (00 44) **0116 234 0205**

Other titles published by Ulverscroft:

THE OLD MAN AND THE KNEE

Christopher Matthew

Although in his seventies, Christopher Matthew is convinced he is not old. He plays golf, he walks the dog, and no one ever stands up for him on crowded buses and Tubes. He has all his own teeth and hair, and does not require a hearing aid. He is, in short, enjoying late middle age. How, though, does one know when one is old? Does old age creep up slowly, or arrive out of the blue like an outsize pigeon dropping? Will one be able to summon up some half-decent last words, and what should they be? No one likes the idea of growing old, but this largely light-hearted guide to life in the last lane will persuade late middle-agers that they have more to look forward to than they might imagine.

ENGLISH

Ben Fogle

Beginning at the top of a muddy Gloucester-shire slope at the Coopers Hill cheese-rolling contest and traversing a landscape of lawns and queues, coastlines and sporting arenas, Ben Fogle takes us on a journey through the peculiarly English: a country of wax jackets, cricket, boat races and jellied eels, by way of national treasures such as the shipping fore-cast, fish and chips and the Wellington boot, not to mention the Dunkirk spirit of relent-less optimism in the face of adversity. The archetypal Englishman — lover of Labradors and Land Rovers, yet holder of two passports — Ben applauds all things quintessentially English while also paying tribute to the his-tory, culture and ideas adopted with such gusto that they have become part of the fabric of the country.

A YORKSHIRE VET THROUGH THE SEASONS

Julian Norton

Julian Norton has been a vet for over twenty years, and in that time he has treated animals of every kind — snakes and lizards, fish and fowl, sheep, goats, alpacas, cows, horses — you name it, Julian has seen it and, most likely, made it better. In *A Yorkshire Vet Through the Seasons*, Julian recounts more inspirational tales from his life, the animals he has treated and the people he has met, including the challenges and surprises that occur at the most unlikely times. Whether he is tending to a domestic pet at his practice in Thirsk, or called out to an injured swan in the middle of a cold Yorkshire night, the animals always come first, and Julian's passion and commitment are always to the fore.

READING WITH PATRICK

Michelle Kuo

As a young English teacher keen to make a difference in the world, Michelle Kuo took a job at a tough school in the Mississippi Delta, sharing books and poetry with a young African-American teenager named Patrick and his classmates. For the first time, these kids began to engage with ideas and dreams beyond their small town, and to gain an insight into themselves that they had never had before. Two years later, Michelle left to go to law school; but Patrick began to lose his way, ending up jailed for murder. And that's when Michelle decided that her work was not done, and began to visit Patrick once a week, and soon every day, to read with him again . . .

THE DAY THAT WENT MISSING

Richard Beard

On a family summer holiday in Cornwall in 1978, Nicholas and his brother Richard are jumping in the waves. Suddenly, Nicholas is out of his depth, and drowns. Richard and his older brothers don't attend the funeral; incredibly, the family return immediately to the same cottage to complete the holiday. They soon stop speaking of the catastrophe, and Nicky is written out of the family memory. Nearly forty years later, Richard Beard is haunted by the missing grief of his childhood, but doesn't know the date of the accident or the name of the beach. So he sets out on a painstaking investigation to rebuild Nicky's life, and ultimately to recreate the precise events on the day of the accident. Who was Nicky? Why did the family react as they did? And what actually happened?